A great man stood in the shadows as this book made its way from idea to possibility to reality. That man is Judge Griffin Boyette Bell, the 72nd Attorney General of the United States and great friend of Judge Anthony Alaimo. Judge Bell provided many of the telling anecdotes, reviewed the book's legal underpinnings and case histories, even contributed detailed pencil-editing when he saw the need. He did this with the unassuming grace, insight and sparkling humor that characterize his life and career. I'm honored to dedicate this biography to him.

Vincent Coppola
September 2008

# Contents

Acknowledgments      vii

Photograph Album      ix

Anthony Alaimo, An American Hero      1

Bibliography      273

# Acknowledgments

This book would not have been possible without the support of three wise and decent men, attorneys all: James Bishop, David Hudson and Robert Steed. In Brunswick, Alaimo hired Bishop straight out of law school. Forty years later, the bond between the two is as strong, vibrant and deeply rooted as the live oaks that populate coastal Georgia. Jim provided the up close and personal insights into Judge Alaimo that bring the biography vividly to life. David Hudson, the judge's erstwhile doubles partner on the tennis court, unfailingly provided the legal expertise and research that guided me through the twisting thickets of the law. It was Bob Steed, that pillar of falstaffian wit and exuberance who first approached me about writing the book. Simply put, fate or destiny sat us next to each other at a luncheon in downtown Atlanta. I can visualize the gears turning in Bob's head as the notion struck him, "Ah, Italian judge... Italian writer!"

In Brunswick, Michelle J. Kim, Judge Alaimo's energetic and efficient law clerk, helped research and coordinate this complicated project with alarming good cheer and endless enthusiasm. Ryan Babcock, Alaimo's senior clerk, provided much background and insight into the complexities of case law I pondered.

I want to acknowledge my editor, Marc Jolley, at Mercer Press for his hard work and support.

And my wonderfully bright and loving children, Gabrielle and Thomas, who have made parenting the great blessing of my life, though an extended one.

And finally, Suzanne Pruitt, proud daughter of Savannah, who has been the most loyal and loving partner any man could hope for.

Vincent Coppola
September 2008

*Judge Alaimo*

*Salvatore Alaimo passport photo*

*(L-R front row) Anthony A. Alaimo (ring bearer) and Constance Tilaro (flower girl); (L-R middle row) Agostino Gust Gerace (Alaimo's brother-in-law), Frances Alaimo Gerace (Alaimo's sister), Jennie Tilaro, Ms. LaMarca, Sandy Alaimo (Alaimo's sister), Angelina Sapienza; (L-R back row) Thomas Tilaro, Ralph Scarintino, Charles Piazza, and friend of bride, at Frances Alaimo's wedding to Gust Gerace.*

*Anthony Alaimo, at nineteen—1939.*

*Jeanne Loy—June 1940.*

*Charles Carcione (uncle), Anthony Alaimo,*
*Francis Carcione (cousin), and*
*(front) Anthony Carcione (cousin).*

*Anthony Alaimo, Philip Alaimo (son), Bobby Bischoff (son), and Jeanne Alaimo, Emory Law School Trailer Village—June 1946.*

*Anthony Alaimo and Mrs. Jeanne Loy Alaimo, on their wedding day—1946.*

*Anthony Alaimo and Bobby Lee Cook—May 1959.*

*President Nixon and Anthony Alaimo—July 28, 1960.*

*1960's Mrs. Jeanne L. Alaimo—1960s.*

*Anthony Alaimo, Venice, Italy—1961.*

*Anthony Alaimo and Philip Alaimo (son), aboard the* SS Statendam, *May 26, 1961.*

*Anthony Alaimo—in his law office in Brunswick, Georgia—1964.*

*Anthony Alaimo and the new Mercedes—1965.*

*Anthony Alaimo, Carolyn Mattingly, Mack Mattingly (future US Senator from Georgia 1981–1987), and Jeanne Alaimo, Madrid, Spain—September 27, 1969.*

*Anthony Alaimo, Spain—1969.*

*Mr. Loy (Jeanne's father), Judge Alaimo, and Mrs. Loy (Jeanne's mother)—December 1971.*

Fred Alaimo (brother), Phil Alaimo (brother), and Tony Alaimo—
Alaimo Reunion August 1974.

Judge Alaimo—1975.

*Judge Alaimo—1975.*

*Judge Alaimo—1975.*

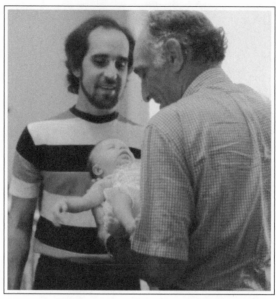

*(L-R) Philip Alaimo, Julie Alaimo (granddaughter),
and Judge Alaimo—July 2, 1977.*

*Judge Alaimo and Judge Tjoflat (Eleventh Circuit Court of
Appeals)—1982.*

*Nikki Bischoff (granddaughter), Judge Alaimo,
and Pammy Bischoff (granddaughter)—July 1984.*

*Judge Alaimo, Cathedral in Sicily—1986.*

*Naturalization ceremony, Savannah, Georgia—September 16, 1987.*

*Judge Alaimo at Juvenile Reformatory in Guangzhou, China, playing tug-o-war—October 3, 1987.*

*Judge Alaimo at Juvenile Reformatory in Guangzhou, China, playing tug-o-war—October 3, 1987.*

*Judge Alaimo and Mindy Bischoff
(granddaughter)—September 1989.*

*Judge Edenfield (US District Court, Southern District of Georgia), Justice Byron White (US Supreme Court), and Judge Alaimo—October 1989.*

*(L-R) Henry Crumley (clerk of court), Judge Alaimo, Judge Edenfield (US District Court, Southern District of Georgia), and Judge Bowen (US District Court, Southern District of Georgia). August 1990 reception celebrating the presentation of the portrait of Judge Anthony A. Alaimo.*

*Justice Clarence Thomas (US Supreme Court) and Judge Alaimo speaking at Ohio Northern University—April 7, 1994.*

*Judge Alaimo in chambers—1995.*

*Judge Alaimo, Don Carter, and James McSwiney, touring King & Prince Seafood Corporation, Brunswick, Georgia—April 3, 1995.*

*Judge Alaimo and 1996 Olympic Torch, Brunswick, Georgia—July 10, 1996.*

*Judge Alaimo and Jeanne L. Alaimo, May 30, 1997, at the Dedication of the Anthony A. Alaimo Parkway.*

*Judge Alaimo and President Carter—1998.*

*Judge Alaimo piloting B-1 Bomber—February 25, 1998.*

*Judge Alaimo and B-1 Bomber, Robins Air Force Base, Warner Robins, Georgia.*

*Judge Alaimo receiving the Emory Medal—September 26, 1998.*

*President Jimmy Carter, Victoria Simms, Judge Alaimo, and Judge Griffin Bell (Fifth Circuit Court of Appeals, 1961–1976)—July 4, 1999.*

*Mrs. Alaimo and Judge Alaimo—December 31, 2000.*

*David Hudson, Jim Bishop, US Magistrate Judge James Graham,
and Judge Alaimo—February 2001.*

*Arnold Palmer, Mrs. Alaimo, and Judge Alaimo—November 7, 2002.*

*Jim Bishop, Judge Alaimo, David Hudson, and Judge Griffin Bell (Fifth Circuit Court of Appeals)—December 3, 2002.*

*Judge Alaimo and Judge Wood—2007.*

*August 2008 Cover of the* Verdict, *commemorating the inaugural presentation of the Anthony A. Alaimo Award for Judicial Excellence to Judge Alaimo. Photograph taken by Michael Shortt.*

*Judge Alaimo in chambers, Brunswick, Georgia.*
*Photograph by Bobby Haven of the* Brunswick
News—*July 17, 2008.*

*Judge Alaimo in Savannah.*

*Memorial Wall at the Mighty Eighth Museum in Savannah, Georgia.*

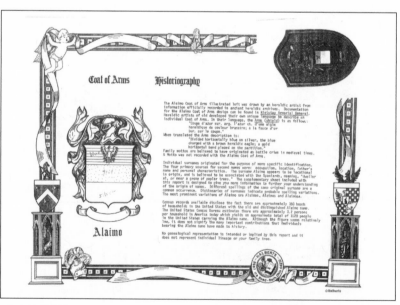

*Alaimo coat of arms*

## THE SALVATORE ALAIMO FAMILY--ELLIS ISLAND RECORDS

Salvatore Alaimo & Santa Rochetta Granza, married Oct. 28, 1905
   b.3/25/82)        b.5/26/84)

  Rosa (Irene) b.1/1/1907 in Termini
  ------------------------------------
The above 3 moved to Bahia Blanca,Argentina in 1907 or 1908.

    Francesca b.11/04/1908 in Bahia Blanca
    Santina (Sandy) b. 11/1/1910 in Bahia Blanca
    ------------------------------------
Salvatore, Santa, and their 3 daughters returned to Italy in 1913

    Filippo b.4/4/1914 in Termini
    Antonino b.3/29/20 in Termini
    ------------------------------------
Salvatore went by himself to Jamestown , arr. Aug.8,1920
------------------------------------
Francesca Liuzzo, Irene, Francesca, ~~Sandy~~ & Calogero Carcione
                  went to Jamestown, June 15, 1921
------------------------------------
Santa took Sandy, Filippo, & Antonino to Jamestown Sept.20, 1922

    Giusepina (Jo) b. 11/5/23 in Jamestown
    Federico b.1/23/1925 in Jamestown
    ------------------------------------


Santa died 5/21/1951    Salvatore died 4/10/57


For some reason, Santa Alaimo is not listed on the ships's manifest, but Sandy, Filippo and Antonino all have entries. I have
tried every possible spelling or mis-spelling of her name.

Log on to  Ellisislandrecords.org  and you will find records of
all immigrants who entered the country through Ellis Island
between 1892 and 1922 (or '24. not sure which).

I gave $100 to the Ellis Island Foundation a few years ago to re-
cord "The Salvatore Alaimo Family, Sicily" on the American Immigrant Wall of Fame" at Ellis Island. If anyone goes to New York,
they might want to go to the Ellis Island Museum to check on this.
I have not seen it.---Jeanne

They could also check with the museum about the missing name of
Santa Alaimo. Perhaps the person who typed up the web site is the
one who left her name out--she might be on the original manifest,
in fact, I'm sure she was. She sailed from Termini on the
"Argentina", with her 3 children, arriving in New York on Aug. 8,
1922.

*Ellis Island records of Alaimo family's arrival in the United States*

## IS THERE NO END TO THESE RANDOM NOTES?

| | PORT | SHIP | ARRIVED | AGE |
|---|---|---|---|---|
| Salvatore Alaimo | Palermo | " Argentina" | Aug. 8, 1920 | 39 |
| Francesca Carcione | Palermo | "Columbia" | June 15, '21 | 59 |
| Charlie Carcione | " | " | " | 24 |
| Rose  (Irene) Alaimo | " | " | " | 14 |
| Frances Alaimo | " | " | " | 12 |
| Santa Alaimo | Palermo | "Colombo" | Sept. 20, "22 | 38 |
| Sandy Alaimo | " | " | " | 11 |
| Philip | " | " | " | 8 |
| Tony | " | " | " | 2 |

I cannot find Antonio Carcione (Fran. Liuzzo's last husband) on the Ellis Island website.  It has changed considerably since I first looked all this stuff up, but I will try again.  Also, still cannot find Santa on the Colombo manifest, but she obviously was on the ship with her three young children.  I have tried every imaginable spelling, including her maiden name.

Correction on Francesca Liuzzo's page:  she died in 1947 at age 85.

Here is the last address we have for the Sicily relatives.  We visited with Rosa and the others when we were there in 1991.She is the wife of Francesco Liuzzo, and at that time owned a small grocery, fruit, and vegetable market in Termini.  She, Pepe, Santa, and all their families live in Termini and are all still living as far as we know.  Rosa has a son named Salvatore Liuzzo whom we met.  I can't remember the  names of the others, but they were all exceptionally nice and very glad to see us.  They got everyone together for a spaghetti supper one night.     Rosa liuzzo
         49 Via Ugo La Malfa
        Termini Immerese
        Sicily,  Italy

I know that she would be delighted to hear from any of the family.   She was a pretty sharp lady and might  know some Alaimo family history-- names of grandparents, great grand-parents, etc.  I would especially like to know how and where Santa and Salvatore met.  Her son or other young people in the family might have a computer and be able to find some of these things  on the internet.

I am sure Italy is covered by the internet; can anyone figure out how to contact the court-house in Campobello di Licata, to try to find records of  Salvatore's birth and his parents and grandparents?  Ditto for Santa Granza in Tortorici.  It only tookTony a short time to find his birth certificate in Termini when we were first there in 1961.  Some of you young folks need to get over there!

One small puzzle is where Santa got the middle name of Rochetta  (or Rochetto).  One Italian dictionary says "rochetto" is a "spool" or a "reel" which sounds more like it would be a last name to me.  And I did find on the Ellis Island site some  passengers with the last name of Rochetto.  Maybe it  was the maiden name of Santa's grandmother.  It must have some meaning, because Italians, at  least back then, did not  just pick names out of the blue for their children.

*Ellis Island records of Alaimo family's arrival in the United States*

# THE SALVATORE ALAIMO FAMILY--ELLIS ISLAND RECORDS

Salvatore Alaimo & Santa Rochetta Granza, married Oct. 28, 1905
    b.3/25/82)          b.5/26/84)

    Rosa (Irene) b.1/1/1907 in Termini
    -------------------------------------
The above 3 moved to Bahia Blanca,Argentina in 1907 or 1908.

    Francesca b.11/04/1908 in Bahia Blanca
    Santina (Sandy) b. 11/1/1910 in Bahia Blanca
    -------------------------------------
Salvatore, Santa, and their 3 daughters returned to Italy in 1913

    Filippo b.4/4/1914 in Termini
    Antonino b.3/29/20 in Termini
    -------------------------------------
Salvatore went by himself to Jamestown , arr. Aug.8,1920
    -------------------------------------
Francesca Liuzzo, Irene, Francesca, ~~Sandy~~ Calogero Carcione
                            went to Jamestown, June 15, 1921
    -------------------------------------
Santa took Sandy, Filippo, & Antonino to Jamestown Sept.20, 1922

    Giusepina (Jo) b. 11/5/23 in Jamestown
    Federico b.1/23/1925 in Jamestown
    -------------------------------------

Santa died 5/21/1951    Salvatore died 4/10/57


For some reason, Santa Alaimo is not listed on the ships's manifest, but Sandy, Filippo and Antonino all have entries. I have
tried every possible spelling or mis-spelling of her name.

Log on to  Ellisislandrecords.org  and you will find records of
all immigrants who entered the country through Ellis Island
between 1892 and 1922 (or '24. not sure which).

I gave $100 to the Ellis Island Foundation a few years ago to re-
cord "The Salvatore Alaimo Family, Sicily" on the American Immigrant Wall of Fame" at Ellis Island. If anyone goes to New York,
they might want to go to the Ellis Island Museum to check on this.
I have not seen it.---Jeanne

They could also check with the museum about the missing name of
Santa Alaimo. Perhaps the person who typed up the web site is the
one who left her name out--she might be on the original manifest,
in fact, I'm sure she was. She sailed from Termini on the
"Argentina", with her 3 children, arriving in New York on Aug. 8,
1922.

*Ellis Island records of Alaimo family's arrival in the United States*

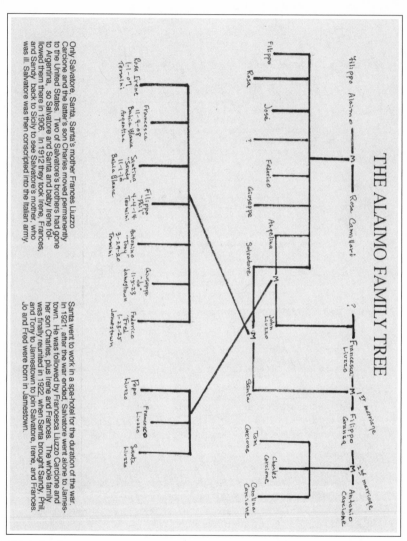

# THE ALAIMO FAMILY TREE

Only Salvatore, Santa, Santa's mother Frances Lluzzo Carcione and the latter's son Charles moved permanently to the United States. Two of Salvatore's brothers had gone to Argentina, so Salvatore and Santa and baby Irene followed them there in 1906. In 1912 they took Irene, Frances, and Sandy back to Sicily to see Salvatore's mother, who was ill. Salvatore was then conscripted into the Italian army.

Santa went to work in a spa-hotel for the duration of the war. In 1921, after the war ended, Salvatore went alone to Jamestown. He was followed by Francesca Lluzzo Carcione and her son Charles, plus Irene and Frances. The whole family was finally reunited in 1922, when Santa brought Sandy, Phil, and Tony to Jamestown to join Salvatore, Irene, and Frances. Jo and Fred were born in Jamestown.

*Alaimo family tree*

# Part I

"Nobility has nothing to do with where you were born or to whom you were born. It has everything to do with the moral choices you make in life."

—Tim Carroll, *The Great Escape*

# Chapter 1

"They were flying suicide missions....There had been
no time; the war came on the country so quickly.
There were navigators who couldn't navigate,
bombardiers who couldn't hit their targets, gunners
who couldn't shoot straight. And their commanders
had no idea...how to stop losing so many men."
—Major Gale W. Cleven,
from *Masters of the Air*

It begins with a simple coin toss.

Two young aviators on the cusp of their first combat mission vie
to see who'll command the pilot's seat. The silver half-dollar spins
and glints in the sunlight. The winner, Lieutenant Joseph H. Jones, a
young airman from Jacksonville, Florida, clambers into the left-hand
seat of the B-26. Second Lieutenant Tony Alaimo slips beside him
into the copilot's seat. If Alaimo is disappointed, he doesn't show it.
There would be plenty of other missions.

It was May 17, 1943. Allied armies had driven Axis forces out of
North Africa. The invasion of Sicily loomed. Hitler was pressing a
massive armored assault on the Red Army desperate to regain the
initiative the Germans had squandered at Stalingrad. The Jewish
uprising in the Warsaw ghetto was in its death throes. D-Day, the
Normandy invasion, any glimmer of the war's end were still more
than a year off.

The skein of history was unraveling around them, but on this
crisp, clear English morning the men of the 450th Bombardment
Squadron were focused on their mission—and, perhaps, the eternal
questions that confront untested warriors.

The night before, Alaimo had written a short V-mail letter to his father in Jamestown, New York. He wrote in Italian, as Sam Alaimo couldn't read English and Tony's mother, Santa, couldn't read at all. The twenty-three-year-old Alaimo was not much of a letter writer—certainly not one to pour his emotions, fears, or hopes out on paper to his family—but this night, the fact that he "was actually going to get shot at" spurred him on. He wouldn't want to leave the world in silence.

Aviators dress with the practiced ritual of medieval knights—in Alaimo's case, khaki pants, brown uniform shirt with his gold second lieutenant's "butter bar" and 8th Air Force shoulder patch, brown shoes, leather bombardier jacket, dog tags, and some currency, "not a lot." He carried no photographs, good luck charms, or other talismans. He purposefully left behind his wallet but couldn't remember why.

The target lay 200-odd miles across the North Sea from the Allied airbase at Bury St. Edmunds: an electrical-generating plant at Ijmuiden in Nazi-occupied Holland that, among other things, supplied a nearby German U-boat pen with power. A dozen B-26 Marauders from the 322nd Bomb Group had attacked the plant just three days earlier. Intelligence reports indicated that the facility remained unscathed.

Eleven of those planes were heavily damaged by anti-aircraft artillery. The worst hit was piloted by Jack Howell, one of Alaimo's squadron mates. Howell nursed his shredded airship back to the coast and ordered his five crewmembers to parachute to safety; as he was attempting to bail out, the plane spun and plummeted to earth. For Tony Alaimo and the others, Howell's death prefigured the inevitable transformation every combat veteran experiences when the exuberance and illusions of youth give way to the bitter verities of war.

Colonel Robert M. Stillman, commander of the 322nd, had led that first futile assault. Now he listened in disbelief as his commander, Brigadier General Samuel Brady, passed on the word that headquarters had ordered a second strike, one without any possibility of surprise against an enemy now on full alert. Stillman was unwilling to order the remainder of his rookie squadrons into a meat grinder. His concerns were passed up the chain of command to Wing Commander General Samuel Egbert Anderson at his headquarters in Marks Hall, northeast of London. Anderson signed off on the mission.

"You'll send them in," Brady warned Stillman, "or another commander will."

"I'll run the mission myself."

As Stillman walked out of that meeting, the major in charge of intelligence called out, "See you later, old boy."

"No," Stillman replied. "We won't be coming back."

He kept these concerns to himself. Standing in front of a scale model of the power plant built on a sand table, he briefed Jones, Alaimo, and the five-dozen or so officers and enlisted men assigned to the attack.

Around 9:30 A.M., Alaimo, Jones, bombardier Norris Kenneth Calkins, and three NCOs—a radioman and two gunners who'd man the .50-caliber machine guns mounted in the tail and dorsal positions—arrived on the flight line in jeeps and clambered aboard the aircraft. Like the others, Alaimo wore a parachute harness and an inflatable "Mae West" lifejacket. Strapped around his waist was a sheath knife and an escape kit containing pressure bandages, burn ointment, gauze, and morphine syrettes.

The Martin B-26 medium bombers the men would fly had been rushed into production, going from the drafting board to the production line in less than two years. No prototype had ever been tested. Its aerodynamics—stubby wings, small swept wing area ("high wing loading"), extreme outboard engine placement—made it a challenging plane to fly. It was tail-heavy. A B-26 landing was essentially a high-speed controlled crash. Takeoffs were treacherous:

loss of power in one of its twin engines—early propeller governors were notoriously unreliable—could result in a violent snap roll that would flip the airplane on its back.

The May 14 attack had been the B-26 bomber's European debut.

Airborne, the plane was fast, sturdy, and highly maneuverable, a formidable weapons platform that could deliver a 3,000-pound payload and shred anything on the ground with twelve .50-caliber Colt-Browning machine guns—weapons so powerful that the aircraft would jar and shudder violently when they were unleashed.

The B-26 had been designed to deliver its payload from 11,000 feet. The Allied Air Command, desperate for a way to hurt the swarming German armies, quickly realized that bombers manned by inadequately trained American airmen thrown headlong into combat were useless. According to the statistics, in perfect conditions only 50 percent of American bombs fell within a quarter-mile of an assigned target. If you believed the hype, the introduction of the Norden bombsight (an innovation so secret that bombardiers were forced swear an oath to guard its workings with their lives) famously allowed them to drop a bomb "into a pickle barrel," a standard that would prove elusive when swarms of Messerschmitt ME109s came screaming at hapless bombardiers through the fog and fury of war.

In any event, the B-26 was not equipped with a Norden sight.

So a new tactic had been developed. Upon arriving in the United Kingdom in March 1943, Alaimo's squadron had spent an exhausting month practicing low-level bombing runs, racing across the rolling hills of Essex at treetop level, flying lower at times than the church steeples dotting the countryside.

The theory was, "You can't miss if you fly at treetop level."

Enemy gunners had come to the same conclusion. They waited by the hundreds in bristling emplacements dotting the coastline.

Eleven B-26 bombers carrying sixty-six crewmembers departed Bury St. Edmunds at 10:00 A.M. The weather was clear and mild. Within minutes, the men were over the North Sea, flying 500 feet above the waves. They headed southeast in a long arc that would swing north once they crossed the Dutch coast, to their target, and then west toward home. Gusting winds pushed the flight further south then had been intended. They flew in javelin formation, Stillman's plane the point of the spear. Jones and Alaimo were at the rear, the "tail-end Charlie" position.

The pulse of the 1,900-horsepower Pratt & Whitney engines would have been reassuring, syncopated to the men's breathing and their beating hearts. There was no fighter escort; the squadron was flying under the radar and maintaining strict radio silence. So no one realized that one of the B-26s had suffered mechanical problems, the pilot pulling up, as he'd been trained, and clawing for altitude, and triggering a telltale blip on German radar.

Ten planes crossed the coast at 200 miles per hour, flying into a torrent of steel and black flak clouds as palpable as a thunderstorm, a "solid mass of firepower." Alaimo and the others watched in horror as 20-millimeter tracer rounds, clearly visible and seemingly traveling in slow motion, groped the underbelly of the bomber—each man instinctively clenching his thighs, the fear of castration more primordial than the fear of death. Alaimo's plane made it past the gantlet of exploding 88-millimeter rounds that filled the air with buzzing shards of white-hot shrapnel. In the madness that ensued, Alaimo watched Stillman's bomber, its rudder shot away, roll on its back and plunge into a canal bank. A second Marauder, moving up to assume the lead position, slammed into his wingman; fragments from the disintegrating aircraft knocked a third plane out of the sky.

Men were dying all around them as Jones and Alaimo, trailing smoke and flame from one of their engines, careened toward the power station. They fought to hold the aircraft steady as Calkins in the nose canopy prepared to release his payload. No bombs found the target.

There were no medics aboard Army Air Force bombers. In the frenzy of battle, shielded by thin aluminum skin and scant armor, the planes became flying abattoirs, the flight decks awash in blood. Surviving crews limped back to the UK firing off red flares to alert ground personnel that injured were coming in.

A round pierced Alaimo's right leg.

Three...four...seven planes were down. Two of the three remaining B-26s were set upon by swarms of fighters based at Woensdrecht as they recrossed the coast and blasted out of the sky.

Alaimo's crippled ship may have been the last aloft.

He "feathered" the burning engine, engaging the propeller's governor to turn the blades parallel to the wind—in effect, shutting down the engine. The risk of explosion was real: the B26 bomber's fuel tanks were in the wings. Alaimo undid his harness, then reached around to grab the fire extinguisher cable located behind his seat. He turned the pointer on its gauge to the distressed engine. Nothing happened. In the confusion, he neglected to rebuckle the harness.

The Marauder was over water when the second engine burst into flames. Alaimo had no choice but to shut it down. Aerodynamically, the 18-ton bomber was not designed to glide. Without power, it dropped like a stone. Alaimo heard Jones, speaking into his throat mike, give the order: "Prepare for ditching."

Parachutes were useless at such low altitudes.

Airplanes die very much like human beings. Vital systems—electrical, hydraulic, propulsion, cooling—begin shutting down, failure building upon failure, each with greater speed and consequence until the organism suffers a catastrophic and irreversible collapse.

In extremis, men do not cry out for wives or girlfriends. Their children's names are not the last words to cross their lips. Not all reach out to God and his mercy. Men in their final moments, in terror or in pain, cry out for their mothers.

A dark-haired woman prays behind a closed door:

*Deo omnipotenti, prego che ave misericordia e pieta per il mio figliio, Tony. Et prego che si puo salvare la vita di questo ragazzo.*[1]

Consciousness explodes into fleeting impressions, shards of memory, the ache of the familiar and what might have been…slipping away. A smiling, fair-haired girl, the thump of a right cross on an opponent's chin, the shameful weight of hand-me-down clothes and worn-out shoes, family gatherings on Easter and Christmas Eve, a saxophone's plaintive wail, an immigrant youth's headlong charge at life abruptly slowing....

Alaimo released the handles of the escape hatch above his head. The wind tore away the Plexiglas panel. All else was drowned out in a deafening roar as the dark, chill waters of the North Sea rushed up to meet him.

---

[1] "Almighty God, I pray that you will have mercy and pity on my son, Tony. And I pray you will save the life of this boy."

# Chapter 2

Io vi ringrazio per sua permesso di noi venire a questo
miraviglioso paese.[1]
—Santa Alaimo

Santa Alaimo's evening prayers were regular and unfailing as Jamestown's many church bells; they were a direct communication from her mouth to God's ear, expressing gratitude for the opportunity to raise and educate her children in the United States of America, this greatest of all countries; beseeching forgiveness for their many transgressions, which they somehow imagined could be hidden from her, if not God's eyes, and the hope that Sam would find a way to keep these hungry mouths fed and clothes on their backs, a near miracle in the depths of the Depression.

Santa Alaimo's prayers were delivered behind her bedroom door at a volume that carried them to each of her offspring in the cramped third-floor apartment at the corner of Willard and Allen Street— what was then the Italian ghetto. Tony, the fifth of her children and one attentive to his mother's every word and desire, swore he could "hear her knee hit the floor." Those prayers, that voice, would remain fixed in his memory, at the locus, perhaps, where divine providence intersects with motherly love.

Santa's husband, Salvatore Alaimo, had arrived in Jamestown from Termini, Sicily, in 1920, traveling along the tenuous strand of familial connection typical of Italian immigrants. Santa Carcione's father Antonio, her uncle Joseph Calavita, and a handful of other family members had settled in northwestern New York a few years earlier, part of the great Southern Italian diaspora that sent more than

---

[1] "Thank you for allowing us to come to this marvelous country."

2,000,000 desperately poor men, women, and children to the United States during the first decades of the twentieth century.

### The Road to America

A chain of coincidences, paths taken or not taken, unexpected turns of events—each random as a coin flip or immutable as the workings of destiny—heralded the Alaimos' arrival in America. In 1908, Salvatore, Santa, and their firstborn daughter Rose had struck out for Argentina to join Salvatore's emigrant brother. They settled among thousands of Italian and Spanish immigrants in Bahia Blanca, a bustling port city that was a transit point for the grain harvests arriving by rail from the Pampas. There, Santa gave birth to two other daughters, Francesca and Santina.

In Argentina, Salvatore, then in his late twenties, taught himself to read and write Italian, no small achievement for a laborer who'd begun working at age seven as a "donkey boy." Thousands of Sicilian children had been impressed into near slave labor, helping guide malodorous cartloads of sulfur ore—brimstone in antiquity, said to feed the fires of Hell—out of the mines, perhaps in the nearby Agrigento and Caltanisetta provinces.

Salvatore was a clever man who could add, divide, and multiply in his head. He became a voracious reader and raconteur who devoured anything he could find on Sicily's convoluted history—a never-ending panoply of larger-than-life rulers, wars, and intrigues.

This hunger for learning and Santa's determination to make a better life for her family were an early expression of a trait that would recur again and again among the Alaimos. This was a family, the salt of the earth, that endured.

In 1913, with Salvatore's mother near death, the family sailed back to Sicily and arrived in Termini, a coastal town 20 miles southeast of Palermo. Soon afterward, Santa gave birth to her first son Philip, a fair-haired child like his sisters Rose and Sandy.

The timing of Salvatore Alaimo's return could not have been worse. World War I broke out on August 1, 1914, and he was conscripted into the Italian army, where he spent the next four years. He possibly fought against the Austrians at the alpine Battle of Caporetto (October–November 1917), one of the war's signal disasters—300,000 Italian soldiers were captured or killed. It was a story he would later tell his sons over and over again.

With her husband gone and four children at her knee, Santa found work in the laundry room of a local hotel. The lower city, Termini Imerese, a former Roman spa, had become a popular resort for the British touring class. There were no public schools in Italy. Though illiterate throughout her life, Santa so "thirsted for education" she scraped together the lire it took to enroll her daughters in a private academy.

Salvatore returned from the war bitter at the lack of discipline and leadership he'd encountered in the military (he claimed he'd slapped a lieutenant who'd "insulted" him). Despairing of the lack of promise Italy held for its poorest sons, he once again determined to escape.

Escape is another recurring theme among the Alaimos. Theirs was a family of escape artists, each generation struggling to free itself—whether from poverty and peasant drudgery, the leaden chains of earthly existence, the iron will of unjust men, or the suffocating weight of others' expectations.

A second son, Anthony, was born on March 29,1920. He bore classic Sicilian features: ink-dark hair and a swarthy complexion. If there were something remarkable about this child, it was his hands— oversized appendages that grasped and danced and fluttered with the delicacy and grace of butterflies.

Soon after Anthony's birth, Salvatore departed Sicily again, traveling to Jamestown, New York, with his brother-in-law Charles Carcione and linking up with his father-in-law. He worked as a laborer, saving what he could to pay for his family's passage.

In the first decades of the twentieth century, Jamestown was a bustling town. It was one of a series of industrial cities—Buffalo, Detroit, Cleveland, Erie—ringing Lake Erie. Jamestown was an archetypal American community with fine schools, imposing stone churches, and tree-lined streets, a place where the American Dream and American dreamers might flourish. The renowned Chautauqua Institution, a Methodist retreat house and conference center, sits on nearby Lake Chautauqua. As the century unfolded, men as different philosophically and personally as Franklin Delano Roosevelt and Ronald Reagan would be speakers at Chautauqua conferences. Lucille Ball was born on Stewart Avenue. Supreme Court justice Robert H. Jackson, who served as chief prosecutor at the Nuremberg trials after World War II, began his career in Jamestown.

Like most American cities, Jamestown was an ethnic mix. In the 1850s, thousands of Swedish immigrants, many of them skilled cabinetmakers, began settling there. By 1920, when Salvatore Alaimo arrived, the city (population 40,000) was a major furniture manufacturing center, and the Scandinavians were slowly being displaced by other waves of newcomers: the Italians and the Irish.

Unlike the Irish, who possessed language, the Italians had no English. Most could not even read and write Italian. (In Italy, as many as half the inhabitants of Sicily and the southern Italian provinces of Calabria and Lucania, wellsprings of emigration, were illiterate in their own tongue.) They had few skills to recommend them beyond manual labor. They were Roman Catholic, distrustful of the Protestants—idolaters whom, they believed, worshipped *testa del cavallo* (a horse's head). Most Sicilians would cross the street rather than pass in front of a Methodist church. They were inward-looking, superstitious, wary of outsiders, distrustful of authority both secular and religious—the bitter harvest of centuries of poverty and oppression in Southern Italy, a place so desperate and hopeless it was said that even Jesus Christ, the Redeemer, refused to tread there.

It took Salvatore two years to raise the money to book his family's passage. In 1922 Santa, along with Sandy, Philip, and Anthony, sailed to New York on the steamship Columbia. They traveled in steerage and made the immigrants' passage through Ellis Island. Salvatore and Antonio were there waiting when they arrived. The two eldest daughters, Rose (later nicknamed Irene) and Frances, had arrived in America with their grandmother a few years earlier—an impetus, Santa hoped, to keep a discouraged Salvatore from returning to Italy.

### The Crucible

Over the next decades, the Alaimos passed through the crucible—to paraphrase Emma Lazarus—where poor, tired, huddled masses yearning to breathe free are transformed into Americans. If there is a word that marks this transformation, a word utterly absent and unknown to the peasants of Southern Italy, it is *possibility*. From possibility flows the other defining American virtues: hope, freedom, faith, thankfulness, conviction.

Over time, Salvatore would become "Sam," a small but significant step in the process of assimilation. Sam Alaimo would become a US citizen in 1928, a status automatically granted to his minor children. Santa, too, yearned to be an *Americana* and did so, swearing the oath she'd painstakingly memorized in English.

Today, the significance of such an occasion is difficult to comprehend. For the Alaimo clan, it was a new lease on life.

As he grew older, the boy Anthony Alaimo would wear his citizenship with pride, invest it with meaning, consequence, and obligation. In May 1943, when Lieutenant Tony Alaimo clambered aboard his doomed Marauder, he was willing, as were millions of his fellows and as hundreds of thousands would, to make any sacrifice, endure any hardship, in gratitude for this precious gift.

In Jamestown, Santa gave birth a sixth and a seventh time to Josephine and Frederick, Americans by birth rather than statute. A span of nearly twenty years separated Rose, the eldest, and Freddie. The Alaimos typified the sprawling, hyper-extended American family in an era without safety nets—when offspring were expected to work in the fields or factories to contribute to the wellbeing of parents and siblings, when elder children served in *loco parentis*, when everyone pulled together or foundered.

Sam soon discovered that the streets of Jamestown were not paved with gold. Throughout the 1920s he struggled to support the family as a bricklayer, a trade he'd picked up in Sicily. At times he failed to keep his frustration and rage from overwhelming him.

In the third-floor apartment, Santa tried to stretch her meager budget beyond the staple *pasta e fagioli* (pasta and beans) and *pasta chutta* (dry pasta) with tomato sauce. She was wonderfully adept, canning tomatoes and other vegetables, making homemade cheeses, transforming stale bread and ground beef into meatballs and eggplant into *melanzane parmigiana*. Occasionally there was *baccala* (salted dried cod), which when soaked in water during preparation gave off an aroma so powerful and unpleasant it would drive her children from the kitchen. Even more infrequent were veal cutlets, which Tony remembered Santa tenderizing by pounding with a milk bottle. Her biscotti—elongated, twice-baked cookies fragrant with almond or anisette—were renowned in the family.

In an Italian family, the husband is breadwinner, authoritarian, arbiter, and interface with the outside world—roles that have faded among today's kinder, gentler fathers. Sam Alaimo was a man of his time, a distant figure who showed scant love or affection to his wife and children. This behavior all too often had consequences beyond the pain and insecurity of the moment. If Sam was proud of his dutiful brood, he rarely showed it. Hard work was a given in his world. If he engendered anything in his children's hearts, it was motivation rather than affection. All did well. Philip and Tony would become lifelong strivers.

The exception—and it was rare—was with his youngest daughter Josephine, who decades later recalled her father's delight as she arrived home from school on winter afternoons, her cheeks rosy with cold. Sam would embrace her, exclaiming in singsong Italian, *Dammi un morso di quelle mele!* ("Give me a bite of those apples!").

Poor as he was, Sam always came up with 50 cents to pay for Josephine's piano lessons.

This was a culture where the man who "worked like an animal" was respected even as he inevitably was broken down. And so Sam was quick to anger, given to shouting and outrage, quick to discipline his sons with his heavy hands. These were storms, Josephine believed, that grew out of her father's frustration at not having English, not being able to make his way in the world, desperately wanting to be a part of things yet not knowing how.

And like storms, they passed quickly.

Santa was her husband's polar opposite, a wellspring of love, concern, and compassion. What little she had she shared, feeding the poor and homeless who clustered in the streets near her tenement during the worst years of the Depression. She ran the household, her domain, like a beneficent monarch, imbuing her children with her ambitions and overwhelming them with her religious fervor, even as she kissed and coddled and tempted them with homemade cookies.

### Paterfamilias

Like all immigrants of a certain age, Sam would remain trapped between two worlds. It would be Philip, the eldest boy, who would exert the most influence on the education, careers, and destinies of his brothers and sisters. Intelligent, ambitious, opinionated, imperious—Philip Alaimo was all these things and more. From an early age he believed he'd mastered the intricate workings of assimilation and success in America and, as *paterfamilias*, would unfailingly and resolutely impart this knowledge to his brothers and sisters—whether they wanted it or not.

Philip was everywhere, involved in everything, a big brother who set the bar impossibly high for everyone and then drove them to clear it. Philip was a dropout who went on to earn a PhD; a barber who became a preacher and later a college professor; a pragmatist who counseled Tony, an academic star, to cover his bets by learning how to cut hair. (Tony did learn and eventually went on to charge double the price of Philip's 15-cent haircuts.)

Philip could be oppressive, even suffocating to his adolescent siblings, who were trying on ideas and identities of their own. He convinced Josephine to anglicize her name to better fit in at college. "He told me to do it and I just did," she said, though the decision still gnawed at her more than half a century later.

"It took me a while to find myself."

As the Depression worsened, Santa was forced to watch her children march off to Willard Elementary, Jefferson Junior High, and Jamestown High in hand-me-down clothes. Tony inherited the shirts and pants Philip had worn seven years earlier, then passed them on to Freddie. He wore side-buttoned shoes so ancient and embarrassing he'd slip them off his feet, preferring to walk the streets in his stockings.

If poverty is a disease, then one of its sequelae is fear. Rich people rarely notice their wealth; no one who has been poor can ever escape the dread of slipping back. In the land of opportunity, proud Sam Alaimo found himself standing in line at the welfare office. Tony would register a similar shame. One of his chores was to walk 2 miles three mornings a week to a farm owned by the Johnson family to pick up a pail of fresh milk for his family.

Early one morning the farmer asked Tony to climb up to the hayloft for a load of feed. Tony, then twelve, clambered up the ladder. His oversized rubber boots slipped on a rung and he fell. Desperate to grab something, anything, he plunged his left arm through a window, gashing his wrist so severely that he had to be rushed to the hospital. The milk runs ended when the Alaimos could no longer pay the bill, and Farmer Johnson cut off the family's credit.

# Chapter 3

Like many Sicilian women of her generation, Santa Alaimo was steeped in the church's penitential tradition, in dread of limbo, purgatory, and hell. Without question her children would be raised dutiful Catholics, receiving the sacraments, the framework upon which a moral life was built. Along with his older siblings, Tony was baptized as an infant, made his first confession after reaching the "age of reason," and wore the traditional white suit and armband at First Communion.

There was an evangelical fervor to Santa Alaimo's faith out of step with the patriarchal canons of a church that frowned on the laity proclaiming the joys or the mysteries of faith. Women had their place in the Catholic tradition (Mariolatry was a preeminent aspect of the liturgy) but did not, and never would, have a place at the head of the table.

Jamestown was neither Rome nor Palermo. In America, how one chose to worship was a right rather than an obligation. Given Santa's intensity, it was inevitable that the age-old fault line running through the Roman church—between worldly priests and impoverished flocks, between immense wealth and the penury of the congregants, between hypocrisy and righteousness—would fissure and split until the foundations of her Catholicism collapsed.

According to family legend, Father Bilerio, a priest who charged parishioners 10 cents to attend mass, was the catalyst (the money was used to keep "Americans," i.e., the Protestants who controlled Jamestown's jobs, banks, and political power, from foreclosing on his church).

Santa's pain, like her joy, may have been personal. As Josephine remembered it, her mother, like many of her Italian neighbors, belonged to sodalities, volunteer organizations—Saint Rita's is one example—that promoted piety and charity, comforted the sick, and visited families in times of grief. Santa was recovering from a gallbladder operation—all surgery was risky and debilitating in those days—and waited in vain for her sisters in faith to come calling. Instead, says Josephine, "The sodality sent a notice that her dues were overdue."

### Vox Clamatis

It is reasonable to imagine the Alaimo family at a critical juncture. After a decade in America, they were pursuing a dream with scant success, employment, shelter, educational opportunity, religious connection, or social acceptance. In this they were no different from millions of other *paesani* , living hand to mouth, crowded cheek to jowl, rushing forward and falling back in the teeming ethnic anthills of New York, Philadelphia, Newark, Buffalo, Providence.

Given Santa's aspirations, Sam's frustrations, and the uncertainty of the time, it is reasonable to imagine a certain agitation and impatience, a yearning to arrive at some better place—if not the biblical land of milk and honey, then at least a more promising spot than Willard and Allen Streets. "Had we stayed there," Josephine reflected, still a devout woman many years later, "our lives might have been likened to a wasteland."

The Bible (Matthew 3:1–12) mentions a *vox clamatis in deserto,* "a voice crying out in the wilderness," an allusion to John the Baptist preparing the way for the Christ the Redeemer. Like those eager followers of John the Baptist, the Alaimos were thirsty for deliverance.

It arrived in 1928, in the form of an unlikely Methodist missionary. According to those old enough to remember him, Francisco P. Sulmonetti was a potbellied, spindly legged, long-winded man who squinted at his bible through horn-rimmed glasses. Born in 1880 in Monteferrante, Sulmonetti was from Abruzzo, a region of Italy whose residents are renowned for intense stubbornness. According to Methodist Church records, he'd arrived in New Jersey around the turn of the century and spent the next forty years as a missionary preaching to Italian congregations in Boston, Denver, Chicago, Portland, Maine, New York and Pennsylvania.

An Italian Methodist is a *rara avis*. Today, approximately one-tenth of 1 percent of the population of Italy is Protestant. Sulmonetti was rarer still, part of an outreach by American Protestant churches to the millions of Italians and other European Catholics pouring into the country during the first decades of the twentieth century. The Italian missions, originally an attempt to convert the immigrants and thus ensure that Protestantism would remain the dominant religious force in the US, wound up serving a higher purpose: accelerating assimilation, opening doors, expanding horizons. As Josephine later recalled, the "Italian Methodist church was literally our salvation."

The young Sulmonetti was not a meek, turn-the-other-cheek Christian but a firebrand willing to confront the Roman church and exploit the suspicion and distrust that existed between immigrant Catholics and mainstream Protestants. Was this not the business of harvesting souls? In those years the animosity was visceral, an afterbirth of centuries of bloody European religious strife.

In 1916, in Denver, Sulmonetti's zeal had nearly gotten him lynched by a mob of Italian-American Catholics after he'd denounced them as living "in squalor equal to that of east siders [*sic*] in New York." The slander was infamous enough to be covered by the New York Times.

Twelve years later, when Sulmonetti arrived in Jamestown as pastor of the Italian Methodist Church, his hair had thinned, he had a new wife, and his modus operandi had shifted. The fire-and-brimstone rabble-rouser had become a shepherd attentive to the earthly as well as the spiritual wellbeing of his flock. Given the economic conditions in 1928, his was an inspired approach.

His congregation was tiny, never more than 150 members, at a time when Jamestown's Saint James Roman Catholic church boasted

4,000 Italian parishioners—80 percent of the city's Italian population.

Sam Alaimo first encountered Sulmonetti at his modest church, established in 1913 in an industrial district of Jamestown. Sam needed assistance applying for welfare benefits, a task made more humiliating by his inability to communicate in English.

This Methodist, obviously an educated man, was willing to guide a fellow *paesano* through the bureaucratic maze. Such *rispetto* (respect) flattered Sam's intellect along with his pride. "Sulmonetti was ingenious enough to go and intercede and be representative in a way that helped my father along," Tony Alaimo recalled.

That simple act of kindness, whether random or calculated; coincidence; or, again, the workings of Providence, would alter the arc of the Alaimo family for generations to come.

Under Sulmonetti's ministering, Sam and Santa converted to Methodism, Sam taking the lead. The children became Protestant, as did members of Santa's extended Jamestown family. Philip, the eldest boy, would be ordained a minister; but it was Tony, studious and intense, in whom Methodism's vision of a better world; its stern exhortations to a just, charitable, and uncompromising life; and its emphasis on tradition, reason, and experience illumined by divine grace would become a command.

Jamestown's Italian Methodist Church (like its Swedish counterpart) demanded a commitment beyond the sacraments and Sunday Mass required of Catholics. Congregants were expected to immerse themselves in a continual round of services, activities, and outreaches that effectively weaned the Sicilian and Neapolitan newcomer, body and soul, from the Catholic Church and the immigrant community.

Sam and Santa embraced this faith with a fervor that bespoke all their worldly and spiritual longings, their frustrations, their hopes for their children, and every immigrant's aching need for a Promised Land, whether earthly or spiritual. Tony, then ten-years-old, remembered the intensity of his parents' new-found faith: "They were exuberant in the fact that they had become Protestants," he recalled. "And very, very devout."

All they'd been before was washed away in a flood of duty and devotion that in Santa outpaced the most devout members of the congregation. "We went to church every time the doors opened," Tony recalled. "We'd go Monday for Bible study; Wednesday for midweek services; on Fridays, we'd have cottage meetings, go round to various houses praying and testifying. My mother used to whisper and nudge—practically bruising my ribs—all the time: *Alzare la voce! Alzati* ("Raise your voice! Get up!"). I'd stand in front of everyone and testify what Jesus or the Church had done for me. Looking back, it was great training. On Sundays, it was off to church with my mother and father. I had to do this throughout my teenage years until shortly before I went to college."

The simple pleasures were swept away along with the sinful. Sam gave up smoking along with *briscola* and *scopa*, Italian card games he'd enjoyed playing with his friends. Antonio, his father-in-law, would no longer take a pinch of snuff. Movies would have been scandalous, but the Alaimos never could afford the picture shows. Sam's sons were forbidden to play with their friends or even venture into the yard on Sundays.

The elder girls, Irene, Frances, and Sandy, who'd spent part of their childhood in Italy, were already grown, hesitant to embrace still another round of sacrifice. Josephine, a sprightly, olive-skinned girl with striking multicolored eyes, was forbidden to dance, ride a bike, or wear a swimsuit or ankle socks—restrictions more severe, she said, than her parents had imposed on her older sisters. "I hated Monday mornings in grade school," she remembered. "Everybody was talking about the great movies they'd seen over the weekend."

Santa's faith burned ever hotter. She committed to memory entire Bible passages that Tony read to her in Italian. When the Spirit moved her, she'd stand up and preach the gospel to anyone around her. "Momma, don't do that," Tony would plead. "People don't care to hear that."

"Oh, I got to do it!" she would say.

Tony later remarked, "In many ways, I resented her exuberance about being a Methodist and being saved. I was becoming a teenager and a little embarrassed by it. I thought she did it too much, you know, prayed the loudest in public and exhorted people to go to church. I rebelled against it, but in later in later years I came to see its value."

For Sam, the Methodist Church satisfied a more basic desire—a need to be acknowledged for intellect and ability, not physical strength. Sulmonetti, assisted by American congregant Harold Smith, arranged Bible study groups. Soon Sam was *capo di classa* (head of class), a position he took very seriously. He pored over his Italian translation of the Scriptures as intently as he'd once pondered history.

There were marvelous Sundays when the unschooled Sicilian, Salvatore Alaimo of Termini Immerse, found himself sharing a podium with the learned Dottore Ugo Crivelli,[1] a minister born in Milan. In Italy, a country as divided by region and class as surely as the American South was separated by race, such an encounter could never have taken place.

The Italian Methodist Church served as an spiritual affirmative action program that opened doors to the opportunities, values, and aspirations of mainstream America and sped the immigrant journey into the middle class. Years later, Tony Alaimo remembered walking "in [his] sparse wardrobe" with his parents, sister, and brothers to services at the First Methodist Church—"the big American church" on Third Street—and staring at the fair-haired congregation dressed in their Sunday finery.

---

[1] Crivelli arrived in Jamestown in 1933 after serving as a missionary in the Italian warrens of Indianapolis.

"They were really at a higher social level than we Italians and generally better educated," he recalled. "It changed our outlook completely. We were determined to be included in that social class."

For some time Philip, Tony, and Josephine were embarrassed by their ethnicity and consciously avoided the "Italian way of doing things, the gestures and mannerisms." Philip would go so far as to change his name from Alaimo to Allen to smooth his passage in the clergy, just as he insisted that Josephine follow suit. As Tony grew older, the pendulum swung in the opposite direction: he became proud of and intensely loyal to his Sicilian roots.

On Willard and Allen Streets—the old neighborhood with its bustling groceries and *salumeria* (delicatessens), street peddlers hawking fruits and vegetables in singsong Italian, men sipping espresso and anisette in social clubs named for half-remembered towns and villages—the Alaimos' conversion was greeted with hostility. How could these *compari* renounce the pope and the blessed Madonna to become idolaters like the *Americani* who worshipped the "horse's head"?

Like all Italian mothers, Santa was sensitive to every nuance, glance, or unspoken word directed at her children. She made sure their behavior was beyond reproach. "We had to mind our P's and Q's because the Catholic community was watching us," Josephine recalled. "We'd abandoned the Church. There were many things we weren't told, but we understood. We had to set a good example."

Father Bilerio, the family nemesis, flunked Philip, a brilliant overachiever, in an Italian class he taught. Tony shrugged off the ragging he got from friends and schoolmates at Jefferson Junior High. Determined to live up to Santa's expectations, he'd begun to distance himself from the pack academically. Sunday School teacher Harold Smith became a "faithful" mentor who, sensing Tony's promise, guided the young man's path. Smith, an assistant manager at Lundquist's Hardware, convinced the owner to hire Tony to walk around distributing advertising leaflets, a job that paid the handsome

25

sum of $5 per assignment. Tony would dutifully tithe 10 percent of his earnings to the church.

At Jamestown High, Josephine recalled Tony being "very focused, very competitive, always pushing himself." His standing with Miss Barber, the French teacher, was so exalted it spilled over: "Tony was the reason I got A's in French," Josephine said.

Tony had a sense of humor that offset his serious demeanor and a taste for occasional mischief at odds with dour Philip and older sister Sandy. Josephine recalled Tony sneaking into the kitchen one night at dinnertime and, out of the blue, "dumping a layer of red pepper over our father's spaghetti, then forking more spaghetti over it to cover it up." In an Italian household, this is an act comparable to regicide or, more likely, suicide.

"Talk about the fur flying!" Josephine giggled seventy-five years later.

Tony's only indulgence was his saxophone. Philip had purchased a used instrument for "maybe $3 or $4" but never got around to playing. It, too, was handed down to fourteen-year-old Tony. Envisioning himself as Benny Carter or Jimmy Dorsey, Tony convinced an instructor named Goranson (whose sister oversaw the Jamestown High School Orchestra) to give him lessons. Jazz, it must be assumed, was a pleasure the Methodists had not yet gotten around to banning. Tony played in the junior high and high school bands. His sax playing was typical of the many avocations he pursued in life—boxing, bridge, pingpong, bowling, dancing, tennis. Vigorous determination supercharged his modest ability.

Tony would later remark, "I wouldn't say I had an affinity. I wanted to do it."

Faith without work, if not dead, is sorely tried. Religious fervor could not deliver food to the Alaimos' table. The family suffered under the emotional and physical strains, the arguments and anguish, characteristic of the impoverished. During the worst of times it was

Irene, then living in Detroit with her husband Sam Archie (born "Arci") who kept them afloat.

Philip had to drop out of high school to help support his parents and siblings. Having taken a job at Anthony Trippi's barbershop on Windsor Street, he was soon advising Tony, then a shoeshine boy, that if he wanted to attend college he'd better learn a trade. Haircutting, like undertaking, is seemingly a recession-proof business.

Soon enough Tony was learning the trade. "I practiced on a lot of the poor kids at our church," he recalled. "I'd show up at their homes with my electric clippers and scissors."

There was a law office right across from one of the barbershops where he shined shoes. Tony would stare through the barbershop window at the important-looking men in ties and suspenders—at the roll-tops desks and green-shaded lamps, the bulging file cabinets, the good-looking young secretaries—trying to imagine what went on in their world.

By 1930, the schism with Jamestown's Italian Catholics had become irreparable. With Irene's backing, the family purchased an old house on Wescott Street, along with furniture for the living room. Sam and Santa finally had their piece—albeit a modest one— of the American Dream.

In terms of distance, 69 Wescott Street was not far from the tenement at Willard and Allen. There was, however, one essential difference—the house sat on "Swede Hill," then a solidly middleclass neighborhood, like thousands of others scattered across the small towns and cities of America. For Tony, Swede Hill would become a proverbial "City on a Hill," a place of hope and possibility rising in his imagination and memory above, but not beyond, the pain and hopelessness below.

Tony shared his room with Philip and later Frederick. "Freddie," the youngest, was a gentle, unassuming boy who had none of Philip and Tony's fire. Not surprisingly, he bore the brunt of their ragging.

"Whenever something went wrong," went the refrain, "Freddie did it!"

Some of the "Swedes" living on Swede Hill did not appreciate a family of impoverished Sicilians moving into the neighborhood. Tony, for all his sensitivity, had a pugnacious streak. The epithet "WOP" ("without papers") was a fighting word. Tony knew how to throw a good punch. He got lots of practice in those days.

Nonetheless, the move to Swede Hill accelerated the Alaimos' assimilation. "We wanted to succeed," Tony later reflected. "I learned very quickly that hard work was key to it. Not the money you had, or anything like that. Hard work."

Like Jamestown's seemingly interminable winters, the hardships of the Depression began to ease even as the winds of war were rising. At twenty, Philip Alaimo was able to return to high school. He earned his diploma in 1934 and, under the tutelage of church elders, applied and was accepted at Ohio Northern University, a Methodist school located among the cornfields in Ada, Ohio, 300 miles west of Jamestown.

Philip was called to the Methodist ministry. The day would come when he would return to Jamestown to preach sermons to the congregation in perfect Italian. Tony would never forget the tears of gratitude and joy running down his mother's cheeks.

In Detroit, Irene, a beautician who'd rebelled against her parents' religious strictures, kept a watchful eye over her younger brothers and sisters. Tony remembered her as a "fairy godmother." She was always there, "hovering over all of us," as Josephine would phrase it, ready to offer the loan of a car, a place to stay, a job lead, or maybe even a little spending money to a kid brother hoping to impress his best girl. Irene's husband Sam had a good job at a Ford assembly plant.

All seven Alaimo children finished high school, a miracle given the hard times. Frances wed in an arranged marriage. Like her mother before her, she focused her formidable energies on her children, producing two sons, Joseph and Sam, who became lawyers and a daughter, Josie, who went on to earn two master's degrees. Frances lived to be ninety-five.

Josephine, the youngest girl, studied at Evanston Collegiate Institute and Roosevelt College, Methodist schools Philip selected for her. At Roosevelt, Josephine glimpsed a fellow student getting into an elevator. At that very moment she sensed that Richard Curry was the man she would marry. After Curry graduated from law school, he and Josephine moved to Cincinnati where they raised three sons: Richard, Sam, and John.

Sandy, a beauty who resembled actress Myrna Loy, and her husband Joseph Ceci also moved to Detroit. Ceci worked for Timken Detroit Axle, an automotive foundry, later Tony Alaimo's employer.

Freddie stayed in Jamestown and married Alberta Hall. He worked for the Gurney Ball Bearing Company, a machine tool manufacturer. Coincidentally, Gurney developed the "radial-thrust angular-contact bearing," an innovation that permitted the pitch of the propellers on Tony's B-26 bomber to be "feathered" in flight. Freddie died young of a heart attack in his mid-fifties.

To a Methodist, Holy Baptism is the sacrament of new birth and regeneration. Baptism marks the sacred covenant between God and man upon which the hope of Redemption is based. Baptism is a mark that sets Christians apart from others. Baptism is the means of attaining grace. In the Methodist Church, the rite of Baptism is administered by sprinkling, pouring...And immersion.

# Chapter 4

The Marauder fell out of the sky, engulfed in flames.

"Prepare for ditching!" Joe Jones ordered from the captain's seat.

Moments later Second Lieutenant Tony Alaimo, shot through the leg and pierced by a spray of shell fragments, lost consciousness as the 18-ton bomber slammed into the unyielding sea at 150 mph. His seat harness was still unbuckled and the G-forces drove him up, up through the escape hatch lacerating his face, smashing his nose and collarbone.

Alaimo came to in the water. Instinctively, he kicked free of a shard of entangling wreckage and swam toward the light. The plane loomed above him, a cruciform shadow, then disappeared beneath the waves—carrying with it, into the depths of eternity, Joseph Jones, Norris Calkins, Marvin Harbour, Robert Steffen, and Milton Littrell.

Gasping, Alaimo pulled the cord triggering the $CO_2$ cartridge on his Mae West and bobbed to the surface. The water temperature was perhaps 50 degrees, cold enough to staunch his wounds and trigger life-threatening hypothermia.[1]

Above him the noonday sun shone. Blinking, he looked around, searching for the distinctive yellow of the bomber crew's lifejackets. He saw nothing. In the distance, Alaimo could make out the Dutch coast and hear the muffled rumble of the bombs the squadron had dropped. The ordinance was equipped with 30-minute time-delayed fuses to allow civilians to escape, a humanitarian gesture still possible at this less barbarous stage of the conflict.

The pain surged as Alaimo pulled and uncapped a morphine syrette from the escape kit on his belt and jabbed himself in the thigh.

---

[1] The average person would survive a little more than fifty minutes in 50-degree water.

He drifted off for a few moments in the morphine's "rosy glow," weightless, inconsequential, alone on a painted ocean. Time passed—minutes, hours.

His thoughts turned to his family, his mother at her prayers.

There! He spotted the shark-grey boat cruising slowly off the coast. He grabbed the police whistle each crew member had tied to his lifejacket and began to blow "the hell out of it." In the midst of so much death, Tony Alaimo awakened a furious desire to live.

"I wanted them to save me," he said later.

A sailor must have spotted him. Moments later, the German gunboat eased alongside. Crewmembers extended a hooked pole and plucked Alaimo out of the water like a landed fish.

An estimated 32,000 downed US Army airmen would be captured by the Germans in the course of the war.[2] For Alaimo and thousands of other flyboys, the ensuing years of captivity typically began with a single German phrase: *Fur sie, der krieg ist uber* ("For you, the war is over"). In response, Alaimo managed the standard reply: *Der Krieg ist nicht gut* ("The war is no good").

The Germans laid him on the deck and cut away his blood-soaked pant leg. A medic carefully dressed his wounds. Someone handed him a shot of brandy. The boat headed north and then east for the Port of Amsterdam—in Alaimo's recollection, a three-hour journey.

Unbeknownst to Alaimo, other crewmembers from the downed bombers were being fished out of the sea to the north. All told, twenty of the sixty airmen who took part in the doomed mission survived.

An ambulance carried Alaimo to Amsterdam's General Hospital, a facility overflowing with both Allied and German casualties. There were no captors or captives, no victors or vanquished—every man was

---

[2] In 1980, the US Veterans Administration estimated the total number of American soldiers captured by Germany during World War II at 95,532. Figures dating from late 1945 indicate that roughly one-third of these POWs were airmen.

treated equally. In the operating theater, anesthesia was in short supply. "You can imagine the screaming," Alaimo grimly recalled.

The bullet, most likely a 20-millimeter round, had pierced his right calf and missed the bone. A surgeon cleaned the wound, dusted it with sulfa powder, inserted a drainage tube, and bandaged him up. Alaimo's broken nose, broken right collarbone, facial lacerations, and shrapnel-pierced knee were injuries considered too minor to treat.

In the wards, Alaimo observed an unexpected affinity between the German pilots and downed Allied aviators—grounded, doubtless, in their elite status and the Prussian martial ideal of officers and gentlemen engaging each other honorably on the field of battle. World War I ace Hermann Goering, now supreme commander of the German Air Force (*Oberbefehlshaber der Luftwaffe*), had taken pains to ensure that his fellow airmen were cared for in POW camps run exclusively by the Luftwaffe. Alaimo recalled a German fighter pilot stopping by to pay his respects to the crew member, hors de combat, of a bomber he'd blasted out of the sky.

"They knew who we were." Alaimo later said.

After a week's recuperation, Alaimo was shipped out with other prisoners on a Red Cross hospital train. The wounded hung in hammocks, like cuts of beef. Their destination was an interrogation/transit center 8 miles north of Frankfort. En route, the train rumbled through Eindhoven, Holland, where Alaimo witnessed pitifully young Dutch conscripts being rounded up by the Germans and shipped off to war amid the screams and cries of the townspeople.

*Durchgangslager der Luftwaffe* (Transit Camp of the Luftwaffe) was known to the thousands of captured Allied air crews who would pass through its gates as Dulag Luft. Alaimo has no recollection of this, but a B-17 crewmember named Roy Livingstone, who arrived at Dulag Luft after being shot down in February 1943, recalled a German attempt to inject a little humor into the prisoners' plight: "My first sight of this interrogation camp was a wooden sign that stretched across the entire gate at the entrance. As miserable as I was feeling, when I read the two-foot letters that had been carved across the sign, I couldn't help but break out in laughter. It read, 'I told you it wasn't a Spitfire!'"[3] Alaimo was confined at Hohemark Hospital, a facility that operated as a unit of Dulag Luft. "It was run by what I later determined were evangelical nuns," he recalled. "At one time, the hospital must have been an insane asylum because it had padded walls. I was locked in a room with no light and shuttered windows for a week."

By the end of the week Alaimo was counting the floorboards to keep from cracking up. "I began trying to reconstruct my life," he recalled. "But I had to be careful not to cover too much on a given day or else I'd exhaust the subject."

Later he would meet a British squadron leader who had knowledge of a revolutionary type of radar, the Decca G-Box, that allowed Allied bombardiers to "see" through the cloud cover that blanketed northern Europe much of the year. "They held him in solitary for six months"

Downed Allied airmen were interrogated at Dulag Luft for up to ten days, then assigned to a permanent POW camp for the duration of their captivity. Alaimo recalled the first time his interrogator, a German first lieutenant, walked into his cell. "He immediately let me know he'd lived in Chicago four or five years. He spoke perfect English and offered me a cigarette. I didn't smoke. He wanted to know where I was trained, how long and the method of training.

"We'd been ordered to provide only our name, rank and serial number, which, when you think about it, is pretty stupid. In any event, I tried to do that. He, of course, got pretty angry and kicked the side of my bed. At the time, I couldn't walk.

"I said, 'What would you do if you'd been taken prisoner?' He thought about it and finally answered, 'Well, I wouldn't give

---

[3] A Spitfire would have been a British fighter plane, i.e., a friendly aircraft. The Germans were indulging in a little black humor. Of course, you had to have survived to appreciate the joke.

anything.' He didn't come back. I believe there were more than enough new prisoners to interrogate so he left me alone."

Alaimo was left alone with his thoughts and his frustration at being taken out so quickly after all the training and preparation. Ashamed of his helplessness, his failure to deliver even one blow against his country's enemies, he tried not to despair at the prospect of months or even years of captivity. "I don't know about other POWs," he later remarked. "War is an individual experience. Personally, I felt useless and depressed...neutered."

Captured aviators were especially susceptible to such feelings. These were highly skilled and motivated men—masters of the air, lords of the sky. They were volunteers, not draftees, carrying a deep sense of duty and soaring egos that came crashing down with them. Aviators were civilized. They didn't crawl around in muddy trenches like grunts. They took showers. They ate hot meals—not, for God's sake, C-rations. They lived in snug barracks hundreds of miles from the front. Missions were measured in hours, not weeks or months. Now their mastery and their illusions had been ripped away in a few vertiginous moments.

Around June 1, 1943, Alaimo arrived at Stalag Luft III (Stammlager Luft III), a prison camp for air force officers. Eight months later, the camp would be the scene of one of the war's most memorable incidents—an act of daring that would resonate, like Gallipoli and the flag-raising on Iwo Jima, beyond the pages of military history into popular culture.

Stalag Luft III sat among the pine forests ringing the town of Sagan (now Zagan, in Poland), 100 miles southeast of Berlin. It was grim and dreary with brutally cold winters, a place where subsistence farmers barely scraped a living out of the sandy soil. Sagan was not chosen for its beauty; it was fully 400 miles from Switzerland, 170 miles from the Baltic coast and neutral Sweden beyond.

Downed airmen, British with a smattering of Australian, French, Canadian, Polish, Czech, and Norwegian, first arrived at the compound in 1942. A year later, as the war decimated the US Army Air Forces, Americans began arriving in great numbers. Ultimately more than 11,000 Allied officers would be housed at Stalag Luft III; 6,800 of them were Americans.[4]

Upon arrival, each man was issued a disk with a number stamped on it. Second Lieutenant Tony Alaimo was number 1514.

Stalag Luft III was no hellhole, particularly compared to the savagery inflicted on POWs in the Pacific Theater. In the early years, the Germans took pains to abide by the Geneva Convention. Later, looming defeat and the intentional Allied bombing ("de-housing") of Dresden, Hamburg, and other cities resulted in downed airmen being treated as "terrorists," often at the mercy of an infuriated civilian population.

Red Cross food parcels packed with SPAM, corned beef, chocolate, cocoa, cigarettes, and "Klim" cans of powdered milk supplemented the black bread, potatoes, "maggoty" soup, and "acorn coffee" that comprised a "Kriegie's"[5] diet. The Germans occasionally served cheese derived from fish waste and a red jam distilled from coal. Blood sausage, a rare treat, was little more than horse meat. Alaimo, like all POWs, took his turn in the barrack's cookhouse. He pronounced the sausage "the strangest meat product. It looked like Georgia mud and would not congeal. Its palatability was in proportion to your hunger."

Operating out of neutral Switzerland, the YMCA provided books, athletic equipment, and musical instruments. Stalag Luft III had softball fields, a theater, an orchestra, a choral group, bridge foursomes, and even "Sagan U," a university where prisoners could take philosophy, Latin, physics, accounting, and other courses.

The theater was a multiplex. Sand excavated from the many escape tunnels the prisoners were constantly digging was dispersed

---

[4] Stalag Luft III was evacuated in the face of a Red Army onslaught in January 1945.

[5] POW, from the German *Kriegsgefangener*

beneath seats constructed from food crates. When Alaimo arrived, a number of German guards had been compromised, usually for not much more than chocolate bars and cigarettes. Radio parts had been smuggled in and crystal sets assembled. A British officer would make the rounds at night, announcing, "Tallyho, soup's on." He'd then give his fellow prisoners news briefings lifted from the BBC.

Like the sullen waters of the Bober River and the gloomy forests, the very permanence of the Stalag and the detailed routines the POWs had established weighed on Alaimo. He was recovering from his wounds, grieving over the deaths of his crew members, and dreading the impact his being reported "Killed in Action" would have on his family.

Equally devastating was the psychological impact of entrapment. "I cannot describe the terrible feeling of claustrophobia that engulfed me when the gates of the camp closed behind me," he recalled. "Loss of liberty is one of the most serious injuries that can be inflicted on an individual. I'd taken my freedom for granted—freedom of locomotion, freedom to go where I pleased, freedom from having to carry identity papers. I didn't appreciate freedom's true import until it was taken away.

"And I vowed, somehow, I was getting out of this camp."

The newness of his circumstances faded as did thoughts of his miraculous survival. Everyone was a survivor. Alaimo's days devolved into rounds of repetitive drudgery and boredom. He convinced himself that the war would be over by Christmas. He'd be released and repatriated. Stalag Luft III was a bad dream that would vanish like mist in the morning light.

"Of course it wasn't and I saw the futility of such thinking."

He saw something else. As he noted many years later, "something I still cannot explain." It was bound up in Alaimo's character and personality, forged in his status as an immigrant son who carried the dreams and, yes, the responsibilities of all immigrants. It would compel him in his long stay at the camps and for the rest of his life: a total commitment to fidelity, unending loyalty and unwavering dedication to one's duty.

In Jamestown, Philip Alaimo spared Sam and Santa the dreaded Western Union telegram expressing the secretary of war's regret that Anthony A.[6] Alaimo had been reported Missing in Action. At Bury St. Edmunds, a squadron mate had sent Philip his kid brother's scant belongings in a chest so fraught with grief, memory, and crushing responsibility it felt like it weighed a thousand pounds. Philip pushed it away.

In war, dead men's belongings are moved out quickly. No warrior wants reminders of what might lie in wait. For months Philip kept the bitter news to himself. Months later, word finally filtered from the Red Cross[7] that Tony was alive in Germany.

Alaimo had sworn to resist his captors using any means possible. Escape was a high form of resistance, forcing the enemy to commit men and resources better used elsewhere to track down fugitives. For most POWs, given the horrors outside the Stalag's walls and the impossibility of making one's way hundreds of miles across the Nazi heartland without knowledge of the language, terrain, or customs, the oath became simply words in the wind. "I always envied the guys who could get up in their sacks and sleep the war away," Alaimo would later say. "I just couldn't do it. This powerful feeling made me keep trying to escape." At Stalag Luft III, there was no shortage of like-minded men.

A good number of the British officers were public school boys, blue-blood adventurers who'd rushed to fill the ranks of the Royal Air Force in the early years of the war. In fact, the Royal Air Force's 601

---

[6] He'd taken the middle initial "A." to get around army bureaucracy. He'd been required to mark "NMI" ("no middle initial") every time he wrote his name on a piece of paper. Later, the initial "A." expanded to "Alfred."

[7] In the camps, POWs were permitted to fill out rosters distributed by the Red Cross.

Squadron was known familiarly as the "Millionaire's Squadron." Preeminent among them was a fighter pilot named Roger Bushell, an Olympic skier who'd read law at Cambridge.

Bushell was an inveterate escape artist. Shot down over France in 1940, he'd already participated in a number of breakouts, the last unhappily coinciding with the May 1942 assassination of an SS general, Obergruppenfuhrer Reinhard Heydrich, by Czech partisans. Hiding in Prague, Bushell was betrayed by an informer and scooped up by the Gestapo. In retaliation for Heydrich's death, thousands of Czech civilians were executed. Bushell never spoke about what had happened to him, but he arrived in Sagan with a burning hatred of all Germans and a warning from his captors that nothing could save him if he tried to escape again.

When Alaimo hobbled into the camp, the POWs lived crowded together in wooden barracks in the North Compound. Twice a day they were summoned to *Appell,* a roll call that could last for hours. To a casual observer, the camp was escape-proof. The barracks were 100 yards from the perimeter, making tunneling out a logistical nightmare. Twin 10-foot fences, the space between them sowed with coils of barbed wire, formed the perimeter of the 60-acre compound. Thirty feet in front of the fences ran a wooden rail about 18 inches high. Cross the rail and Maschinengewehr 42 gunners in the towers overlooking the camp would cut you in half with weapons that shrieked like ripping canvas and fired 1200 rounds a minute (the gun's off color nickname was "Hitler's zipper").

"Ferrets," specially trained enlisted men, swarmed through and under the barracks, plunging "prangs" (long rods) into the soil hoping to uncover telltale signs of tunneling.

The camp's *Kommandant,* Colonel Friedrich-Wilhelm von Lindeiner-Wildau, a decorated World War I cavalryman, was a fair-minded and honorable man. He ordered his underlings to conduct themselves accordingly—no easy task in a compound packed with thousands of intransigent warriors whose intentions directly opposed his.

Lindeiner-Wildau was also an aristocrat (he'd married a Dutch baroness) who extended to his charges the courtesies and privileges of rank. He would host dinners for senior POW officers and encourage them to behave, if not like gentlemen, like honorable schoolboys.

Despite von Lindeiner-Wildau's attempts to create tolerable living conditions, Stalag Luft III was a place that reeked of hopelessness. If one were to come upon it on an evening blurred by rain and mist, its helmeted guards leading fierce German Shepherds in the glow of floodlights that swirled and probed, its bleakness would be overpowering.

As Alaimo discovered, there are worlds within worlds. An Escape Committee led by Bushell (code name "Big X") had authorized the construction of three tunnels—Tom, Dick, and Harry—30 feet below the sandy ground, each intended to run hundreds of yards into the forest beyond the perimeter.

Before Bushell arrived, escape had been a haphazard undertaking. Prisoners in clothing crudely altered to resemble German uniforms marched out the gate at the change of the guard; they clung to refuse carts and "honey" trucks moving in and out of the camp; or they headed for delousing showers in the custody of bogus guards and ran off.

The Geneva Convention specified that escape was a legitimate, even appropriate, response to confinement in a POW camp. Punishment was typically light: two weeks of bread and water in the "Cooler" (*Kittchen*), or punishment block.

The exception, seemingly ripped from the Iliad, began around the time of Alaimo's arrival. A Royal Air Force lieutenant named Eric Williams convinced the Escape Committee that he'd found a way to build a tunnel much closer to the camp's perimeter—a wooden horse.

The Germans considered exercise an appropriate way for POWs to work off excess energy and frustration. Sure enough, Williams and his conspirators were granted permission to construct a vaulting horse out of scrap lumber. A cadre of carpenters designed a secret cavity in the horse's belly large enough to conceal Williams and another tunneler.

Each day, Williams's fellow Kriegies, straining to appear nonchalant under the 300 additional pounds they were lugging, carried the horse to the same spot on the exercise field. While men hurtled overhead, Williams, Michael Codner, and a Royal Air Force officer named Oliver Philpot descended through a trap door and commenced digging. At day's end, the excavated sand was carried off in sacks hung inside the horse and the tunnel's entrance was carefully concealed until the next exercise shift.

In October 1943, the three men escaped through a 100-foot tunnel. Armed with fake identity papers and a compass manufactured using a section of a gramophone record, they successfully made their way to Sweden.

Bushell's Great Escape was more complex, bold and fraught with risk. Not two, not two dozen, but 200 POWs would break out. They would have new identities and cover stories, masterfully forged travel documents, tailored civilian clothing, maps, compasses, and even high-energy meals. They would be familiar with train schedules and border crossings and would be provided with contacts in the Resistance.

Bushell and his committee assembled teams ("departments") of engineers and former coal miners, printers, tailors, graphic artists, and other craftsmen—a beehive of intricate activity operating full tilt yet in total secrecy. He recruited "Penguins," volunteers who strolled and scuffled around the camp surreptitiously dumping telltale yellow sand from sacks hidden in their trousers. An estimated 8,800 pounds of sand were disposed of each day.

Hundreds of men who had no desire to participate in a breakout gave up the bed boards supporting the paper and wood-shaving mattresses in their bunks, lumber used to shore up the loose sand through which the dig progressed.[8]

Other volunteers, "Stooges," kept track of every move the Germans made using elaborate alert systems to warn their fellow conspirators that danger was eminent. The trap doors into the tunnels were masterpieces of deception. The Germans had built the barracks on stilts to preclude escapees burrowing through the floors; the tunnelers instead cut through concrete foundations sunk into the ground to support washrooms and cooking stoves.

In block 123, Tom's trap was a thin, wire-handled slab that replaced the original concrete. In block 122, Dick's entrance was under water, a waterproof panel concealed in a drain beneath the washroom. In block 104, Harry descended from a section of tile beneath the stove. Each tunnel was assigned a *Trapfuhrer*, an overseer armed with cement, ash, dust, and whatever else it took to render the entrances invisible.

One of the men working on the escape was an American named George Harsh, who'd enlisted in the Royal Canadian Air Force. Harsh was a Southerner, a scion of a wealthy Atlanta family who in what seemed like another life had been convicted in what the newspapers labeled "a thrill killing."

In 1929 Harsh, one of a group bored teenagers, had attempted a "perfect crime." During the course of a botched robbery, two men were shot and killed. Harsh, the triggerman, was convicted despite an elaborate defense[9] underwritten by his family's fortune. Spared the gallows, he drew life on a chain gang. He eventually became a prison trusty and, as Harsh tells it in his biography, *Lonesome Road*, drew the approbation of the parole board after he'd saved another prisoner's life in a medical emergency.

---

[8] The size of the bed boards effectively defined the dimensions of the tunnel as roughly 2 square feet.

[9] Six psychiatrists testified that Harsh suffered from "psychological responsibility and hereditary taints."

After serving twelve years, Harsh was paroled. In 1940 he turned up in Canada. Commissioned as a RCAF pilot, he flew missions over Europe, where he was shot down, captured, and imprisoned a second time.

Life is as unpredictable as a coin toss. Thirty years later, US District Court judge Anthony A. Alaimo would spend years reforming the same brutal prison system George Harsh had passed through.

Work on the escape tunnels progressed into the fall of 1943. The tunnels were so deep that diggers had to be supplied with fresh air. Air pumps were developed using stitched-together kit bags, wire hoops, tar paper seals, and valves made of leather. The devices were set in wooden frames resembling a child's cradle. An operator sat in a sliding wooden seat and pushed and pulled on a handle that drew air from a line running to the surface, forcing it out through a line running the length of the tunnel. The air lines were constructed joining together a series of empty powdered milk cans.

Alaimo was "small fry" compared to the higher-ranking and endlessly ingenious plotters, but he was eager to join and immediately accepted. "It was organized to a 'T,'" he recalled. "Whenever a ferret got close, someone pulled a string tied to a can filled with pebbles to alert the diggers to stop. We knew where every ferret in the compound was at any time. My job was the air pump. I sat in that bucket seat and pushed that thing back and forth four hours a day for three months."

Alaimo's pump was housed in a hollowed-out section near the bottom of the tunnel's entrance. By then the engineering was so sophisticated that the tunnel was illuminated by pirated electric bulbs, run by a cable tapped into the camp's power lines. Wooden trolleys shuttled diggers and excavated earth back and forth on tracks set in the tunnel floor. There were workshops and turnaround stations in the tunnel designated "Piccadilly Circus" and "Leicester Square."

Time, however, was not on Alaimo's side. The numbers of downed Yanks had begun to overwhelm the prison camp. Russian slave laborers cleared the forest and began building a separate compound to house the bloated ranks of Americans.

Roger Bushell ordered a speedier pace to the construction of Tom so that the Americans would have a fair chance to escape. Unfortunately, the activity tipped off the Germans. Ferrets began raiding the barracks. An hours-long search of block 123 turned up nothing. In the next phase of what had become a chess game, the Germans sent in horse-drawn wagons to crisscross the compound, hoping the weight would collapse the tunnel they knew lay somewhere below.

Tom was approaching the forest's edge when workmen began clearing a stand of trees directly above the spot the tunnel was to emerge. Was another barracks being constructed? Another gambit to counter the plotters? Tom would have to be extended dramatically. It was not to be.

In September 1943, during another raid on block 123, a ferret dropped his probe near the section of floor that concealed the tunnel's entrance. As the histories record it, he reached down and noticed the joint that marked the edge of the trap door. Sergeant Major Hermann Glemnitz, the Stalag's stone-faced chief of ferrets, is remembered smiling broadly at the discovery. An explosives expert was brought in to collapse the tunnel. Tom was so heavily reinforced that the backwash from the dynamite required to destroy it blew the chimney off block 123. Checkmate.

A month later, the Americans were marched off to the new South Compound, Alaimo among them. They played no further role in the Great Escape.

Five months later, on March 24, 1944, Roger Bushell's dream of mass escape became reality. On a moonless night, seventy-six men scrambled out of the tunnel designated Harry into freezing cold and immortality. Bushell, a "French businessman" in overcoat and grey suit, was among the first out.

Tactically, the escape was a disaster. Three men—Norwegians Per Bergsland and Jens Muller and Dutch pilot Bram van der Stok—made their way to freedom. The others were recaptured in a manhunt involving thousands of German police, soldiers, and security men.

As Bushell had hoped, the Great Escape did outrage and infuriate the Nazis. Hitler personally ordered the Gestapo to execute fifty escapees. The men were escorted from police stations and holding pens, then killed by a bullet to the back of the head. The Gestapo recorded the murders as actions taken against men caught "trying to escape." Roger Bushell was executed on March 29, 1944. Ironically, the German commandant Von Lindeiner-Wildau was later courtmartialed.[10]

The killings would later be prosecuted at the Nuremberg Trials.

In 1963, Steve McQueen starred in Hollywood's version of the *Great Escape*, a reenactment that remains one of the most popular films of all time.

The live-and-let-live atmosphere of the early years gave way to threats and punishment. "That first morning they hauled us out to the Parade Grounds," Alaimo recalled. "They ordered us to stand out there all day long. A bunch of 'goons'[11] with submachine guns strapped to their shoulders kept watch over us. They warned us if it happened again, everybody would be shot."

D-Day, June 6, 1944, came and went, sparking hope and then the realization that there would be no quick end to the war. Like the pent-up young men around him, Alaimo grew more frustrated and inevitably reckless, ever more determined to escape. Living month after month in close quarters, constantly cold or hungry, deprived of

---

[10] The next commandant of Stalag Luft III, *Oberst* (Colonel) Braune, permitted the POWs to erect a memorial to their comrades.

[11] "Goons" is the term the POWs assigned to their German guards.

even the sight of a flesh-and-blood woman brought out the worst in men. Idiosyncrasies were exaggerated until they became intolerable. Tempers flared; vicious fights broke out.

"I grew more committed to escaping," Alaimo remembered.

POW George Harsh captured the feeling precisely in his autobiography: "Not the least of the ordeals of prison life is the ordeal of never being able to be alone, of never being out of the sight and hearing of other human beings."

Alaimo would pace the circumference of the camp, restless. He'd stare at the unfeeling stars, or through the rusting barbed wire into the forest, visualizing the towns and rivers, the clashing armies, the devastated cities, and the great expanse of ocean that separated him from everything he longed for. On one of these walks into the depths of winter, along a narrow exercise track cut through the drifting snow, he encountered Sergeant-Major Glemnitz, the escapees' chief antagonist, walking toward him.

"The question became, 'Who's going to step aside?'" Alaimo recalled. "I didn't move. I told him, 'You're a sergeant, I'm an officer. Out of my way.'"

Glemnitz listened in astonishment, then motioned, "Come with me."

He marched Alaimo to the commandant's office in the *Vorlager* (German compound). Von Lineinder-Wildau was facing serious problems of his own. "He was very gentle, telling me I should show more respect," Alaimo recalled. "I realized it had been a totally ridiculous thing for me to do."

The Americans formed an escape committee of their own. Colonel Charles Goodrich, the ranking officer,[12] had to sign off on any breakout attempts by the men under his command.

Alaimo would remember Goodrich as "the finest solider I've ever met." He was that rarest of officers, a man who inspired loyalty and

---

[12] Goodrich's B-25 bomber had been shot down over North Africa in 1942.

discipline by personal example. He shared every hardship with his men, even at those moments when his rank would have afforded him privileges.

"He would have weekly inspections in the camp," Alaimo remembered. "Some officer would go through our rooms to see that everybody was keeping them clean. We pressed our uniforms with irons made of sardine cans. At Colonel Goodrich's insistence we tried to keep ourselves looking pretty neat."

Another of the intriguing characters in Stalag Luft III was intelligence agent Jerry Sage, a member of William "Wild Bill" Donovan's swashbuckling Office of Strategic Services. In the postwar years, the OSS would evolve into the CIA. Sage had been captured in North Africa and managed to pass himself off as a downed airman. In Stalag Luft III he went on to hatch innumerable, occasionally half-baked, escape schemes. In the *Great Escape*, Steve McQueen's indomitable character Captain Virgil Hilts is based, in part, on the real-life Sage.

Alaimo recalled being one of twenty POWs who took part in one of Jerry Sage's more hair-raising escape attempts. "There were cables carrying current for the electric lights in and around the compound. Sage planned to construct ladders that would get us over the fences at night. The idea was to throw a wire across the cables and short out all the lights. Of course, we had to practice jumping because the fences were more than 10-feet high. We did all kinds of practices beforehand. Two days before the escape was supposed to be run, there was an Allied air raid or some damned thing.

"It became immediately clear that there was a backup circuit and the escape was called off. Had we gone ahead, not only would we have been electrocuted, we would have been electrocuted with the lights on."

Not long afterward, Alaimo and buddy "Ace" Langberg, from Jensen Beach, Florida, went before the committee with a plan of their own. It's no understatement to suggest that it lacked the sophistication of the British schemes.

"They had gates for provision wagons to come in," Alaimo remembered. "One particular gate was within 10 or 15 feet of a guard tower which faced the parade grounds where, twice a day, we were counted. These gates were always locked, but looking at them, I noticed deep ruts where the wagon wheels had cut into the ground. I thought we could squeeze under."

Goodrich signed off on the escape, which was set to take place during the 4:00 P.M. *Appell*. The distraction Alaimo thought up to draw the attention of the guard in the watchtower came straight from his Jamestown childhood, a mass snowball fight on the parade grounds.

At the appointed time, Alaimo and Langberg, who'd been hiding during the roll call, took off for the fence. "We're were supposed to round this one barracks about 30 feet from the barbed wire and walk along the warning rail," Alaimo recalled. "There were two signals to be given. When we left the barracks, a lieutenant colonel named Bud Clark was assigned to signal us 'On' or 'Off.' Clark gave us the 'On' signal. The next one was supposed to be at a corner of the barracks. If it was 'On,' another lieutenant colonel was supposed to be standing; if 'Off,' he'd be crouching. My job was to check on him as we came around. Hell, I just had a split second to have a look see."

Alaimo saw a group of prisoners milling around the barracks— no one crouching. And here, one of the army's familiar snafus— "Situation normal, all fouled up"—unfolded. Unbeknownst to him, the escape had been called off. Goons were patrolling outside the fence. There was no snowball fight—and, unfortunately, no signal.

Alaimo stepped over the warning rail into no-man's land, Langberg trailing a few yards behind. He wriggled under the first gate, realizing to his dismay that the space "was not as generous" as he'd estimated. He scuttled to the second and, as he tried to squeeze under, shook the fence.

The tower guard whirled. He trained his machinegun on Alaimo, now scrambling to his feet, throwing his arms in the air and shouting, *Kamerad! Kamerad!*

Without a word, the man squeezed the trigger.

# Chapter 5

"I'd be delighted boys!"
—Josephine Baker to Tony Alaimo

If it is true that in moments of dire jeopardy one's life flashes before one's eyes, if neurons deep within our brains unload their caches of prized memory, then the panorama of Anthony Alaimo's existence as he stared into the muzzle of the guard's machine gun, as he watched with perfect clarity the German's fingers squeezing the trigger, would have flared briefly, yet exceedingly bright.

In Ohio, Alaimo had met a girl, dazzling and high-spirited, whose wit, charm, and beauty had stirred him deeply. He'd graduated from college—Santa Alaimo's impossible prayers had been answered—and was serving his country honorably, risking all he had struggled to achieve. And he had, however briefly, tasted the sweetness of life and sensed its seemingly irreconcilable injustices.

A year earlier, on the 322nd Bomb Group's flyover to Europe, Alaimo's squadron had crossed the Sahara, swept across the snow-covered peaks of the Atlas Mountains, and bivouacked in Morocco to await orders. War to the young aviators was still a romantic illusion and Marrakech a dreamscape, its boulevards lined with orange blossoms, rose bougainvillea, and every variety of exotic flower. Alaimo, a man who'd never ventured beyond the cornfields of Ohio, found himself exploring the mysterious confines of the Casbah. The squadron had been billeted at La Mamounia, an Art Deco and Moorish jewel, surrounded by ocher walls and luxuriant gardens. It was a retreat favored by Winston Churchill and Franklin Delano Roosevelt and, half a century later, Ronald Reagan.

One morning Alaimo glimpsed General George Patton, decked out in his riding boots and pearl-handled revolvers, striding through the hotel's marbled dining room. It was January 1943, and the battle of the Kasserine Pass was raging. "Patton's 1st Armored Division was getting the hell kicked out of it by Rommel," Alaimo recalled. "I wondered what he was doing at the hotel. Of course, I'd never know."

Another night at the Mamounia, Alaimo and fellow aviator Norman Harvey were mesmerized by the appearance of "a beautiful, striking black woman in a white robe and turban. We didn't know who she was," Alaimo recalled. "But she was with El Gloui, the mayor of Marrakech. Norman and I decided to ask her to sign our short snorters." Short snorters were WW II collections of foreign banknotes that reflected a GI's passage from country to country as the war progressed. The souvenirs were especially prized if they bore signatures, dates or other inscriptions.

"I went over to her and said in my broken French, 'Would you please sign this?' She gave us a big flashy smile and answered in English, 'I'd be delighted boys!' I didn't know she was Josephine Baker until I saw her signature." Alaimo had no inkling that Baker, a star who'd enthralled legions of men—Ernest Hemingway and F. Scott Fitzgerald among them—was working undercover for the French Resistance. Sixty-five years later, Alaimo confided in delight, "You know, I still have that bill!"

So strong was the memory of those halcyon days in Marrakech that, decades later, Judge Alaimo and his wife Jeanne returned to La Mamounia. They stayed in the same room "Second Lieutenant" Alaimo had enjoyed, strolled the same perfumed garden paths, and marveled at the warble of songbirds Alaimo had listened to once upon a time....

Anthony Alaimo graduated from Jamestown High in 1936. He'd done well in his studies, pursued his saxophone playing, and mastered sufficient French to get by conversationally—though, barring a trip to Quebec, that skill didn't seemed likely to be put to much use.

People stayed close to home in those years. Like his brothers and sisters, Tony was fiercely loyal to his parents.

Young Tony had an eye for the girls but scant resources. The Italian Methodist Church was not fertile ground for adolescent romance. "We had some pretty girls in the band," he recalled wistfully, "but I had no money to go out on dates and spent a lot of time at home."

Philip, true to his word, had opened a barbershop on Main Street in Ada, Ohio. The shop, located above the college bookstore, generated sufficient money to cover his tuition and expenses. He'd encouraged Tony to follow his lead, and his dutiful kid brother enrolled at Ohio Northern University.

The day Tony set off for college, Philip showed up in a Model T Ford he'd bought for $30—it had a crank starter that could kick like a mule. Santa cried profusely. Sam gave his second son an embrace Tony remembered as "austere." And then they were off.

Tony replaced Philip, who'd graduated a few years before, as Ohio Northern's favorite barber. Even as a seventeen-year-old freshman, a proverbial fish out of water, Alaimo exuded confidence tempered by his charm, churchboy humility, and humor. He'd playfully tease the faculty members who frequented his shop ("My tuition is paying your salary!"), or grump when a girlfriend's father declined his services. He wanted to be a part of things. He was a joiner, a mixer who sang in the school's Methodist choir. Beneath the still surface of Alaimo's outward demeanor lurked a fierce competitor eager to test himself in the world.

"My brother had given me confidence in that I knew about the town and the college," he recalled. "I knew who the important people were and so on, which gave me an advantage. One of the faculty members, Dean Potter, became a mentor to me, really a father figure. Another part of it was my conversion to Protestantism. That experience, my interaction with a higher level of people in Jamestown, gave me confidence I otherwise might not have had."

Alaimo's wardrobe was "quite limited," though he later pointed out, "Everybody's was in those days." As befitted a barber, he was well groomed and meticulously dressed with a strong, if malnourished, fashion sense. He had a secret advantage over his non-Sicilian classmates: he shipped his soiled laundry all the way to Jamestown, where his mother lovingly washed, starched, and ironed it.

Soon enough Alaimo met a girl—a blonde, vivacious highschooler with a personality as bright and engaging as her startling good looks. He first laid eyes on her as she sat with a group of friends in a booth at Balish's, a local ice cream parlor. Students frequently gathered there for sodas and fountain drinks, their schoolbooks scattered on the marble tabletops.

"Well, she was cute you know," Alaimo recalled, laughing and sounding once again like that long-lost seventeen-year-old. "I guess you could say she stood out in a crowd."

Even in high school, Jeanne Loy was more than a match for any college boy. Her father, Frank Loy, was a dean at Ohio Northern. He and Jeanne's mother, Elsie Geer Loy, had raised an independent and strong-willed young woman. Jeanne's best friend was Florence Williams, another free spirit, whose father Robert Owen Williams was the university president.

"We were inseparable," Jeanne recalled. "And we did some crazy things back then. Once, Flo and I got out on the highway and hitchhiked all the way to Fort Wayne across the border in Indiana, and, you know, came back home. Don't ask me why. We must have been fifteen or sixteen years old. I don't think either of our parents ever knew we did that."

There was no shortage of young men—both townies and college students—eager to date the dazzling Jeanne and Flo. It was clear that the overwhelming majority of the college boys would move on to jobs and careers in other places after graduation, and it was equally evident that local suitors represented stability, familiarity—no small attributes even in the tail end of the Depression.

Jeanne's father was an academic dean, but he also cultivated hundreds of acres of farmland.

For Jeanne, that first encounter with Tony at the sweet shop did not go unnoticed. "He kind of looked different from the other kids on campus," Jeanne recalled during a 2007 interview. "Definitely Italian-looking, with this pompadour and pouty look. He was adorable. All the girls thought so!"

To a visitor's surprise, Jeanne pulled out a daily journal, blurred by rain and too many years' storage in an attic. "This is from the first day I met him," she said. She read an entry dated January 15, 1938: "We went to Balish's ice cream parlor tonight after some meeting or other. I met the cutest boy. He's in college. His name is Tony."

The two became friends and, given the tenor of the times, Jeanne's popularity, and Tony's overriding commitment to his studies, they began dating very casually. "I felt that I shouldn't be serious about anybody," Alaimo recalled. "I hadn't finished school and I had an obligation to my parents which I felt strongly."

The two took long bike rides together and attended school dances, where Tony attempted to keep up with Jeanne's adept jitterbug. "I'd never gone to a dance in my life before I went to college," Alaimo recalled. Jeanne was also a terrific ping-pong player and Tony was no slouch. "She was maddening," he said. "She could always hit the ball back." They played mixed doubles in Ohio's Mid-Atlantic League tournaments, piling up a string of victories.

Tony had had his share of fights in Jamestown. At Ohio Northern, he joined the Boxing Club and honed his pugilistic skills, at the time scarcely more advanced than his dancing abilities. He was drawn to the excitement and the toe-to-toe challenge of the "sweet science." In those days, Alaimo stood 5-foot-8 and weighed 147 pounds, a muscular welterweight with more slugging ability than real skills.

He was never afraid of taking a punch if it allowed him to set up his best weapon, a right cross that could stagger his opponent. Beneath the pillowy 16-ounce gloves, his hands—those oversized appendages—packed a tremendous wallop. He boxed for three years in college, each year signing up for the local Golden Gloves competition. The first year he was outpointed. During the following years he advanced to second rounds in Lima, Ohio. He won both times but decided not to move on. "That would have required transportation, all kinds of stuff," he said later "Those were different days."

In Jamestown, Santa had no idea what her son was up to. She imagined Ohio Northern a safe and secure Methodist bubble. Had she known her Tony was in a boxing ring pounding heads with unsavory, even unchristian characters, she would have hopped on the next train headed west. Jeanne Loy, on the other hand, lustily cheered Tony on.

When asked what attracted her to Tony, Jeanne's simple reply was, "He was really, really smart." She continued, "Believe me, it was easy to tell if a guy was dumb. Tony had good grades, a good record. He came to college when he was barely seventeen, and he'd read an awful lot of good books, classics."

Jeanne's mother Elsie first met Tony at an estate sale—Ada was a very small town—and took to him immediately.

### "So I Went to Law School"

The college years, as they always do, passed quickly. Tony and Jeanne continued to date, but not frequently or exclusively. Alaimo had already begun a flirtation with the enduring love of his life. It began, as romances often do, by coincidence. After graduation Alaimo stayed on in Ada, working in his barber shop. His decision to attend law school was largely one of convenience. "When I first started school," he recalled, "I was able to get all my classes in the morning and run the shop in the afternoon. The same thing was possible with the law school. So I went to law school. It's funny how things happen."

He sensed that whatever dreams he might be pursuing, whatever future he might plan or hope for, were, for the moment, illusory. In Europe, the dogs of war were being unleashed. In September 1939, Hitler invaded Poland, triggering the Second World War. In the spring of 1940, 350,000 desperate British, French, and Belgian troops were trapped at Dunkirk. Paris was being overrun; the Battle of Britain was unfolding over the English Channel. The United States was inevitably being drawn into the conflict.

Anthony Alaimo did not do well in his first attempt at law school. He candidly reflected, "I didn't work. You know, you have to at least read the cases." In the year following college, Alaimo had lost focus. Perhaps he needed to escape the rigors of academia. Perhaps he was tired of being broke. Whatever the reason, he departed Ada and moved to Detroit to await the draft board's inevitable call-up.

Alaimo's sisters, Irene and Sandy, were living there with their husbands, Sam Archie and Joe Ceci. Tony moved in with Sandy and Joe. Ceci got him a job at Timken-Detroit foundry. In summer 1941, wages were good and the work mindless, repetitive—a respite from the rigors of pursuing perfection.

That fall, Alaimo would borrow Irene's car, a spiffy two-tone Buick, and drive the 125 miles to Ada to take Jeanne Loy out on a date. He could afford it now. Once, with "her parents' frowning consent," Jeanne rode back to Detroit with him to visit one of her girlfriends, Louise Peterson, who was living there. "We had a wonderful time," Alaimo remembered.

On Sunday, December 7, Tony was bowling with a group of friends when news of the attack on Pearl Harbor flashed over the radio.

# Chapter 6

The next morning, December 8, Tony Alaimo borrowed Joe Ceci's car and drove to Selfridge Field near Mount Clemens, Michigan, to enlist in the US Army Air Corps.[1] When he arrived, he found eighteen prospective volunteers ahead of him in line, all college graduates determined to do their part in the looming conflict.

The Japanese attacks stirred deep emotions in Alaimo. "I doubt I would have enlisted without the war," he later said. "Now, I had to get into the fight. I had certain feelings of loyalty to our country and people. Later, I realized there were suspicions about Italians' loyalty"—suspicions Anthony Alaimo was eager to dispel.

He sailed through his physical and placement exams. Two weeks later, a letter arrived ordering him to report to San Antonio for pilot training. "It was a desired placement," he later recalled. "Just the excitement of flying. The girls all were drawn to pilots. Of course, I had no clue as to what it was really like."

He rode first class all the way to Texas in a Pullman coach. Along with a thousand other cadets, he found himself back in a classroom—immersed in meteorology, communications (the long and short sequences of Morse code would become second nature), navigation, armaments, and, for combat aircrews, the identification of Axis aircraft—forgetting for the moment that he'd never even been on an airplane.

Cadet Alaimo was so green that when an upperclassman shouted, "Fall out, there on the floor, dodo," he dropped to his knees.

Alaimo first went aloft with an instructor in a 200-horsepower, single-engine Fairchild PT-19. He soloed at Pine Bluff, Arkansas,

---

[1] The United States Air Force would not become a separate branch of the military until September 1947.

where he had his primary training: "You go up and you go around the field, you know, and then you come in and land."

He loved the challenge and exhilaration of flying—the freedom, the hushed beauty of pillowed clouds, the complex and confusing world below his wings reduced to a series of checkerboard squares. Railroads, the "Iron Track," provided direction. At night and in foul weather, he winged his way home on radio beams.

Alaimo recognized that the true test still lay ahead. "I was competing with the other air cadets on marksmanship and cross-country flying," he recalled. "But I knew, soon enough, I'd be competing with the enemy."

On September 6, 1942, Anthony A. Alaimo earned his wings and was commissioned a second lieutenant in the Army of the United States. "Of course we were all following the course of the war," he recalled. "It was right around this time that Rommel was beating the hell out of the British. We were eager to get in."

Alaimo drew a week's leave and flew home on a commercial airliner, another first. He went through a second ("medium") phase of training at Sherman, Texas, then moved on to advanced training at Parker Field in Victoria, on the Gulf of Mexico between Galveston and Corpus Christi. Texans opened their hearts to the young warriors. "They would give us the keys to their beach homes to come and spend the weekend there," he recalled. "It was a marvelous experience."

On weekdays, Alaimo flew the 550-horsepower AT-6, a sleek, nimble aircraft with retractable landing gear.

"We had dogfights," he recalled, laughing at the memories. "We'd go up and play in the clouds, maneuver and all that kind of stuff. We were kids. We'd go and tap wings, dive down, bounce over fences and fly under bridges. It was just crazy. One time we got caught and they made us run around the air field hauling our parachutes."

*The Widowmaker*

Alaimo wanted to be a fighter pilot, but the Army, in its infinite wisdom, had other plans. Many levels above Alaimo's rank, General Henry Harley "Hap" Arnold, a World War I aviator, commanded the renamed US Army Air Forces (USAAF). Arnold and his 8th Air Force commanders, Major General Carl "Tooey" Spaatz and Brigadier General Ira Eaker, were eager to put their new theories on "strategic" bombing to the test.[2]

In simple terms, Arnold was convinced that massive, "round-the-clock" bombing would bring Germany to its knees, making a land invasion (D-Day) unnecessary. The Royal Air Force (RAF), under Air Marshall Arthur "Bomber" Harris, had seized the night, indiscriminately fire-bombing ("city-busting") civilian population centers like Cologne and Dresden—bloody payback for the German blitz on London.

The 8th Air Force would cripple the enemy using precision daytime bombing. This would prove a murderously flawed strategy in the early years of the war due to inclement weather, poorly trained crews, inadequate fighter support, overwhelming German air defenses, and the furious waves of Messerschmitt and Focke-Wolfe fighters that swarmed up to blast the lumbering bombers out of the sky.

Second Lieutenant Alaimo reported to MacDill Field outside Tampa, then to Drane Field (Lakeland Army Air Field). The Army Corps of Engineers had improved Drane's three runways and constructed a training facility for bomber and P-51 Mustang crews. "We lived in tents, slept on canvas cots out in the middle of a sandy

---

[2] "In modern warfare there are two main types of aerial bombing—strategic and tactical. "Strategic bombing," as defined by the Air Force, "strikes at the economy of their enemy; it attempts to cripple its war potential by blows at industrial production, civilian morale, and communications. Tactical bombardment is immediate air support of movements of air land or sea forces.'" (Donald Miller, *Masters of the Air*, 31).

field," Alaimo recalled. "I don't know how they maintained those planes with all that damned sand."

The 322nd Bomb Group was undergoing training on the Martin B-26 medium bomber. Officially, the B-26 was known as the "Marauder." In the weeks ahead, Alaimo would come to know it intimately as the "Widowmaker," "Flying Coffin" and "Flying Prostitute." As the jokes going around the base had it, the stubby-winged craft had "no visible means of support."

In earlier training sessions, fifteen B-26 bombers had crashed in thirty days. Owing to the graveyard humor of the military, the catchphrase became "One a day in Tampa Bay!"

Ten hours of flight time on the difficult, often unpredictable aircraft qualified an airman as "First Pilot." The designation had less to do with the learning curve than with the military's urgency to propel the young aviators into combat.

"We were just not trained properly," Alaimo recalled, the amusement so typical of his reminiscences vanishing. "We had bombardiers who hadn't dropped a bomb, navigators who hadn't navigated anyplace. Our bombing runs consisted of dumping sacks of flour on the Gandy Bridge between St. Petersburg and Tampa. Later on, honest to goodness, our navigators really misdirected us. That's how it was in the early days. Good people paid the price."

On January 1, 1943, Alaimo's element of the 322nd Bomb Group took delivery of twenty-four new Marauders and departed Florida for the European Theater of Operations. Each pilot had to sign for his plane, making him personally responsible for a difficult-to-control $425,000 albatross. Tony remembered "wondering what in the world was I going to do if I crashed."

War was at hand, and with it unimagined and terrible consequence; but luck or destiny had decreed that the passage of these American boys, these twentieth-century Huck Finns, would be memorable. A picaresque journey awaited, filled with unexpected twists and fantastical adventures.

"The whole trip was a tour director's dream," Alaimo recalled. "War was farthest from our minds. Most of us had never been more than 100 miles from our home towns."

They flew what military planners had designated the Southern Route, a wildly indirect passage with a series of refueling and rest stops in ever more exotic places. The first leg began with a departure from Morrison Field, in West Palm Beach, for Borinquen Field in Puerto Rico.

"We immediately went through a very violent front that depleted our fuel supplies," Alaimo remembered. "We had to make a forced landing at a Pan American airfield outside Ciudad Trujillo in Santo Domingo. Unfortunately, the runways were very short and our commanders were dubious about being able to take off again. So we were ordered to strip all the planes of their armament. (The B-26 carried a dozen .50-caliber machine guns that, loaded with incendiary shells, could literally burn up anything on the ground.) The crews were sent to Puerto Rico on the Air Transport Command's DC-3s. The pilots stayed behind to ferry the planes over."

The next scheduled stopover, Trinidad, was less arduous. Alaimo and his buddies spent two days among the "mountain pools and tropical waterfalls." Next came a southeasterly passage to South America—Atkinson Field near Georgetown in British Guyana. "Unfortunately, we were vectored into Venezuela," Alaimo said. "We missed our target by a 100 miles." It was a telling mistake that the men, in their excitement, glossed over.

From Guyana, the crew made their way to the port of Belem in Brazil. Located on the Para River, a branch of the Amazon, Belem had once been home to rubber barons who'd amassed fortunes during the nineteenth-century boom. It retained the faded trappings of past glory. One of the squadron pilots borrowed a Tiger Moth (de Havilland DH82 trainer) from the Brazilian Air Force for some sightseeing. He got caught in a thunderstorm and had to make an emergency landing in triple-canopy jungle. "It took three days to get him back," Alaimo later said. "And he was just a mile and a half from the road."

For the adventurous, Belem's enticements included horsemeat steaks and a visit to Madame Zeze's famed bordello. Over the years, when the inevitable question—"Did you try it?"—was put to Alaimo, he always answered, "The line was too long!"

"From Belem, flying over the Amazon estuary at 2,500 feet, you could see the color of the water some 50 miles out into the ocean," Alaimo remembered. "From there we went to Natal, the easternmost point of Brazil, to refuel, then jumped across the Atlantic to Wideawake Airfield [a RAF base], on Ascension Island. We encountered 'wide-awake birds,' gulls that would congregate on the end of the runway. You had to radio ahead to have them shooed off."

They flew 1,220 miles northeasterly to Accra on the Gold Coast, now Ghana. The beautiful beaches glimpsed from on high gave way to the stench and misery of abject poverty on the ground. This was equatorial Africa—the cradle of mankind—but the crews, treated to hot meals in the mess halls, an outdoor movie theater, and screened-in barracks, might have imagined themselves descending into a serene and civilized planet. The illusion would soon be shattered.

The men moved on to Bathurst (now Banjul) in West Africa, at the mouth of Gambia River. Dakar, Senegal, was the next stop on their itinerary, but the city was in German hands. A command decision was made and the warbirds flew north over the desert to Morocco. Alaimo and his buddies spent three glorious weeks in Marrakech, living royally at La Mamounia—they were, after all, officers and gentlemen. They moved on to Port Lyautey, north of Rabat, where a few months earlier in November 1942 troops from Operation Torch, the British-American invasion of North Africa, had stormed ashore. The squadrons' bombardiers surrendered their flour sacks and now practiced bomb runs using crates of Moroccan oranges.

*"Hell, we're going to France!"*

The squadrons crossed into the United Kingdom at Torquay, barely escaping disaster when a navigational error vectored them into Brest in occupied France. One of the pilots shouted, "Hell, we're going to France boys!" barely averting disaster. "This was the second time the lead navigator had made a bad mistake," Alaimo recalled. "It was terrible."

The Marauders touched down in Bury St Edmunds in March 1943. The airbase, one of dozens sprouting up like weeds in the English countryside, was in Suffolk, about 40 miles northeast of London. The town's single point of historical interest was a ruined abbey, a shrine to the Saxon king Saint Edmund, who was slaughtered by the Danes in A.D. 869.

England was a fortress nation. Alaimo remembered eerie ranks of barrage balloons floating on the horizon like silent sentinels. The balloons, tethered to the ground by thick metal cables, were used to protect cities, industrial complexes, and ports against low-flying German dive bombers, shredding their wings as they hurtled toward their targets.

Alaimo and his fellow pilots struggled to master the new low-level bombing tactics. The men were ordered, essentially, to execute reckless stunts that would have washed them out of flight school. Alaimo practiced pulling his shrieking, shuddering ship into violent spins and twists.

"For thirty days we trained," he recalled. "The theory being you couldn't miss if you flew treetop level with these damn planes, these big planes. And what you did, you flew what they called evasive flying, which meant that you'd pull the plane up and push it down and skid it to prevent being tracked. It was exhausting to fly this way, but the theory was you'd come in under radar, go up maybe 500 feet, bomb, and come back. Unfortunately, it didn't work out."

On May 14, 1943, Alaimo's squadron mate Jack Howell was killed in the initial attack on the Ijmuiden power plant. Three days later, on his first and final mission, Anthony Alaimo's Marauder crashed in flames into the North Sea.

# Chapter 7

"And the damned thing jammed."
—Anthony Alaimo

Alaimo and Langberg were marched off to solitary confinement in the Cooler. They spent two weeks living on black bread ("very nutritious," according to Alaimo) and water. Sixty-three years later Alaimo, nearing ninety, still tries to unravel his skein of good fortune—and, perhaps, to come to terms with a much deeper question: "Why was I spared when so many others, better men than I, died?"

Was it just luck? The German Maschinegerwehr 34 and 42 weapons did have a tendency to jam when not well maintained. The suggestion that Santa Alaimo's prayers had saved her son's life yet again is pure speculation. In any event, Tony was more outraged by the snafu than grateful for his life.

The escape attempt had taken place sometime in December 1944. At the time, the Battle of Bastogne was raging in the Ardennes. Hitler's desperate gambit was threatening to split and encircle the stalled British and American armies, seize vital supply facilities at Antwerp, and snatch an impossible victory from the jaws of defeat. This was the last news a thoroughly miserable Alaimo wanted to hear. D-Day had come and gone, the Russians were on the move, and POW hopes had soared only, once again, to be dashed. The war seemed no closer to an end.

Alaimo later recalled a memorable conversation with one of the German "goons" guarding the Cooler. "A sergeant came in and told us the Germans 'had taken 20,000 prisoners.' They were 'going to push the Allies into the sea.' Then they were 'going to take care of the Russians.' In the course of this, we got to talking. After a while, I asked him why he had become a Nazi and he told me, 'You know, when I was coming along right after World War I we were in terrible shape. My wife died in childbirth of malnutrition. When Hitler appeared on the scene, I had a job. Eventually, I was able to buy a car. The state provided my family with medical services. Life was better.' That's an answer that's pretty hard to refute."

Alaimo's spirits sunk further when another POW told him the debacle under the fence had blown his chances of having another attempt approved by the Escape Committee ("You guys have had it!"). He was so upset that upon his release from the Cooler he wrote Colonel Goodrich, demanding a redress of his grievances.

"Goodrich had the wrong information," Alaimo later said. "I asked for a hearing because I felt what was happening was unjust. Well, the witnesses testified that the lieutenant colonel (charged with green-lighting their final dash under the fence) didn't do what he was supposed to do. In the end, Colonel Goodrich absolved us and chewed that guy out to a fare-thee-well."

In retrospect, it was the classic Alaimo approach: bring to bear unimpeachable evidence, expertise (in this instance, nascent), sufficient outrage and indignation; pursue justice above all other considerations. On the other side of the scale, it's fair to say his "victory" was, for all intents and purposes, Pyrrhic. He won the right to put himself in harm's way next time around.

Alaimo wasn't much of a letter writer. Like so many World War II GIs, he was more concerned with assuring the folks back home that he was in good spirits than with pouring out his heart on a scrap of heavily censored V-mail or Red Cross communication. On the other side of the Atlantic, Tony's status as a POW allowed his big brother Philip—ever a wellspring of familial love, overbearing advice, and opinion—to lecture a truly captive audience. On November 30, 1944, Phil wrote:

We haven't received word from you for quite some time. I suppose that poor transportation facilities there may account for our failure to get your letters. I haven't received even a card from you for more than three months. I trust that all is well. I am continuing to send you the parcels (both book and other). I hope you are receiving them regularly. From this end everything looks encouraging. Keep your hopes high & your candle of faith burning brightly. I imagine that monotony is the chief problem you have to meet. Some kind of variation in your daily routine is imperative—in athletics or otherwise. If you wash clothes & play ping pong one day, try reading and checkers the next. Some variation is imperative. Even in your reading, balance your diet. Alternate the heavy with the light, the serious with the amusing. Use good judgment here and you will, not only be able to hold yourself better integrated, but you will be able to help some other boy there who is not so well-equipped as yourself. Remember: the law of self-sacrifice works always & everywhere. Put yourself out to help some other boy in need, and inevitably, those inner resources of the spirit will well up within you to help you meet the need of the hour. Jesus said that when a man loses himself, he then finds himself. Everyone is well here, and we're all looking forward to that grand reunion. I'm keeping your needs in mind. I'll have a definite program worked out for you, when you return. Our deepest love to you. Our prayers and thoughts are of you always.

Being a POW puts a man directly in line for a "Dear John" letter. In this respect Tony, who had no real sweetheart, was spared. Some recipients made light of what has to be the most egregious example of insult added to injury. "They'd tack them up on the bulletin board for everybody to see," Alaimo recalled with a laugh. Others were devastated. "The worst was a married guy whose wife wrote and told him he was divorced and she'd married somebody else."

Alaimo's friendship with Jeanne Loy had not yet deepened into romance. "I don't think either one of us thought about that," he said. "Anyhow, it didn't happen." This was not surprising, Jeanne would point out, since Tony had graduated, moved to Detroit, enlisted in the service, and wound up being reported as KIA, MIA, and POW.

Alaimo did stay in contact with Elsie Loy, Jeanne's mother, and one day a letter arrived advising him that her daughter had married a boy named Bob Bischoff, whose family ran a local shop in Ada. "All my friends were getting married," Jeanne later recalled. "I was twenty and I decided it was the thing to do…. Later, I realized I'd made this huge mistake."

First among a prisoner's dreams is what he will do when he finally gets out—after, of course, the thick steak, the cheeseburger, or the steaming bowl of pasta, or perhaps the encounter with a sweetheart left behind. The future is all such a man can hold on to. Significantly, the seed of Alaimo's future in the law took root in Stalag Luft III's sandy soil.

Alaimo was in good company. Among the thousands of interned officers at Stalag Luft III were lawyers, former law school students, and academics—including Nicholas Katzenbach, a navigator who'd been shot down over the Mediterranean in February 1943.

In the run-up to the Great Escape, Katzenbach, who'd dropped out of Princeton to volunteer in the USAAF, had been a "penguin" helping to disperse sand excavated from the tunnels. Katzenbach later wrote that he kept his sanity in Stalag Luft III by reading hundreds of books and breaking down his captivity into manageable segments. "I said, 'I'll only be in prison for ninety days,' and when the ninety days were over, I'd say it again, and when those ninety days were over, I'd say it again. And eventually, I was right."

Katzenbach returned, earned his degree with cum laude honors from Princeton (legend has it that he convinced the university to accept his POW reading as an accredited extension course), and in 1947 graduated from Yale Law School. As Deputy US Attorney General, Katzenbach confronted segregationist Alabama governor George Wallace when he attempted to "stand in the schoolhouse door" in June 1963.[1] He went on to serve as US Attorney General and Under Secretary of State during Lyndon Johnson's presidency.

According to the 2002 film *Hart's Law* (adapted from a book of the same name written by Katzenbach's son), Nicholas somehow got a hold of a copy of Edmund's *Principles of Common Law* during his stay in Stalag Luft III. The book became the basis for an informal course he taught.

"Word got out that some of us were interested in the law," Alaimo recalled. "Nick let it be known that if anyone was interested.... Well, about seven or eight of us began to get together."

Unlike the camp's softball games or theater productions, the law class was more than a way to speed the petty pace of day-to-day prison time. "It was something to hold on to," Alaimo recalled. "Soon, the thought that I'd go back to law school took root and it never left me."

There was something more, something tied to the utter barbarity of war. Liberty and justice had been uncivilly ripped—not only from Alaimo, but from untold millions of innocents. Institutions had crumbled, but the law glimmered in those dark days—a beacon of hope, personal and universal. "I became intrigued with its majesty and logic," Alaimo later said, "the brilliance of the human intellect and the interchange of humans beings in a civilized society."

### Stalag Luft III Abandoned

At 8:45 PM on Saturday, January 27, 1945, Colonel Goodrich walked into the South Compound's theater and announced to his

---

[1] Katzenbach persuaded Wallace, who had made his pitch to the cameras, to stand aside.

assembled officers that the Germans had ordered all 10,000 POWs in the camp to gather their gear and report to Stalag Luft III's front gate in thirty minutes.

Elements of the Russian Army were within 12 miles of the camp. Hitler had personally ordered the evacuation, hoping either to keep the aircrews from reentering the conflict or to use them as pawns in negotiations. Ironically, the Germans had cooked up a legal justification for the move. Article 19 of the Geneva Convention required POWs to be moved out of harm's way.

It was bitterly cold. Six inches of fresh snow covered the ground when the bewildered men, Alaimo among them, formed their ragtag ranks. They were accompanied by their shouting captors, police dogs straining at leashes, and overloaded supply wagons creaking against the frozen earth.

They'd wrapped themselves in layers of whatever clothing they had and filled their packs—pairs of trousers tied off at the waist and legs—with Red Cross foodstuffs and whatever tobacco or chocolate bars they'd hoarded. Their worn and tattered footwear would fail first, speeding the onset of frostbite, hypothermia, and lethargy that, among already malnourished men, could prove fatal.

At midnight, 10,000 POWs moved out into the blackness beyond the double fences they'd so desperately dreamed of fleeing. They marched westward for the next twenty-six hours through the cold and whistling wind, some of the men dropping, exhausted, until even their captors lost the will to beat them to their feet.

Given his rank, Colonel Goodrich could have ridden in one of the wagons. Alaimo would remember him marching alongside his men, exhorting the strong to support their faltering comrades. It was an image of duty and responsibility Alaimo would never forget.

A POW named Harold E. Cook, who'd served with the 722nd Squadron, 450th Bomb Group, captured that terrible march in his journal: "The cold was unbearable; tears froze upon my face. I told myself if I could make the next minute, the next hour, the next mile perhaps I would make it home. Down the column came the message over and over, 'Only 6 more kilometers to go!' More men were falling now, motionless in the snow. At 4 A.M. a group of us were herded into a barn. How grateful I was to God for the privilege of lying on the hay and closing my eyes...."[2]

Sometime around 2:00 A.M. on January 29, Alaimo staggered into the town of Muskau on what is now the Polish border. The men had traveled 30 miles through harrowing conditions. Staggering alongside them were hundreds of old men, women, and children fleeing the onrushing Soviets. "I remember a man, his beard literally frozen, holding his few possessions in his arms," Alaimo recalled. "I asked myself, what have these people done to endure this?"

The Germans allowed the exhausted men to take shelter in a factory. "It was a ceramic tile or glass factory with working kilns," Alaimo remembered. "We spent two nights there. The heat was so intense that my damned blanket was scorched and I never felt it. I finally thawed out. I think it saved my life."

The men were marched 15 miles further to the Spremberg rail yards. On January 31, they were packed into cattle cars. They spent two days and nights sealed in the stinking boxes, traveling southwest, blind to the bombed-out cities and devastated towns, the streams of refugees and defeated German soldiers along their route.

Alaimo emerged from a boxcar, blinking in the pale winter light. This was Moosburg, north of Munich in southern Germany. He was marched along with thousands of other Kriegies into Stalag VIIA.

At the start of the war, Kriegsgefangenen-Mannschafts-Stammlager (Stalag VIIA) was designed to hold 10,000 men. When Alaimo arrived in February 1945, 80,000 Allied soldiers and forced laborers were imprisoned behind the wire. There was only one water

---

[2] See http://www.450thbg.com/real/biographies/450/038cook.shtml.

spigot for every 500 men. Infestations of lice, fleas, and vermin had reached epidemic proportions.

# Chapter 8

"Justice delayed is justice denied."
—William Gladstone

Tony Alaimo was not a man to wait around. Within hours of arriving at Moosburg, he was plotting another escape.

On December 26, 1944, Patton's Third Army ended the siege of Bastogne, though the battle would seesaw for weeks. The Luftwaffe was no longer an effective fighting force, and Allied bombers filled the skies pounding the remnants of German resistance. Hitler and Mussolini would be dead within ninety days. Disorder and disintegration had opened the gates of the Nazi slave state. Millions of forced laborers, impressed Axis soldiers, and refugees of every stripe were on the move.

The dying Reich was still a murderous place. Alaimo's plan was, at best, reckless. He recalled:

> Ace Langberg, a guy named Schrefler, and I decided to escape. We were in the delousing area of the camp and were supposed to get a hot shower. The unusual thing about this compound was that it only had a single wire fence around the perimeter rather than two. I checked with Colonel Clark, the officer we called "Big X," and told him we wanted to cut the fence. He approved and gave me a pair of homemade wire cutters. At dusk, we got some German-speaking POWs to divert the guards. I cut the fence and the three of us ran off.
>
> Schrefler spoke German. That's the reason we had him along. We walked that night dressed in old, bedraggled GI stuff. The fields were muddy and we quickly got bogged down. We slept in a damn pigsty. God, it was awful.

We decided to walk to Munich during the day. Sure enough, a young soldier, a German private, stops us. He couldn't have been twenty years old. Riding a bicycle! He demands our papers. Of course, we didn't have any. I tried to tell him we were French workers and all that kind of stuff. He didn't buy any of it.

He hauled us off to a local jug, a terrible old lock-up with six locks on the door, and shut us in for the night. Next morning, he was going take us back to Stalag VIIA.

At 7:00 A.M., It was still dark. The private turned his back for a moment to lock the door. Somebody shouted, "Let's go!" We ran. Dumb me, I should have stayed put. He came out and started shooting with his pistol. As I was rounding a curve, I ran into a damn telephone pole. Knocked me to the ground. I thought I'd been shot! Ace and Schrefler quit running and threw their hands up. Oh Lord! It was just like the Keystone Kops!

At the camp we were locked in solitary.

# Chapter 9

At Moosberg, officers were segregated from enlisted men. Under the Geneva Convention the Germans were prohibited from using them as forced labor, a last remaining concession to their rank. Alaimo quickly realized that this "privileged status" was keeping him behind the wire, limiting his chances of escape. Freedom had become an obsession, to be pursued at any cost, a singularity of purpose that recalls Ahab's mad pursuit of the White Whale.

Alaimo wasn't a guy who could "sleep the war away," even with the end of hostilities clearly in sight. "A powerful feeling made me keep trying to escape," he recalled many years later. What Alaimo sought that bleak February was not escape—not then, and not for the remainder of his life—but transcendence, a "state of existence above and beyond the limits of physical experience." Death holds no sway over a transcendent spirit.

A few weeks after being released from the Cooler, Alaimo encountered an enlisted man, part of a detail working in the officers' compound. The NCO was convinced that living conditions for officers were less onerous than starvation rations and overcrowded barracks. Alaimo struck up a conversation:

> I say to the guy, "Well, how about switching? I'll go out with your group and you stay here." He thought it was a good deal, so we switch dog tags. We didn't have a lengthy conversation. Afterward, I look at his dog tag and realize I'd missed something. "Greenberg." He's Jewish.
>
> I go to Munich with the next work party. I turn up some badly torn civilian clothes that could be useful. Afterward, I spend a couple of days in the enlisted men's barracks. Boy, it was filled with lice and fleas. Awful German fleas. The

morning I'm going to try to escape, I pack what provisions I have, socks and things like that, in a knapsack. I'm wearing my civilian clothes underneath my GIs. The knapsack is strapped to my back.[1]

The Germans round us up at 5:00 A.M. It's pitch dark. There are no lights because of air raids. As we begin marching to the boxcars that will take us to Munich, guards begin checking us out. I don't know what to do. If they look in my knapsack—I have chocolate bars and so on—they'll know something is up.

Then I luck out. A guard is examining the guy ahead of me which takes a few seconds, so I walk around them and continue marching to the boxcar. I get to the boxcar. I'm a son of a gun! They have somebody else checking, this time inside the boxcar. Now, I don't know whether to enter at the front or the back of the car. I go up to the front just as he's searching somebody else and toss my knapsack into a corner. He never sees it.

I arrive in Munich with lots of other prisoners. Our work detail is assigned to a military academy that's been bombed. So we're hauling concrete and rubble until noon when there's an air raid and we all rush to the basement. There's a big room down there where everybody's congregating, and a couple of small ones off to the side. I head for one of the small ones. It's four or five feet below ground level with a row of shattered windows level with the sidewalk. I take off my GIs and start to crawl through one of the windows. I'm halfway out when I spot the sergeant in charge of our detail walking up the damn sidewalk!

---

[1] Article 93 of the Geneva Convention specifies "disciplinary punishment only" for nonviolent military escapees recaptured carrying false papers and/or wearing civilian clothing; however, the Gestapo typically viewed such men as spies subject to summary execution.

I don't know how in the world he misses me but he does. I crawl out the window, dust myself off and walk south, just an ordinary worker going about his business. The hardest thing to do when you're walking down a road is not to look back

After a while, I hit Route 2, which runs down to the Brenner Pass (the border between Austria an Italy). I know the location of what were called "kommando"[2] camps where impressed French workers operated big state farms. The first was near a town called Gruenwald about 7 kilometers south of Munich. I show up, talk my way, in high school French, into seeing the barrack's chief (*chef de casernement*) and tell him who I am. I ask if he'll help me.

*Bien sur!*

That night, when the Germans arrived to count the French workers, Alaimo lay hidden in the attic. After they left, his newfound compatriots, who were putting their lives at risk, invited him to share their dinner.[3] "Believe it or not," he recalled, "we played bridge. For the first and only time in my life I made a grand slam, no trump, which is the best you can do! Doubled and I redoubled!"

The next morning, he set off for the next camp, about 15 kilometers south near the town of Traubing. "My instructions are to go to the southernmost part, to a fork in the road. In that fork 'there would be a Frenchman pitching hay.' I think, 'Oh hell' this can't be.' I'm a son of a gun, sure enough, there he is! You couldn't mistake Frenchmen. They all had berets."

---

[2] *Arbeitskommandos*, officially *Kriegsgefangenenarbeitskommando*, were sub-camps holding POWs of lower ranks who worked in industries and on farms. This practice was permitted under the Geneva Convention, provided the prisoners were accorded proper treatment.

[3] Alaimo doubts the camps were part of an organized escape pipeline run by the Resistance. He believes his appearance was an "oddity."

In this camp, the chief decided that Alaimo's hair was "too long" for him to pass as a civilian. He trimmed it before passing Alaimo on to a third camp in Starnberg. Alaimo was exhilarated, experiencing what the civil rights activist Andrew Young would one day describe as "freedom high." After so many false starts and bitter disappointments, Alaimo was making progress. Even being out of uniform and carrying a Jewish soldier's identification didn't phase him. "I didn't think about such things," he later said.

At Starnberg, a lakeside resort in southern Bavaria, things grew complicated. "The Frenchman there is a very intelligent guy," Alaimo recalled. "We discussed whether I should try for Switzerland from the German side or, since I know Italian, make my way to Italy. We decide Italy is my best shot."

The two strolled down to the town's bustling railroad station. The barracks chief made his way to a ticket window and used his own money to purchase a ticket for Alaimo, who waited in the crowd, trying to blend in. The Frenchman walked past, slipped Alaimo the billet, and whispered: *Bon chance!*

Alaimo again slipped past the Gestapo men checking travel papers. He rode the train to Garmish-Partenkirchen,[4] a resort town at the foot of Zugspitze, Germany's highest mountain. Alaimo felt like he was traversing entire continents, but today, Garmish-Partenkirchen is just an hour's drive from Munich on the Autobahn. "We arrive at this great, elaborate train station," Alaimo recalled. "And we all have to disembark."

On the platform, he heard a sound as welcome as a choir of angels. A group of Italian workmen were chattering away, waiting for a train that would return them home. Alaimo walked up to them and impulsively discarded the half-formed alibis swirling in his head. He identified himself as an American pilot. The move was not without risk, since the fascisti and Nazis controlled northern Italy. "One of

---

[4] In happier times, the city hosts one of Europe's best-known Passion Plays.

the Italians tells me to try for Milan and then make my way into Switzerland."

The stranger gave Alaimo something precious—the name and the address of a partisan in Milan who might assist him.

*"77 Corso de la Porta de Ticinese."*

Ticino, as luck would have it, is the name of the Italian cantonment in Switzerland.

At Innsbruck on the border, everyone was again forced to detrain, elevating the risk of Alaimo's being detained by an Austrian border guard or overzealous fascisti. Even in peacetime, Europe is a place where one's papers—one's internal passport—are constantly in demand and must be in order. The Nazis elevated this predilection for bureaucracy, passes, and papers (e.g., Humphrey Bogart in *Casablanca*) to obsession.

Alaimo had no papers.

*"I never killed anybody in the war that I knew about. He could have been the one."*—Anthony Alaimo

"We were in a big warehouse run by the Italian government," Alaimo recalled. "There are cots all over and a guy at a table handing out bread stamps. I thought about the audacity of my going up there, but I did." He lingered for two full days, waiting for his chance. Finally he encountered a group of Italian POWs[5] being repatriated into Italy, escorted by just two German guards.

---

[5] Mussolini was deposed and arrested in July 1943. That fall, a new Italian government headed by Pietro Badolgio signed an armistice with the Allies and declared war on Germany. The Nazis then forced the surrender of thousands of Italian troops and took control of much of the peninsula north of Rome. They quickly freed Mussolini and appointed him head of a puppet government, the Italian Social Republic. In April 1945, en route to sanctuary in Switzerland, Il Duce was captured and executed by Italian partisans.

"They were split into two groups," Alaimo recalled. "One eighteen men, the other of seventeen. One German covered each group as they boarded the train. I kind of merged into the group of seventeen. The guard must have figured he had the eighteen."

*Kind of merged....*

The phrase is archetypal Alaimo, reducing a delicately timed and potentially fatal maneuver into a walk in the park. He had no idea what offenses these prisoners had committed or what fate awaited them—or no longer cared.

At one point, Alaimo fell into a deep sleep in the narrow corridor of a passenger car. "I was kicked awake by somebody," he remembered. "He was a Death's Head[6] storm trooper. He began was cussing me out."

"I don't understand German!" Alaimo exclaimed.

"It seems you don't understand Italian!"

"I thought the jig was up with this fellow. I was prepared to be very violent if he pushed me. I never killed anybody in the war that I knew about. He could have been the one."

The man moved on. The train inched its way along bomb-damaged tracks into the Brenner Pass. Alaimo was often forced to walk for miles or hop aboard big "carbon-burning"[7] trucks. Finally he arrived in Bolzano, an irreducibly Italian town in the South Tyrol. Like an orphan encountering his biological mother for the first time, Alaimo was reduced to tears: "There are these beautiful Italian women who'd cooked spaghetti. Wonderful women who fed us." Nearly a lifetime later, he remembered this meal as though he'd dined on honeydew and the milk of paradise.

Once again, invisible and unbound by physics, Alaimo escaped the notice of the German guards and slipped off. The Italian POWs

---

[6] A *Shutzstaffel* (SS) trooper. These were typically assigned to oversee the concentration camps.

[7] Wartime vehicles equipped with "generators" that converted burning wood or coal into a combustible gas.

were taken to a military compound in Brescia. Alaimo stayed on the truck, concealed among a group of workers. Milano lay 150 kilometers ahead.

There the dead-enders of the Italian Republican Army[8] roamed the streets, ill-disciplined, trigger-happy, and uncontrollable. "They were worse than the Germans," Alaimo recalled. "They couldn't stand the air raids. They wouldn't go into the shelters for fear of being buried alive. They were emotional, afraid of their own shadows. They'd shoot you if you were out on the streets after 9:00 P.M. Shoot you on the slightest notice."

A sergeant was waiting as Alaimo clambered off the truck. The man searched his fellow passengers but Alaimo ducked behind another man and slipped away. How many times could he roll the dice? "I wondered what in the world was going on," he recalled. "I began to think my mother's prayers—or some such thing—had suspended the law of probability."

As he made his way into Milan, Alaimo struck up a conversation with an elderly woman. He told her he was a Sicilian laborer trying to make his way home, a story aided by his swarthiness and the traces of Sicilian dialect that escaped his proper "church" Italian. "This woman, abjectly poor herself, gave me a 50 lira note," he recalled. "I've often wondered if I would have had the same compassion."

Alaimo used the scrap of money to hop a streetcar. In the pale spring sunlight, he passed through a massive gate, La Porta de Ticinese, and onto the avenue (*Corso*) beyond. Number 77 turned out to be the Pasticceria DeMarco, a pastry store. Alaimo recounted the story:

> I went in and asked the proprietor if he knew this person.
> "I'll go see if I can find him."
> "Thank you."

---

[8] The Italian Republican army was the military arm of Mussolini's puppet Italian Social Republic, installed by the Nazis in 1943.

A few minutes pass. It seems like hours.

"He's gone. What can I do for you?"

After a moment, Alaimo decides he'll put his trust in this stranger. He explains his situation, and adds, "If you can't help me, just let me go."

The man was Vincenzo DeMarco. In 2007, like so many of the extraordinary individuals that have peopled Alaimo's life, DeMarco is long deceased. "I'll help you."

He got me Italian papers. I needed a pass to move around. He got me a suit of clothes. Clothes were pretty scarce at the time. He put me up in an apartment. During the day, I'd walk to the pastry shop, and in the course of our conversation, eat some delicious cookies. He gave me money. In the evening, on my way to the apartment, I could stop at a restaurant. Dinner cost 30 lira and they gave me a pint of wine with it. Money was nothing.

DeMarco knew all along that if he was caught with me, the reprisals would be horrible. Not only would they kill him, they'd kill his family.

Man has an endless ability to adapt to changing circumstances. Within a week, Alaimo and DeMarco attended a performance of Rossini's *Il Barbieri di Siviglia* at Milan's La Scala opera house. The Nazi SS colonel who sat down next to Alaimo was terrifying enough to transform the most wanted men into sopranos. "Of course, he had his young blonde girlfriend with him," Alaimo remembered. "He was much more interested in her than me."

## The Road to Switzerland

After two weeks, Alaimo asked DeMarco for help getting to Switzerland. The Germans still clung to control in northern Italy, but their days were numbered.

"I'm sure Demarco wants to keep me as a sort of an intermediary when the Americans arrive," Alaimo recalled. "But he agrees to help me. I ask him to get a typewriter and I type out a letter addressed to the Commanding General of the Army of Occupation.[9] In substance, I describe how much he's done to help me and write him a draft for $1,000."

The two traveled by train past Lake Como to Ponte Chiasso on the Italian-Swiss border. There they were met by one of DeMarco's associates, a Turkish woman whose name and raison d'etre have been lost in the mists of time. After a "great, big dinner and a big bottle of wine," Alaimo and DeMarco, close as brothers in the crucible of war, embraced and said farewell.

A guide led Alaimo to the border. The air was crystal. In the distance beckoned the lights of Chiasso, the first illuminated city he has seen in two years. On the border, the double gates, guards, and electrified fences of the stalags and slave camps gave way to a chicken wire fence. This border, so permeable yet out of reach of Europe's desperate and doomed masses, was both risible and tragic.

"I pull it up, crawl under, and make my way into town."

---

[9] POWs had been advised that if they escaped and received help, they could promise their benefactors a reward of as much as $1,000.

# Chapter 10

If Alaimo expected to be welcomed by the Swiss, he was sorely mistaken. (He later remarked that he possessed neither looted art nor numbered bank accounts; had no gold bullion in safekeeping with the gnomes of Zurich.) He was rumpled, hollow-eyed, drastically underweight, and tightly wound. He carried the false Italian identity papers DeMarco had provided him and made the mistake of addressing the Swiss border guards in Italian.

"I had a time with them," he recalled. "The Swiss interrogated me more intensely than the Germans ever did. They favored the Germans. The Swiss sure did. They questioned me for hours, then decided, 'You're not American.' They were going to intern me!"

Alaimo continued, "Well, I about flip my lid! I begin raising hell, maybe more hell than I should have. Finally, a major walks over and says, 'We're sending you to Geneva. They'll know whether you're an American.' In any event, I spend my first night of freedom in a jail cell. And these are Italians! I'm in the Italian canton!"

The next morning, a private arrived to escort Alaimo on another train ride, this one to Geneva and the nearest US Consular Agency. Once he passed through the embassy doors, he was home free. However, neither the embassy staff nor Marine guards rushed over to accord him a hero's welcome—nor did Alaimo expect one. In the grand scheme of things, he was simply another GI, one of 11,000,000 men and women serving in the US Army during World War II—albeit a fortunate one. More than 400,000 Americans from all branches of the military and merchant marine died in the war.

No one was intrigued by the details of Alaimo's escape. Decades passed before he evidenced any interest in sharing them. "I'd typed that letter to DeMarco for the Army of Occupation," he recalled.

"Other than that, I don't know if there was any other verification. Besides, there were so many other matters of more importance."

To paraphrase Tim Carroll, author of *The Great Escape*, if there is a deeper significance or nobility in Second Lieutenant Alaimo's escape ("Hell, I just wanted to get out of there!"), it may lie in the moral choices he made, the worthy people he met, the cruelty and kindness he encountered along the way. These lessons and models would inform and guide him for the remainder of his life.

Alaimo departed Geneva on a deuce-and-a-half truck packed with other soldiers; like him, the flotsam and jetsam of war. "Some of them couldn't speak English," he recalled. "But I really didn't concern myself with talking to other people, not yet. Some guys were in civilian clothes. I was wearing a turtleneck sweater that my sister Irene had knitted and sent to me via the Red Cross."

What Alaimo does remember about his three days in Switzerland—and this is consistent with every soldier who ever returned from war—is the food. The "beautiful table with napkins" set before him in Geneva, and later, after being transported via Lyons into liberated Paris, "Practically eating myself to death." It was not bifteck or canard a l'orange Alaimo desired but "peanut butter and jelly," a craving he finds outlandishly funny when he describes it sixty-odd years later.

There were GIs everywhere. Alaimo drew his backpay and a fresh uniform. It being unseasonably cold, Alaimo gave his beloved turtleneck sweater to a chambermaid at the hotel where he was billeted. "She was so appreciative," he recalled, "because everything was short in those years."

In turn, Alaimo was rewarded with good news. Two of his buddies, Alvin Vogtle and Harold "Shorty" Speirs, had also escaped from Stalag VIIA (Alaimo himself had provided the diversion). They were en route to the US. The doughty Vogtle, nicknamed "Sammy from Alabamy," had literally swum to freedom across Lake Constance on the German and Swiss border. After the war, he went on to become president and CEO of Atlanta-based Southern Company, one of the largest utility corporations in the country.

Alaimo boarded a C-54 "Skymaster" transport bound for Lajes Field in the Azores. After refueling in Bangor, Maine, he traveled on to Washington, DC. In Maine he literally kissed the ground of his homeland. A line from Sir Walter Scott's "Lay of the Last Minstrel" ran through his head: "...Breathes there a man, with soul so dead, / who never to himself has said, / this is my own, my native land!"

His next stop was northern Virginia. "A base called 'The Farm,'[1] which I later learned was OSS land." He was debriefed and told to await further orders.

On a greater stage, on April 29, 1945, Patton's 14th Armored Division liberated Stalag VIIA. On May 7, General Alfred Jodl, chief of staff of the German High Command, authorized the unconditional surrender of all forces, a scene repeated outside Berlin the following day when German commanders surrendered to the Soviets.

Two years had passed, but the words of the German sailor who had plucked Alaimo from the North Sea finally proved true: "For you, the war is over."

---

[1] Camp Peary, outside Williamsburg VA, was the Office of Special Services' clandestine training facility.

# Part II

## A Middle Passage

"I saw a look on their faces. It went through my mind they were thinking, 'Why my son and not you?'"
—Anthony Alaimo, home from the war

# Chapter 11

He'd received no hero's welcome, but Anthony Alaimo couldn't have been happier. He rode the Erie Railroad into Jamestown, a duffel bag slung over his shoulder, his hungry heart bursting with emotion. He'd planned to treat himself to a sleeper car but a conductor talked him out of it, saying it wasn't worth the extra expense ("You'll get there tomorrow morning anyway"). Alaimo "went on the coach."

Alaimo was merely a drop in an ocean.[1] Nearly 78,000 POWs would be repatriated from the European Theater. After September 2, 1945, the date of the Japanese surrender, the trickle became a flood as the men of the "Greatest Generation" came home to reclaim their lives.

At the OSS camp, Alaimo had been vetted by men already engaged in a new, "Cold War" and the scattered brushfire conflicts that were its afterbirth. He could offer his interrogators only the location of some German 88-milimeter antiaircraft batteries he'd noted in Milan. He did put in a kind word for Vincenzo DeMarco. Sixteen years would pass before the two friends would meet again.

In Jamestown, no one knew Alaimo had escaped and was on his way home, a surprise he'd intentionally planned. He arrived at 7:30 A.M. and caught the streetcar to Lake Chautauqua, where his sister Frances lived with her husband August Gerace. Alaimo knocked on the door as calmly as though he were delivering the mail. Frances wasn't so calm: "She was just absolutely overwhelmed."

Together, brother and sister made their way to their parents' home on Swede Hill. Alaimo's memory of his first encounter with his mother is so powerful that at age eighty-eight he is stricken mostly

---

[1] Sixteen million Americans served in the armed forces during World War II.

speechless. Carried on the wings of memory and deposited back on that doorstep on an unforgettable spring morning.

"I knock on the door," he says. "My mother answers. And, well, it's just remarkable. The warmth...the multitude of kisses...my mother and Grandmother Francesca standing there. Mother got down on her knees and thanked the Almighty for bringing her son home to her."

The lyrics of "Mama," a ballad beloved by generations of wandering Italian sons, may approach the tenor of that meeting: "...Mama, you'll be with me, you won't be alone any more / These words of love are from the bottom of my heart / Oh Mama, you are the most beautiful song / You are life and I will not leave life any more."

Word of Anthony Alaimo's arrival quickly spread. His father hurried home from work, brother Freddie close behind. Church friends and neighbors appeared carrying plates of Italian food. "There was a big get-together that night," Alaimo recalled, "visitors arriving just like they would at a funeral."

He was treated to his favorite pasta and veal braciole—savory strips of meat stuffed with Parmigiano cheese, garlic, parsley, and bits of boiled egg, then rolled, tied with thread, and sautéed in tomato sauce. "A real delicacy," he recalled, "I can taste it now." At the time, he weighed only 130 pounds. He'd soon regain the twenty pounds he'd lost in the camps.

Alaimo spent two weeks in Jamestown catching up on sleep and visiting with friends, sensing surely, as millions of other vets would sense, that the familiar and routine were no longer satisfying. Like his former comrades he was conscious of the pull of career, the urge to start a family, and the possibility of new challenges, unfamiliar places, and greater opportunities. Reinvention is, after all, a fundamental American virtue. "I knew what I wanted and never wavered," Alaimo later said. "To become a lawyer." He paused, then added, "And also get married."

In Jamestown, someone mentioned a POW camp[2] near Dunkirk on Lake Erie. Curious, Alaimo rode up to see for himself. "I was really interested in seeing how we were treating these prisoners," he recalled.

He got an eyeful. There were American women—the pretty, vivacious girls every GI had ached for and dreamed about—gathered at the gate, chatting and flirting with German POWs. The few women he'd even seen in the last two-and-a-half years were dressed in rags and spent their days digging for blackened potatoes in the frozen soil of Silesia.

The women were young and lonely—silly, self-interested creatures who had no understanding of the larger world and the sacrifices being made to guarantee their safety. Most eligible American men were off fighting the war. POWs could be tragic, even romantic figures. Despite himself, Alaimo flashed back to the "Dear John" letters the jilted POWs had pinned to the barracks' walls.

In the vernacular of the day, Alaimo "blew his stack" and rushed up to the women at the gate, shouting and gesticulating as he "cussed them out."

On extended leave, he headed to Atlantic City for a week, where he mingled with thousands of other soldiers, strolled the boardwalk, ducked in and out of nightclubs—he was a teetotaler—and admired the pretty girls trailing schools of fawning GIs. To his delight, he discovered that former POWs were accorded special treatment in billeting and received other benefits, a sop to ease the rigors of repatriation.

His orders arrived. He was directed to Dodge City Army Airfield, a training facility in Kansas, to be assigned to a new aircraft, the Douglas A-26 twin-engine attack bomber. Upon arrival he

---

[2] During the war more than 380,000 German and Austrian POWs were interned in the United States. Dozens of small camps were scattered throughout Central and Western New York state, satellites of a central command camp at Fort Niagara.

discovered that the base was being shut down, and was transferred to another base, this one in Frederick, Oklahoma, where he spent the next four months flying above the soybean and cotton fields that carpeted the prairie.

Alaimo was part of a class of fresh pilots being prepared to wage war in the Pacific. Already a grizzled veteran to the youngsters around him, he kept his experiences to himself. "Nobody was an idol in those days," he remembered. "There were no heroes."

He'd wanted to be assigned to the Army of Occupation in Europe, but here his POW status worked against him. "They would not permit you to go back for fear you'd take reprisals," he recalled.

Around this time another Alaimo idiosyncrasy emerged, heartfelt and long-lived. "In the Air Corps, when I'd be passing through some big city like Chicago," he remembered, "I'd always pick up the phone book and look up the Italian names. On occasion, I'd even call and introduce myself. Some people reacted positively; others didn't have any interest in me at all. It wasn't loneliness. I was proud of my background and I wanted to share the pride."

Generations later, that pride was still very much apparent. Visitors to Sea Island on Georgia's coast may cruise past the luxurious residences, the live oaks hung with Spanish moss, the lantana, bougainvillea, and narcissus blooming everywhere, but no one misses Anthony Alaimo's home. It's the one, the only one, with twin flags—American and Italian—on the front lawn.

In January 1946, Colonel Douglas Freeman, a good friend and former squadron mate who'd risen through the ranks, contacted the newly minted First Lieutenant Alaimo. The war was over. Like millions of other GIs, Alaimo was eager to get on with his life. At the time, the army had implemented what was called the Green Light Points System, an order-of-discharge system based on a man's length of service, citations received, and other criteria. "Freeman called me from headquarters and asked, 'Would you like to get out?'" Alaimo remembered. "I said, 'What about these points? I'm two shy?' He told me not to worry."

Freeman was as good as his word. A week later, on February 2, 1946, a Saturday, Alaimo was discharged. He remained in the Officers Reserve Corps for the next five years, narrowly escaping the Korean War call-up.

# Chapter 12

Within weeks, Alaimo was back working his old job[1] at Timken Detroit Axle, the war receding gradually into the ebb tides of memory. He visited the family of Norris Kenneth Calkins, the bombardier killed with the rest of his crew on May 17, 1943. "I wanted to let them know what happened," Alaimo recalled. "They were wonderful people, but I saw a look on their faces. It went through my mind they were thinking, 'Why my son and not you?' It was understandable. I was not bringing any joy. I decided then and there, 'No more.' I wouldn't contact any of my crew's families."

He worked afternoon shifts and attended morning classes at Wayne University (now Wayne State University) law school, at the time located in "a big, old house." He tried it for a month, but his mind was elsewhere.

Alaimo reconnected with Elsie Loy, in Ada, and learned that her daughter Jeanne's marriage to Bob Bischoff had fallen apart when he'd returned from the service. "Something was missing from the very beginning," Jeanne later explained. "Passion." Jeanne had a two-year-old son, Bobby.

Mrs. Loy was uncomfortable with the idea of her daughter's divorce—this was 1940s Ohio, after all—but at the same time she'd been as taken with Tony Alaimo's fierce work ethic as her daughter had been with his good looks. Mrs. Loy was familiar with the years he'd spent toiling away in his little barbershop, mastering his studies, puzzling out his future. These were sturdy Midwestern virtues.

"Elsie invited me to come and spend a weekend at their farm in Sydney, Ohio," Alaimo recalled. "Dean Loy had retired from school

---

[1] The Selective Service Act of 1940 guaranteed returning veterans the right to reclaim their jobs with no loss of rank or seniority, provided they reapplied within ninety days of their discharge.

and was now principally a farmer." Soon enough, Tony was on the phone with Jeanne, asking her to lunch. Fate, destiny, or some benevolent deity smiled on two seemingly star-crossed individuals. Jeanne was in the final stages of the divorce. Tony began driving down from Detroit on most weekends so the two could date. Law school temporarily took a back seat.

Marriage was a pillar of Alaimo's world, but it was not the only pillar. He felt the "cold hand of poverty" clutching at him. The notion that he'd find himself unable to support a family created an unshakeable tension, an "obsession" that shaped his thoughts and behavior in ways he would not comprehend for decades. He was not alone in his fears. In the 1950s, the term "workaholic" did not carry a negative connotation.

"The fear of poverty is something you never lose," he recalled. "All us Depression kids felt this way. You never forget when they cut off your milk because you can't pay a bill. I can't explain why it persisted, other than the experiences were so vivid in my life. After I bought our first house, I never borrowed money again. Never before and never after."

He'd always been competitive and he performed[2] well under pressure. Tony Alaimo didn't want to be a lawyer, he wanted to be the best lawyer—the hardest-working lawyer, and, if the fates smiled upon him, the richest lawyer.

At Stalag Luft III, Alaimo had met Nicholas Katzenbach, a Princeton man. He'd also met a POW named Brown who'd graduated from Harvard Law School and a number of other Ivy Leaguers. "These were superior individuals," he recalled. "Obviously, it was because of their academic background."

If he overlooked the fact that Katzenbach came from a Main Line Philadelphia family and had graduated from Phillips Exeter

---

[2] The washout rate among World War II pilots was more than 50 percent.

Academy, perhaps it was because, as Alaimo freely admits, he was a dreamer.

"I chose Yale Law over Harvard Law,"[3] Alaimo recalled with no small irony. "Yale was smaller and I felt I'd get more individual attention." He sent out his admissions application and went back to work at the foundry. When the rejection notice arrived in the mail, he was out the door in a flash.

"I took the train from Detroit to Connecticut," he added, drifting back in time. "I went and interviewed whomever the admissions guy was. I wanted to see if I could change his mind. He'd taken a look at that bad year I'd had at Ohio Northern, and he'd decided I couldn't make it. I told him, 'If I can't at least make straight Bs, I'll voluntarily resign.' He turned me down again. I said, 'You'll accept me one day.' I really was depressed." He was politely shown the door after another fruitless interview at the University of Virginia.

In Ada, Ohio, a professor named George Patton told him about a law program at a Methodist university in Atlanta that might be worth a look.

### A Deep and Committed Romance

Alaimo's relationship with Jeanne Loy was blossoming into a committed romance. Like Tony, Jeanne was more than a dreamer—as it turned out, much more. "Besides being beautiful, she was smart, which I was really interested in," Alaimo later explained. "At the time, I was thinking about a person who would push me. I typified her as being one such person."

Ironically, this dispassionate assessment comes from a man who claimed "a full head of wavy hair" as one of his selling points. The

---

[3] Decades later Alaimo's great friend, former US Attorney General Griffin B. Bell, a dreamer himself, told Alaimo that Harvard Law School had an open admissions policy for returning WWII veterans. Alaimo never knew it and didn't apply.

truth seems to be that Tony was smitten, so smitten that he proposed to Jeanne over the telephone in route to proposing to her in person at lunch in Lima, Ohio. "'Will you marry me?' was practically the first thing he said in that conversation," Jeanne recalled with a laugh. "I guess I wasn't too surprised. I said I would."

It would be a love affair for the ages, still vigorous, full of fun, and going strong sixty-one years later. When asked those many years later what had drawn Jeanne to him, Alaimo had responded without missing a beat: "my personal magnetism."

The two were married in Detroit on June 11, 1946. Jeanne's parents and Tony's entire family showed up for the occasion—a measure of the event's significance to the Alaimo clan, since Santa and Sam Alaimo rarely traveled beyond Jamestown. Brother Philip conducted the ceremony. Younger sister Josephine, herself a few months away from marriage, served as maid of honor. Like all weddings, this one had its memorable moments, often not the intended ones. Tony's sister Irene, a beautician, spent so much time arranging Jeanne's long blond hair that the bride was late for her own wedding. She was so late, in fact, that the church organist left and Josephine had to fill in at the keyboard.

### Southbound

The newlyweds left Detroit that night in Jeanne's blue '41 Nash Ambassador. They'd rolled the dice, decided to make a fresh start, and were leaving behind Jamestown, Ada, Detroit, and those frigid winters. They headed for Atlanta, 750 miles to the south, a city and a region neither of them had ever visited and about which they knew nothing. In retrospect it was a prescient move, arriving in the Sunbelt before it existed, in a South on the cusp of momentous change and dislocation.

Jeanne and Tony were at the forefront of a great postwar migration out of the small towns and crowded cities of the North into the West and South, out of the small towns of the South into magnet cites like Atlanta, Birmingham, and Nashville. Like so many others in their day, they pursued the dreams, opportunities, and sometimes fantasies men had clung to in hellholes like Guadalcanal and Anzio.

Jeanne was the perfect companion for such a journey. "I seem to have been happy wherever I put my head and whatever I was doing," she said.[4] "When I was a young girl, I'd be out at a church camp or something like that and half the girls would be crying, wanting to go home. I never could understand them. I've never been homesick in my life, no matter where I was. I didn't have any stereotypes. I didn't care where I lived. Everything was an adventure."

The proximate reason for the move was that Tony had followed Professor Patton's advice and decided to enroll in law school at Emory University. At the time, Emory was a "respectable regional school"[5] with strong ties to its Methodist founders, as well as the Candler and Woodruff families, founders of The Coca-Cola Company.

After Alaimo's traumatic experience at Yale, Emory seemed almost too friendly. "All I did was walk up to the registrar and say, 'I've got a bachelor's degree,'" he recalled. "He admitted me right then and there without credentials or anything like that. In retrospect, all of this was quite strange."

The quarter was to begin in a week. The newlyweds drove to Detroit, picked up Bobby from Jeanne's parents, and headed straight back.

The campus was located in Druid Hills. A tranquil, almost bucolic residential enclave, it was laid out by landscape architect Frederick Law Olmsted, the visionary who designed New York's Central Park. That summer, the only jarring notes were the scores of house trailers squatting among the azaleas and magnolias. A trailer

---

[4] This is from a 2007 interview
[5] From *A Brief History*, Emory University website, http://emoryhistory.emory.edu/history/index.html.

would be the Alaimos' home for the next two years, an experience that remained fixed in Jeanne's memory more than half-a-century later.

These were old trailers, 26 or 28 feet long. In the front was a couch that folded out into a bed. One part was much higher than the other part. When I was pregnant with Philip, I rolled right off that horrible bed onto the floor. There was a tiny oak table, a kerosene heater. Every once in a while a trailer would catch on fire, fortunately not ours.

There was a little sink with an icebox. Ice was delivered once a week. I hated that. The sink only had cold water. When I had to bathe Bobby, I'd sit him in the sink and put a teakettle on to heat up the water. The sink was so small he could barely fit.

The trailers had no bathrooms. There were boardwalks running in different directions. I had to walk down 50 feet then up another boardwalk to take a shower and go to the bathroom, a real drag when I was pregnant.[6] Tony built a little crib in the back of the trailer. I don't know where we put or clothes or the pots and pans. I washed the kids' clothes on a washboard until the university installed a washer and dryer.

Having said all this, I never seemed to mind it. To me it was more of an adventure, like camping out—something that was going to end. As for Tony, well, he was used to cramped spaces. He could sit there in that trailer and read his law books."

As for financial resources, they had Tony's back pay, one unexpected benefit of being a POW, plus some bonus money from his retention in the Officers' Reserve Corps. Ultimately, Tony's law

---

[6] On the plus side, Emory University Hospital, where Jeanne gave birth to Philip in July 1947, was just yards away.

school education would be underwritten by a landmark piece of legislation—the Servicemen's Readjustment Act of 1944, or more familiarly the GI Bill. The law funded tuition costs up to $500 per school year and provided married vets with a $90 monthly living allowance

The impact of the GI Bill would reverberate for generations. It lifted millions of men and women into the middleclass, kept those same millions from flooding the workplace as the economy slowed after the war, and, ironically, nurtured and shielded the baby boomer generation from the deprivations and sacrifices of their parents.

In 1947, a peak year, veterans accounted for half of all college admissions. In 1956, when the original legislation expired, 7.8 million of the 14 million World War II vets had taken advantage of an education or training program. "It was one of the best things the government has ever done," Tony Alaimo later remarked.

Rent on the trailer ran $19 a month, leaving $71 for food, clothing, and other necessities—approximately $18 a week for what would soon be a family of four. "It was hamburger every night," Jeanne recalled. "I knew fifty-seven ways to do hamburger." At the time Jeanne was not much of a cook (she "had to learn to boil potatoes") and Tony, a "traditional Italian male," had never mastered even the most basic pastas, hearty dishes that could be prepared for pennies.

One Thanksgiving, Tony caught a cantankerous old rooster that lived on the campus. Jeanne served him up with noodles for dinner. After four hours of boiling in the pot, the rangy bird was still too tough to enjoy.

It's not difficult to imagine the "cold hand of poverty" on Tony's shoulder as he hunched over his books in the library. One could easily imagine the ferocious self-reliance that had fueled his escape from the camps reemerging. This complex mix of duty, responsibility, pride and stubbornness (*ostinato*), would define him in the decades to come.

"He never wanted my folks to help us," Jeanne remembered. "And they would have. My mother would send me $50 on my birthday and Tony would kind of frown. I'd say, 'Tony, she's always given me birthday presents and she's not going to stop.' He didn't want anybody in the world to think he couldn't support me."

There were thirty-six students in Alaimo's class, among them future Fulton County district attorney Lewis Slaton; superior court judge Elmo Holt; jurist and environmental activist Ogden Doremus; Jeptha Charles Tanksley,[7] who'd graduated from West Point in 1943 and lost both legs and an eye in the Italian campaign; Macon's John Sammons Bell, who would later serve as chief justice of the State of Georgia Court of Appeals. Bell, a Purple Heart recipient, had been seriously wounded in the Solomon Islands.

For the next two years Tony would measure himself against such men. Poring over endless cases, he slowly and painstakingly developed the skills necessary to systematically apply logic and precedent to a problem—and, as he would emphasize, "dispose of it."

When all is said and done, this is the essence of a lawyer's job.

Something else was driving Alaimo, inchoate and as of yet unformed: a love of the grandeur and majesty of the law. A realization—underscored by the horrors he'd witnessed—that the rule of law is key to an ordered society.

Many years later, Alaimo would point to a 1978 Harvard commencement speech made by the Soviet dissident Alexander Solzhenitsyn that deepened his love by broadening it:

> I have spent all my life under a communist regime and I will tell you that a society without any objective legal scale is a terrible one indeed. But a society with no other scale but the legal one is not quite worthy of man either. A society which is based on the letter of the law and never reaches any higher is

---

[7] Tanksley would serve for more than twenty years as a Superior Court Judge in Georgia's Fulton County.

taking very scarce advantage of the high level of human possibilities. The letter of the law is too cold and formal to have a beneficial influence on society. Whenever the tissue of life is woven of legalistic relations, there is an atmosphere of moral mediocrity, paralyzing man's noblest impulses. And it will be simply impossible to stand through the trials of this threatening century with only the support of a legalistic structure....

"Once we've complied with the rule of law, we think we've satisfied our obligations to society," Alaimo remarked in 2007. "Solzhenitsyn considers that too sterile a concept, suppressing human desire and compassion that go above and beyond the rule of law.

"And he was right."

On a less magisterial plane, the prizefighter in Alaimo appreciated "the logic of the law...the discipline of it...getting up earlier than the opposition and overwhelming them with hard work." He discovered he prized these things more than most men.

He would need these virtues in the lean years ahead.

# Chapter 13

Alaimo graduated from Emory in June 1948, ranking second to a budding lawyer from Albany, Georgia, named G. Stewart Watson.

"You'll accept me one day!" Alaimo had vowed to the Yale Law admissions officer who'd rejected him. Sure enough, his sterling work at Emory opened the doors to Harvard, Yale, Columbia, and New York University, each offering Alaimo a coveted spot in their graduate law programs.

Nonetheless, "unsure about stepping out into the competition," he'd doubled his bets, applying and earning admission to MBA programs at Penn's Wharton School and Northwestern University.

That summer, Tony delivered Jeanne, Bobby, and baby Philip to the Loy family's farm in Sydney, Ohio, stopping to stand for the Ohio bar along the way. He traveled back East and enrolled at New York University in Greenwich Village only to discover that there were no accommodations for a family of four. He made his way uptown to 116th Street and Broadway and matriculated at Columbia University only to run into the same problem. "They halfway promised they'd find us a place to stay," he recalled, "but after a month or so at the King's Inn, I concluded a Master of Laws (LL.M.) degree was just not worth the time I'd have to spend. I went back to Ohio, picked up Jeanne and the kids, and drove back to Atlanta."

## Job Hunt

The weather in Atlanta would have been mild, even balmy, compared to the icy blasts that roll off the Hudson River and howl through the concrete canyons surrounding Columbia University. Another chill, however, had begun to spread in Tony Alaimo's guts: the all-too-familiar feeling that he—pilot, POW, escapee, law school overachiever—did not command his own destiny.

He installed Jeanne and the boys in a $4-a-night motel on Ponce de Leon Avenue and drove into downtown Atlanta every morning to search for a job. He dressed in his only good suit, a double-breasted gray sharkskin he had purchased, along with an overcoat, at a sale in Jamestown.

There were no "law fairs" bringing recruiters and prospective hires together, and networking opportunities were scant unless your family name was gilded on the door. Alaimo was reduced to door-to-door canvassing, cold-calling, hardly different from a Fuller Brush or encyclopedia salesman—as hard on his pride as it was on his polished shoes. Given the realities of postwar Atlanta, it would have been exceedingly hard for a salesman with swarthy complexion, unmistakable Yankee accent, and unpronounceable name to prosper.

At the time, Atlanta was hardly the "capital of the Southeast" and certainly not the "buckle on the Sunbelt." The Sunbelt didn't exist, and Birmingham, Alabama, with its steel mills, and Chattanooga, Tennessee, home to rail and heavy industry, seemed better positioned to achieve first-tier city status in the Southeast. Savannah and New Orleans had ports and navigable rivers; Atlanta's genius was endless boosterism and self-promotion.

The city owed its existence, and its original name, "Terminus," to an 1830s railroad junction. Atlanta's notoriety, in fact, derived from its connection to a Hollywood blockbuster, *Gone With the Wind,* and to a fizzy soft drink that became one of the world's most powerful and enduring brands. Atlanta's second name, Marthasville, did not carry the excitement and prosperity its citizens wanted to project, so it was jettisoned.

When Alaimo appeared on the scene, Atlanta had adopted the phoenix as a symbol of its rise from the ashes of the Civil War. It was verdant and unpolluted, a commercial and financial hub. The Coca-Cola Company and the Trust Company Bank dominated the scene, but a number of national and international corporations had regional offices there. White-shoe law firms like Powell Goldstein Frazier &

Murphy and Spalding, Sibley, Troutman & Kelley (today King & Spalding), staffed by fewer than ten attorneys, serviced these growing businesses.

Atlanta's population was then 331,000.[1] Metro Atlanta, the enormous "donut" that would surround the city over the next half-century, had a population of 792,000.[2]

In Atlanta a Sicilian was as rare as a hen's tooth. Alaimo, forever seeking connection to his roots, could actually count his fellow Italians. "There was a tile-setting company of Italians (the Mion Brothers)," he recalled, "some architects, a fruit and vegetable grocer, and four Italian-American lawyers."

African Americans made up a quarter of the metro Atlanta population, reflecting the dramatic exodus of rural blacks over the first half of the century. The city of Atlanta would be majority black by the early 1970s. What set Atlanta apart from urban centers elsewhere in the US was a solid black middle class and a strong leadership cadre, both characteristics traceable to its historically black colleges—Clark, Spelman, Morehouse, Morris Brown—founded at the end of the Civil War. What would make Atlanta resonate with people everywhere was the presence and legacy of Martin Luther King Jr.

Mid-century Atlanta was a segregated city. Unlike Birmingham, Selma, Montgomery, and Oxford, Mississippi, Atlanta would integrate peacefully, never suffering the social and economic consequences of snarling police dogs, church bombings, and schoolhouse posturings broadcast around the globe. Atlanta would become, as the boosters liked to say, "The City Too Busy to Hate." There was some truth to the statement but also a helping of what would later be called "Sunbelt dynamics"—cheap labor, mild winters, scarce unions, and good transportation. Atlanta would attract

---

[1] US Census bureau statistics.

[2] By April 2007 that figure had soared to 5.1 million.

millions of new residents and untold billions in investments, birth a Ted Turner, and host the Olympic Games.

Many have written and debated about power sharing and deal making between the entrenched but reasonable white power structure and an onrushing, irresistible black political engine as key to Atlanta's resurgence. Alaimo was a young attorney during these tumultuous years, but he would have reduced all the Sturm und Drang to an indisputable fact: the rule of law prevailed.

### "You Don't Have the Right Background"

By Christmas Alaimo had tramped the streets of Atlanta for a solid month, interviewing at more than two dozen firms "without a strike." At Sutherland, Tuttle & Brennan he encountered Elbert Parr Tuttle, a man who'd survived a grievous combat injury at Shima Island, near Okinawa. Tuttle would go on to an appointment to the US Court of Appeals for the Fifth Circuit in the tumultuous years following Topeka's *Brown v. Board of Education* case. He and his brother-in-law, William A. Sutherland, were sympathetic but not helpful. "They were nice, gave me good advice, you know, and all that," Alaimo remembered, "but no offer."

The law was hardly a growth industry in late 1940s Atlanta, but Alaimo sensed ghosts and shadows swirling in the background. At Gambrell, Harlan, Barwick & White, he encountered the aristocratic Harvard Law grad E. Smythe Gambrell,[3] who after interviewing Alaimo informed him, "You don't have the right background."

In the South, family, place, and social connections run exceedingly deep. They are an integral element of the workplace, particularly in professions like the law. It's likely Gambrell and the

---

[3] Gambrell, Eastern Airlines General Counsel, would later serve as president of the American Bar Association. His son, David H. Gambrell would be appointed US senator by Governor Jimmy Carter to serve out the term of Richard B. Russell Jr., who died in office in 1971.

others decided the corporate clients that were their bread and butter would balk at a stranger such as Alaimo.

"I knew what he meant," Alaimo later recalled. "I was a Yankee. I was an immigrant. I talked funny."

He soldiered on, returning to the hotel each night to Jeanne and the children a little worse for wear. "Demoralized" is the word he would use to describe himself at the time. "I'd had a fair shake in the army," he said. "A fair shake in law school. I thought excellence would do it. I was still pretty much an innocent."

Patience is one of the seven virtues identified by the fourth-century poet Aurelius Prudentius Clemens. It's no coincidence that Prudentius, also a lawyer, listed patience next to diligence in his *Psychomachia*.[4] Alaimo didn't realize it at the time, weary as he was of struggling, but his ill treatment in those days provided lessons to be drawn—meditations on fairness and justice that would guide him in his time on the bench.

### *"Rube" Garland*

In any event, had things gone more smoothly, Tony Alaimo might never have encountered Reuben A. Garland. To say that Garland was a flamboyant, larger-than-life criminal lawyer would be an understatement. White-maned and florid of face, Garland was a character whose thrust and demeanor would have stretched Mark Twain's imagination. The next generations of defense attorneys, the "Racehorse" Hayneses, Melvin Bellis, and Johnny Cochrans seem like choir boys compared to Garland. He was a peacock with a raptor's eye and jugular instincts, an absolute master of persuasive argument and linguistic flourish (what once was called "the colors of rhetoric"). Garland could seduce a jury, drive an opposing attorney to despair, and bait and infuriate the most patient of judges.

---

[4] "Contest of the Soul."

In the course of Garland's long career, there would be times when his clients would walk away free men while Garland, a lightning rod for all the emotion and tension stirred in the courtroom, would be jailed for contempt by judges whose forbearance he had stretched beyond the breaking point.

Griffin B. Bell, the former US attorney general, remembered a typical Garland run-in.[5] At the time, Bell was a partner with the Atlanta firm King & Spalding.

Well the judge gave him twenty days in jail. And he (Reuben) had something else to say, so he gave him twenty more. Reuben came to see Mr. Spalding and wanted Mr. Spalding to represent him. Mr. Spalding called me to his office. We talked a while and I said, "Rube, I think you need to apologize to the judge in some way. I don't think you're capable of apologizing." He said, "Not only am I not capable, I wouldn't apologize to him." I said, "Well, he is a judge. In your heart, you've got to figure out how to do that. Mr. Spalding will do it for you, or I'll do it because I know you can't do it." He sat there a while, and he said, "I believe I'll take the forty days."

Garland lived in an aging mansion on West Paces Ferry Road, drove a long black Cadillac, and dressed like an English lord. The big house had once belonged to a corporate attorney, Rembert Marshall, who'd disliked Reuben intensely—an irony that would have pleased Garland. He was renowned for taking on sensational cases, defending his clients to the utmost, and extracting the heftiest of fees.

In *The Temple Bombing*,[6] a reassessment of the infamous 1958 attack on an Atlanta synagogue, Melissa Fay Greene would capture a somewhat older Garland, one who would win the acquittal of the

---

[5] *The Journal of Southern Legal History* (12:1-2) 208.
[6] Melissa Fay Greene, *The Temple Bombing* (New York: Da Capo Press 2004).

alleged white supremacists accused in the attack. "Carrying a gold-headed walking stick and giving it a twirl, he was no stranger to the fresh flower in the lapel, the gold pocket watch, the black cloak for the opera. He was outfitted in breathtakingly expensive suits by London clothiers…. Garland saw to it that the cut of his broad-bellied figure and the ornate trappings of his person made the point that here was a man of wealth, worldliness and distinction…."

This is the man who awaited Alaimo as he walked into the second-floor office at the Candler Building on Peachtree Street.

The two felt each other out. The forty-two-year-old Garland, who could read a man at a glance, no doubt ran a cost/benefit analysis on the eager young man sitting across from him. "We got to talking about army life," Alaimo recalled. "About my being a POW and that kind of stuff. He was impressed that I'd gone to Emory and had finished second in my class."

For all his brilliance, Garland was admittedly no master of the legal nuances. In *The Temple Bombing*, Greene recounts a story told by Garland's son Edward, now a prominent criminal defense attorney in Atlanta: "Dad told a story about being in class one day in law school, with the professor calling on everyone about, 'What is stare decisis?'[7] And he asked different people and he finally asked Dad what stare decisis was. Dad gave some answer and the professor said: 'Mr. Garland, if you were standing in the middle of the road and the law came down the road and the law ran completely over you, you would never have known that it had come nor that it had gone.'"

When the job offer came, Alaimo didn't know whether to laugh or cry. "Rube offered me $35 dollars a week," he recalled. "This was less than the elevator operator made, but it was all that I could get."

So began a relationship, a partnership—a long, if occasionally prickly, friendship between two men who were in many ways polar opposites. Alaimo, careful and painstaking, prepared the research and

---

[7] "To stand by that which is decided," literally, the legal concept of precedent.

legal arguments Garland would marshal in the courtroom. He countered the many demurrers[8] filed by the opposition. "These cases were prepared a hell of a lot better than he'd ever had before," Alaimo reflected. "And I was becoming a pretty damn good lawyer." Over the course of his career, the indefatigable Garland tried an endless parade of cases—by one count, his murder cases alone totaled more than 400.

Alaimo sensed something profound in Garland, something that mirrored his own fierce passions. "What Rube was unparalleled in," Alaimo recalled, "was belief in his client's cause. By God, he really was loyal. He'd do anything in the world he thought would help his case. There's a story that he'd lost one guy to the electric chair and was so despondent, he quit his Georgia practice and moved to Oklahoma."[9]

The defendant in the case was Mell Gore, a twenty-two-year-old convicted murderer whose appeal (*Gore v. Humprhries*) was denied by the supreme court of Georgia. On June 3, 1927, Gore was put to death in the electric chair. Reuben Garland, according to his son Edward, filed the first challenge to the constitutionality of the death penalty in Georgia.

"Rube was a marvelous speaker," Alaimo continued. "He'd learned certain euphonious phrases. The man would make my spine tingle even though I'd heard the same argument any number of times. He was brilliant at cross-examination. He could ask a question infinitesimal in time. With difficult witnesses he would do that to the point where they'd finally say, 'I don't remember, I don't remember!'

---

[8] In simple terms, a demurrer indicates that the objecting party will not proceed with a pleading because of insufficiencies in the other side's pleadings; instead the objecting party will await the court's judgment as to whether he is bound to answer.

[9] The anecdote was confirmed in January 2008 by Reuben Garland's son, Edward T. M. Garland. Reuben Garland practiced law in Oklahoma City for a year before returning to Atlanta.

"He loved to stir people up. For example, he'd brag that he cheated on his income tax. But he damn sure didn't. I know he did not."

One of Garland's perennial adversaries was E. Smythe Gambrell, the Harvard-educated lawyer who'd dismissed Alaimo as not having the "right background."

"When Gambrell got up to make his argument before a jury he'd usually introduce himself as, 'a little country boy,'" Alaimo recalled, beginning to chuckle. "When it was Rube's turn, he would look at the jury and say, 'Who ever heard of a country boy being named—and he would draw out the word—Smmmmyythe?' You can imagine what Gambrell thought. He despised him."

Alaimo laughed at the memory.

Humdrum cases blur and disappear into dusty filing cabinets—or, in today's world, onto servers and hard drives. Others live on to be told and retold. Alaimo particularly liked to recount the story of a memorable "breach of promise to marry" action he and Garland had handled:

My client was a beautiful brunette who'd been "stood up" by a fairly prominent, well-heeled Atlantan. One of the legal requirements in such a case was proof that the lady had a virtuous past. I called my client to the stand, and as I have said, she was very attractive, the best part of my case.

I asked her the usual, preliminary questions eliciting who she was, her family history, and her current home. Following that, I asked her the key question: "Well now, have you lived a virtuous life?"

She responded very quickly as if indignant that such a question had even been asked. "Of course, I have!" And then she turned to the jury, batted her beautiful, long-lashed eyes two or three times, and said, "But I haven't been a fanatic about it."

There was the case of a salesman from Texas, a Mexican named Cohen, who "sold lingerie to whorehouses." Garland and Alaimo represented the illegal alien before the federal Board of Immigration. After various and sundry criminal charges against the man were sorted out, the two managed to get the board to grant the client resident alien status thanks to what Alaimo recalled as "one of those pet bills tacked onto another bill in the US House of Representatives. There was a local judge who'd been elected to Congress from our district," Alaimo explained, "a guy Rube supported by hundred-dollar bills every now and then. He got the bill tacked on." Alaimo got to plead Cohen's cause before the immigration board. He began his arguments with a memorable (if seemingly cryptic) phrase, "Yesterday, I was picking corn in a snowstorm...."

### "A Pretty Good Guy"

Garland's animosity toward opposing attorneys was so fevered ("They were devils with horns sticking out") that the junior lawyer found himself approached when compromise or conciliation might be in order. "I didn't play the game the way Rube did," he recalled. "So lawyers on the other side probably placed greater emphasis on me than they might otherwise have done. They thought I was a pretty good guy."

Such rich experiences were offset by Alaimo's slow but definite slide into poverty, a repeat of his parents' struggles a generation earlier. Thanks to a loan from Jeanne's parents, the couple was able to purchase a modest house on Chelsea Circle near Emory University. "In my family, that meant having a note all done properly and paying it back in full," Jeanne Alaimo remembered. "Which we did."

Frank Loy, Jeanne's father, was not particularly impressed with the deal. He referred to the property as "the house on the side of a ditch."

112

"At least we didn't have a mortgage expense," Alaimo later explained. In those days, "nickel and diming" was more than just a phrase. "For 10 cents I could ride the bus to work. I'd eat hamburgers at the White Castle across the street from the Candler building for 10 cents. We lived on my $35 a week. We didn't go to the movies or eat out. We played bridge with the neighbors for entertainment."

Increasingly anxious, Alaimo began to spend more and more hours at the office, a pattern that would stay with him for the rest of his life. Though it would drive many successes, he'd later lament that it cost him dearly. "I became obsessed," he admitted. "I'd get home after the kids had eaten and gone to bed. In the morning, I left before they got up."

Early in 1951, Alaimo had had enough. For the second time in his life he was becoming a prisoner, so he walked away. To Reuben Garland's astonishment, Alaimo resigned, packed up Jeanne and the kids, and drove to Ohio to become a farmer. For nearly two years he worked the fields alongside his father-in-law and his strapping brother-in-law, George Burrey. The three planted, tended, and harvested corn, wheat, oats, and soybeans on Frank Loy's 1,000-acre farm. "There was a certain appeal to farming," he mused many years later. "Being close to soil has a spiritual benefit that you can get no other way. I watched what I planted grow, admired the beautiful wheat fields in the wind." One could easily imagine Tony, escaped from the mountains of briefs and depths of his disappointments, freed of suit and tie, big hands cradling a delicate seedling or shoot.

That year Alaimo suffered a devastating loss. On May 21, 1951, just two days before her sixty-seventh birthday, Santa Alaimo died of a cerebral hemorrhage. She was in her bedroom when afflicted and died instantly. According to her daughter Josephine's account more than half a century later, "Father found her on her knees in a position of prayer."

Santa had recently been voted president of the Women's Society at the Italian Methodist Church, a signal honor. "It's what God wants," the Italians liked to say of tragedy. One could take solace in that.

Tony picked up his sister Josephine and her husband Richard in Cincinnati and drove to Jamestown for the funeral. He felt that a vital part of him had died and, no matter his worldly successes, would remain beyond reach. "I worshipped my mother…we all did," he recalled. "You know, she never came to Georgia to visit. She never had the money, though I can't remember a time when she wasn't working."

Literally on the day she died, according to Alaimo family tales, Santa's refrigerator was packed with veal cutlets, meatballs, and other delicacies. She'd prepared them in anticipation of some family gathering.

Alaimo's plan to work part-time as a lawyer—he'd passed the Ohio bar a few years earlier—never panned out. Even in the age of mechanization farming was grueling, a dawn-to-dusk endeavor. And the certainty he sought still eluded him, like wheat chaff passing through his fingers. Family interactions are exceedingly complex, particularly in close quarters, and to a degree Tony felt himself an outsider. Burrey and Loy had been working together long before he and Jeanne had arrived. The three families ate what they grew and lived off a communal fund, which unfortunately did little to grow the Alaimos' finances.

Two years later, in November 1953, Tony was out in the stubbled fields harvesting the last of the corn crop when the corn picker on his tractor broke down. The stroke of bad luck was a turning point. Winter comes early and fiercely in Ohio, just as it does in Poland and Germany. Perhaps, then, it's no stretch to imagine Alaimo sensing himself trapped, the urge to escape building.

"I was down there on the ground trying to fix one of the gathering chains on the damn thing," he recalled. "I spent four hours working on it and just about froze to death. Finally, I said, "Hell, I'm going back to practice law!"

Reuben Garland had been pleading with Alaimo to return to Atlanta for months. Edward Garland, then a boy, remembers his father vowing to fly to Dayton and haul Tony back personally.

In a Georgia courtroom, Alaimo wasted little time putting his experiences to good use.

*"Yesterday, I was picking corn in a snowstorm...."*

Things improved. Over time, Garland offered Alaimo a partnership. The sign on the door now read "Reuben A. Garland & Anthony A. Alaimo." Tony was earning one-third of the firm's income—not a fortune, but enough to buy a house at 414 Hildebrand Drive in Sandy Springs, not far from the Sandy Springs United Methodist Church.

The two partners attended Atlanta Bar Association meetings together. Garland was blithely oblivious, Alaimo acutely aware of the glares the other attorneys would shoot at Reuben.

Tony and Jeanne attended fabulous Christmas parties hosted by Reuben and his elegant wife, Fauntleroy "Faunty" Winston Moon Garland. Her father Edward T. Moon was a judge in Troup County. On weekends, they'd drive down to the sprawling farm Faunty had inherited from her family and ride horses.

Edward Garland recalled Alaimo, trim and vigorous, regularly visiting his parents' house when he was a child. "He'd make me flex my biceps for him and always make a big fuss." Ed remembered babysitting the Alaimos' two boys, Bobby and Philip.

Tony began to indulge his own taste for fine clothes. He wore a fedora, an affectation admittedly copied from Garland, that would become his trademark over the subsequent decades. Anthony Alaimo's middle initial, originally added to escape army paperwork, now suggested a "Triple A" practitioner. His skills had become sharper, his confidence building.

# Chapter 14

"If you were the last man at the table, you always got
the smallest slice of bread."
—Anthony Alaimo, January 2008

The men who marched home from World War II had come of
age during the Depression. They craved stability and financial
security. They did not suffer malaise or question their raison d'etre—
the Japanese and Germans had already done that. They didn't
challenge authority or mock the status quo. Status quo felt pretty
damn good compared with foxholes, snipers, and K-rations. It meant
you had an excellent chance of waking in the morning in one piece.

In the 1950s, the measure of a man was hard work and earning
power—food on the table, the ability to a put a down payment on a
house, money set aside for the kids' education, and the occasional
family vacation. The humblest of virtues defined the Greatest
Generation. "Being a material success was the criterion," Alaimo
recalled. "Not the fact that you were brilliant or stuff like that.
Success meant the money you earned to support your family. Oh my,
yes. The fear of not being able to do it was in the back of my mind
for many years; long after it didn't need to be there."

Other voices swirled in Alaimo's head—what the old pastor
Sulmonetti would have called *una vocazione piu alto*, a higher calling.
Alaimo held them off, seeking an easier path. Over time the calling
would compel him, refocus his energies, fire his spirit when he might
otherwise have faltered.

For all his training and self-discipline, idealism surged through
Alaimo like an electric current. The tension between the real and the
ideal, between "what should be" and "what was," energized him.
Using the law to bridge this yawning gap would be a worthy

endeavor, a life's work Sulmonetti and Santa Alaimo would have been proud of.

In war, Tony had learned bitter lessons:

"There's nobody any more defenseless than a prisoner."

"Humans are selfish. If you're the last man at the table, you always get the smallest slice of bread. Always."

"Heroes cannot remain heroes for any protracted period of time."

In peace, these lessons would serve him well.

In hindsight, it was obvious that a professional alliance between men with the outsized egos and disparate personalities of Reuben Garland and Anthony Alaimo would inevitably rupture. The proximate cause was Garland's decision—out of the blue—to seek an appointment as a judge to the Fulton County superior court. "Reuben had the capacity of a hummingbird," Alaimo recalled. "He could switch course 180 degrees without the beat of a wing."

By 1956, Alaimo was ready to test his own wings. He departed Garland & Alaimo to rent space on the thirteenth floor of the Fulton National Bank from Roscoe Pickett, an attorney and would-be politician from North Georgia with close ties to the former governor and newly minted US Senator Herman Talmadge. Pickett was another rara avis: a Southern Republican.

The firm Pickett, Alaimo & Lawson existed more in name than substance. Alaimo spent the next twelve months "settling lawsuits," mostly referral work from attorneys he'd impressed during his partnership with Garland. His good work came to the attention of a prominent attorney named Huston White, but to Alaimo's disappointment the two could not come to terms.

The outsider treatment Alaimo had encountered years earlier reemerged, this time among jurors. "When I went outside Atlanta to try a case, I just could not win," he recalled. "I was a Yankee and, on top of that, a foreigner."

While working with Garland, Alaimo had made the acquaintance of E. Way Highsmith, an attorney from Brunswick, Georgia. Midway between Savannah and Jacksonville, Brunswick is the gateway to Georgia's "Golden Isles" resorts—St. Simons Island, Jekyll Island, and Sea Island.

Like Bobby Lee Cook in Summerville, Georgia, the six-foot-five Highsmith was a small-town Southern lawyer with major-league credentials and Hall of Fame batting averages: Rhodes scholar with two double firsts at Oxford, Phi Beta Kappa graduate of the University of Georgia, special assistant to the US attorney general, former general counsel to the chemical manufacturing conglomerate Hercules Inc.

"Way had gone to the University of Georgia at the same time as Rube, so they knew each other," Alaimo recalled. "He came to Atlanta every so often to attend Bar Association functions. He was a great big guy who'd dominate a courtroom, simply overwhelm everybody. He'd read Melvin Belli's[1] books—they were damned revolutionary—on how to try a case and had a history of getting tremendous verdicts."

As Alaimo remembered it, Highsmith had recently tried a railroad case with the assistance of another courtroom magician, James P. "Spot" Mozingo of Darlington, South Carolina. The case had won a $100,000 verdict, a judgment almost unheard of in those days.

---

[1] Known popularly as the "King of Torts," Melvin Belli's six-volume *Modern Trials* became the textbook for plaintiff's attorneys.

Among the legion Mozingo stories[2] was that the attorney had once billed a "Yankee corporation" $10,000 for services rendered. When the company's accounting department demanded an itemized bill, he'd fired back: "Telephone call—$100; knowing who to call and what to say—$9,900."

"Now," Alaimo continued, "Highsmith had this case involving a man named Johnson, an antiques dealer from Newburgh, New York. Mr. Johnson was involved in a head-on collision near Woodbine[3] driving home from Key West. Spot didn't much want the case, so Highsmith asked Rube to come down and assist at the trial."

Soon enough, Alaimo and Garland were driving the 300-odd miles to Brunswick in Garland's Cadillac. Highsmith's house sat on 20 acres on Sea Island's Frederica Road. Alaimo, who by now hated cold weather, was taken with the area's extraordinary beauty and mild climate. Yet something else struck him—something beyond the innate courtesy and hospitality of the South.

Brunswick was a port city, a tidal city, and like Savannah with its enormous and unexpected Irish Catholic population, it reflected the ebb and flow, the divergent streaming, of humanity. It was a small town, a place where you could get to know your neighbors, make friends, shoot the breeze in the barbershop or at the courthouse, attend PTA meetings, start a garden club...a place where a man willing to work hard, no matter his accent or how many vowels in his name, might make his way.

"I came on down, prepared that case for trial," Alaimo remembered. "I had questions with respect to each witness. And Highsmith was very impressed with that. Rube made the final argument, a really fine argument. We got the biggest verdict ever rendered in this state at that time."

---

[2] See http://legalblogwatch.typepad.com/legal_blog_watch/2007/12/ wachtells-10-mi.html.

[3] Camden County is south of Brunswick near the Georgia-Florida border.

Jeanne Alaimo remembers Tony and Rube Garland collaborating with Highsmith on a "big land case." She and the boys would occasionally drive down to Brunswick to spend weekends with Tony as he prepared for trial. Jeanne too grew fond of Brunswick. "I was from a small town," she later said, "and I liked this place."

The big land case was memorable for a number of reasons. For one, Alaimo and Highsmith represented a real estate broker and former state senator named Hadley Brown. Brown had brought suit in the City Court of Brunswick against a joint venture partnership that included, among others, Frances Myers of the Bristol-Myers pharmaceutical family.

Myers and her partners had sold 3,000 acres to Rayonier, an international forest products conglomerate that owned or leased millions of acres of timberland. Brown claimed they had refused to pay his 5 percent commission on the $3.3 million.

Brown contended that his commission had been negotiated in an oral agreement. The defendants' lead attorney was John Gilbert of Reese, Bennet & Gilbert, an eminent law firm whose blue-chip clients included Sea Island Company, Hercules Powder Company (a manufacturer of naval ordinance), Brunswick Pulp & Paper, Metropolitan Life Insurance Company, and a number of area banks and hospitals.

Years earlier, Highsmith and Gilbert had been partners and, as Alaimo recalled, "a certain tension" existed between the two men. John Gilbert is remembered as a severe and proper Baptist, a teetotaler who'd hold up his glass at parties and announce to all within hearing distance, "This is a Coca-Cola." What he thought about the newly arrived attorney with the swarthy complexion and odd accent is not known.

Alaimo and Highsmith had only one witness—plaintiff Hadley Brown—to present to the jury. Seated in the jury box was a vice president of the American National Bank, another of John Gilbert's clients.

The jury found for the plaintiff, awarding Brown $167,000—his original commission plus 7 percent interest over the two years it had taken for the case to run its course. (The case was eventually settled for $150,000.) This was a staggering sum for the time and an embarrassment for John Gilbert, a man with a long memory.

"He never really recovered from that loss," Alaimo reflected.

As for the banker, he voted his conscience (his name is lost in the mists). And his chances of becoming president of the American National Bank faded dramatically. As the story has it, the man argued, "I would have been the only juror to vote against the verdict and I wasn't about to do it."

Gilbert moved to appeal the disastrous verdict. However, certain pleading strictures had to be adhered to. A bill of exceptions[4] had to be served on the opposing lawyers (Highsmith and Alaimo) before the judge could certify it and then, after certification, be served again on the attorneys.

Alaimo was all too familiar with the intricacies of appellate procedure; his years in Atlanta had assured that. Gilbert neglected to serve his notice of a appeal, a procedural error that opened the door to dismissal. In a panic, he began phoning the two suddenly scarce lawyers, even "ferreting out" Alaimo in a bowling alley. "I didn't say anything, but I refused to acknowledge service," Alaimo recalled. "He should have had the sheriff do it, but I guess he didn't know that." John Gilbert's appeal was dismissed.

In April 1957, Sam Alaimo passed away. Life is unkind to men who make a living with their hands. He'd hurt himself on a job and become partially disabled. Sam also suffered from arteriosclerosis and type II diabetes. He died in Jamestown General Hospital the night

---

[4] A bill of exceptions is a statement of exceptions to the decision, or a judge's instructions in the trial of a cause, made for the purpose of putting the points decided on record so as to bring them before a superior court or the full bench for review.

before his leg was scheduled for amputation. He was seventy-five years old.

Tony was now an orphan, no longer anyone's son. With the death of his parents, it would seem that the connection between himself and the immigrant past might begin to wither. Instead, it blossomed. Sam and Santa's simple faith—their patriotism, belief in hard work, trust, determination, and gratitude—were his inheritance.

The year 1957 was the one in which Way Highsmith convinced Tony to pull up stakes and head for the coast. The two men entered into a partnership—Highsmith, Highsmith, Alaimo & Knox—that lasted until Way's retirement in 1961.

The move infuriated Reuben Garland, a man whose notions of *fidelta* (loyalty) and vendetta would have made a Sicilian proud. "Rube thought I was being disloyal and did everything he could to defeat me in the practice," Alaimo recalled. "By then I understood the man, all his plusses and minuses."

The relationship between the two would remain complex and enduring. In 1962, the solicitor general of the Atlanta Judicial Circuit moved to have Reuben Garland disbarred. Judge Jeptha Tanksley and the rest of the local judges who'd instigated the action disqualified themselves. Garland's fate now lay in the hands of Judge Bowie Gray of the Tifton Judicial Circuit. According to the records, "Various demurrers, motions and pleas, as well as an answer, were filed by the respondent. On the trial of the case, at the conclusion of the evidence, the trial court directed a verdict of disbarment and rendered a final judgment thereon disbarring the respondent...."[5]

"Some of Rube's clients had complained about being overcharged and other kinds of stuff," Alaimo later explained. "The real issue was Reuben as judge-baiter. They thought he was an obnoxious lawyer, not properly respectful to the bench. They were looking for an opportunity to do something to him."

---

[5] *Garland v. State of Georgia* 40922, 110 Ga. App. 756, 140 S.E.2d 46 (1964).

Garland didn't have to look far to find the one attorney he'd trust to handle his appeal, and it didn't matter that he'd been doing his best to disrupt the man's practice. Anthony Alaimo drove up from Brunswick to handle the case but insisted, sticking a needle in the distraught Garland, that he'd only consent to work if it were "without a fee."

To Sicilians, revenge is a dish best served cold.

"My attack on appeal was laid upon the fact that the judges were recused, and thus disqualified from signing the initial order," he remembered. "The complaint should have been dismissed." And it was.

Reuben Garland kept his law license. Was he grateful? "It never came up," Alaimo recalled with a grin. "But I'm sure Rube would have said it was no big thing."

# Chapter 15

"The last man into the jury room met the first guy
coming back out."
—Anthony Alaimo

In 1957, the Alaimos bought a home at 628 Neptune Way, located on St. Simons Island a mile or so across the Atlantic Intracoastal Waterway from Brunswick. The purchase price was $22,000.

The three-bedroom ranch had a double carport. Later, Tony and Jeanne would add a big room with a fireplace and ample space for Tony's oversized desk and growing library.

Alaimo, now thirty-seven, threw himself into his work. He operated out of an office on Gloucester Street, Brunswick's main commercial strip. This was a time before law offices began to resemble the Duke of Marlborough's country estate. "Most of us were in the upstairs of houses and shops," Alaimo recalled.

In Brunswick, the plum defendants' cases went to firms like Reese Bennet & Gilbert and Gowen or Conyers, Fendig & Dickey. Tony was forced to become a rainmaker. Crisscrossing the rural counties that made up Brunswick's superior court circuit—Glynn, Wayne, Appling, Camden, Jeff Davis—he picked up what work he could find: workman's compensation cases, insurance cases, criminal cases, traffic court cases.

Alaimo's name got around—not surprising, since Brunswick was a small place. The fellow knew the law, worked hard, and was always prepared to try a case whenever it appeared on the calendar. Alaimo developed a lifelong aversion to the lazy lawyer's first defense, the continuance. "Lawyers made more money continuing cases than trying them," he recalled. "Nobody was trying cases. One time in

Camden County there were 101 cases sounded by the judge. I had two of them and I was the only one prepared."

At 5:00 A.M., you could find Alaimo at the Forks Restaurant on Highway 341, an establishment run by an old bootlegger named S. O. Jenkins. There Alaimo would be, in his crisp suit and tie, dunking donuts in coffee with the sheriff's deputies, Georgia State Patrol troopers, and assorted good old boys who were regulars.

"I realized that the sheriffs, court clerks, the guys at the state patrol were very valuable people," Alaimo remembered. "Usually, lawyers sort of look down on them. I made friends with them. They were the best friends I had. They'd recommend people to me. They'd help me with the little things you need to know to try a case effectively. I'd give them the jury list. They'd go over it and say, 'No, don't get this guy.' And I'd be sure to strike him."

In the courtroom, Alaimo eschewed histrionics, simplified complex matters, and built logical arguments embellished with the right personal touch. Jurors responded; in fact, they remembered his name when the time came to hire a good attorney.

Come to think of it, Anthony A. Alaimo had a ring to it. It sounded solid, like a silver half-dollar spun on a table.

Not everyone knew his name. Alaimo was admittedly speeding one afternoon near Jesup, Georgia, when a state patrol trooper pulled him over. In the 1960s, motorists were taken directly before a local magistrate, made their plea—inevitably guilty—paid a fine, and were sent on their way. Alaimo had no cash on hand and his offer to write a check was laughed off. He spent the next several hours cooling his heels in the Wayne County jail. Fortunately, a local attorney sent word of Alaimo's plight to one of his friends, then-superior court judge Wineburt D. Flexer.

As the story goes, no doubt embellished over the years, the Wayne County sheriff eventually showed up (Alaimo had contributed to his reelection) and asked the hapless deputy, David Conner, what was going on. Conner supposedly replied, "Nothing much, but there's a WOP back there name of Alamo [*sic*] making a hell of a racket."

Judge Flexer had Alaimo released. He is remembered telling the deputy, "You were just doing your job."

Alaimo was a lawyer, but he traveled the same paths as all the preachers, salesmen, itinerant workers, reformers, purveyors of patent medicine and political bromides, who'd ever trod the South. He saw the chain gangs on the sides of road and registered the clang of pick and shovel against rock, the shotgun shacks, the children with their sugar teats and rag dolls, old folks on listing porches, cotton fields, and clinging kudzu.

He took in the crowded churches and one-room schoolhouses, the railroad tracks that divided black and white in every town large enough to have a grain elevator, the decaying antebellum mansions, the encroaching suburbs, the aging mills, and the chemical plants that spewed toxic waste.

Alaimo was a lawyer out to make a good living. And he did. Yet he couldn't help but notice these things, just as he couldn't separate himself from the starving Russians and dying Jewish slave laborers on the other side of the stalags' barbed wire. Maybe that's why he had to keep moving.

He was a lawyer, increasingly prosperous. He played tennis but he was still Santa Alaimo's son, the boy who'd walked miles in the cold of morning to pick up milk for the family, who'd sang in the Methodist choir, who'd seen his illiterate father's aspirations beaten down.

He still dreaded the cold hand of poverty and injustice, but increasingly these were things that clung to other men's shoulders.

"It used to happen in state practice where a man was indicted in the morning and I'd be appointed to defend him,"[2] he remembered. "The trial was set for that same afternoon. I was outraged and expressed my objections about due process in the record, which you had to do, but that was basically it. Of course, I needed more time. Of course, the case should have been continued. There was a saying around here, 'The last man into the jury room met the first guy coming back out.'"

A decade later, Robert Cullen, a Georgia legal services attorney whose path would cross with Alaimo's, experienced this same revolving door justice in Burke County, outside Augusta. "One of my first cases after being sworn in by the Georgia Bar was a furniture repossession action," Cullen remembered. "There were four murder trials ahead of me, all seeking the death penalty. So being young and stupid and not understanding Burke County, I stood up and said, 'Your Honor, may I be excused. I was not given notice that these death penalty cases were underway.'

"'Don't worry about it,' the judge answered. 'We'll reach you by noon.' And they did indeed convict in four separate trials and sentenced four men to death that day.... Fortunately the Supreme Court struck down Georgia's death penalty within a few weeks so I didn't have to try to figure out how to appeal them."

By 1961, Alaimo was doing well enough to take Jeanne and the boys on a three-month European vacation. He bought a used Mercedes-Benz and drove to Sicily to visit his relatives. He stopped at a family touchstone, the hotel in Termini Imerese where Santa had worked in the laundry room to earn a few lira to put her daughters

---

[2] The courts would regularly appoint attorneys to defend indigent defendants. This was considered an obligation that came with bar membership, and no remuneration was forthcoming.

through school. In Milan, Tony visited Vincenzo DeMarco, the partisan who in 1945 had sped his escape into Switzerland. DeMarco had never seen the $1,000 bonus money Alaimo had promised him, but the US government did send him a certificate of appreciation. DeMarco had become prosperous in the postwar boom. "He owned a couple of movie houses," Alaimo remembered. "This was an enterprising Sicilian."

The families spent a few days together, sat down at bountiful dinners, and drank good wine before making their final farewells. Tony and Vincenzo embraced a final time. The wartime *compares* would never see each other again.

Three months is a long time to be away from one's practice. By the end of the trip, a familiar edginess had begun creeping up Alaimo's spine. "I was scared to death," he recalled. "When I got back, it was if I'd never left. This, I decided, was my security...the law practice. As long as I was healthy."

Had he been a superstitious man, a true Sicilian, Tony would have knocked on wood.

Life on St. Simons Island was good. This was an era when you knew your neighbors and never locked the doors. The Alaimos socialized with Frances and Bill Cofer, who lived across the street. "Frances was one of my best friends ever," Jeanne Alaimo recalled, "the most fun-loving person I've ever known." Coming from Jeanne—a woman who'd accompany her son Philip to the Beatles' 1964 concert in Jacksonville and attend (with her future daughter-in-law Pam Paxton ) the 1969 Miami Pop Festival headlined by Jimi Hendrix and the Rolling Stones—Frances must have been fun-loving indeed. Alas, as Jeanne noted many years later, Frances went on to develop "a serious case of religion."

The Alaimos would get together with schoolteachers Pat Medlin and her husband A. V. for potluck dinners and games of charade. Jeanne, a skilled seamstress, sewed most of her own clothing, along with "many a cuff on Tony's pants." She started the Neptune Garden Club and remembered herself "always busy and amused."

As a couple, Tony and Jeanne shared what later generations would call "core values": love of country, religious faith, commitment to each other and their family, and a determination to contribute in ways large and small to their community.

As individuals, two people could not have been more dissimilar. In the 1940s, Jeanne had been a bobbysoxer whose musical tastes ran to Frank Sinatra, a man Tony and other veterans considered a draft-dodger who'd weaseled his way out the service.[3] In the 1960s and 70s, Jeanne loved Led Zeppelin and Pink Floyd; Tony, she said, preferred "Linda Ronstadt and all those vocalists who sang pretty songs."

In later years, Tony traded his Cadillac for a Lincoln Town Car and listened to classical music on NPR. Jeanne clung to her Mustang convertible and a box of old rock and roll tapes she'd kept "for going on trips."

They traveled. "Tony liked to stay in posh hotels a lot more than I did," Jeanne remembered. "That doesn't do it for me. I'd just as soon be out with some natives in a tent, which I've been a few times."

They revisited La Mamounia in Marrakech, journeyed on the Trans-Siberian Railroad, traveled to the Soviet Union (Tony started a ruckus over the lousy service in a restaurant), and the Far East. "Jeanne's been to China five times," Alaimo would later complain. "To me, that's at least four times too many." Jeanne went on to visit the ruins of Ankor Wat in Cambodia, travel to Vietnam, and hike the foothills of the Himalayas, lugging back carpets and tapestries, statuettes, artifacts, and trinkets that would give their home a distinctly exotic flavor.

---

[3] Sinatra was granted 4F status because of a punctured ear drum; however, the evidence suggests that he made every effort to avoid induction, including labeling himself as "neurotic" and "afraid to be in crowds."

*The Sons of Bach*

Growing up, Bobby and Philip roamed the island's marshes and beaches like Peter Pan's Lost Boys. They attended St. Simons Elementary School and Glynn County Junior High. Jeanne remembered Bobby as bright and self-absorbed, always off in the woods "catching rattlesnakes." Bobby spent his summers in Ohio with his father, who was later elected mayor of Ada. Philip was a lifeguard, a gifted athlete, a right fielder on a championship Little League squad, and a promising halfback. When he later wrecked his knee, he said he "cried for weeks."

As a parent, Tony Alaimo was proving himself his father's son: distant, aloof, and imperious—convinced that the love and concern he felt for his boys could be expressed by fiat. This was a folly, amidst all the good, that would grieve him in the years ahead. "I didn't hug them," he recalled in 2007, "didn't play with them or go on picnics. I never was a buddy." The rare exception may have been in Atlanta, when he grimly donned a Cub Scout Leader's garb and immersed himself in the lore of Wolf Packs and Webelos.

"I don't remember a lot of communication," Philip recalled many years later. "My father is a very serious person. He didn't approve of my brother and I cutting up. If you were having fun, something was not right. You were not serious about life."

At suppertime, Tony wasn't there, *signore del maniero* ("lord of the manor"), seated at the head of the table, savoring forkfuls of curling pasta, nodding appreciatively at his sons' hearty appetites, asking pointed questions about schoolwork that the boys would dutifully answer. He rarely attended Philip's Little League games. When the circus came to town, Jeanne was the one who took the kids.

The boys were coming of age in the rebellious 1960s. Bobby had an adventuresome streak. As a boy, he and a pal had packed some supplies, commandeered a boat, and set sail down the Chattahoochee River, a Huck Finn misadventure that triggered a search-and-rescue mission and a front-page story in the Atlanta papers. As a teenager, Bobby hit a rough patch and moved to Ohio to live with his father. Philip traded his dreams of athletic glory for aspirations of becoming a rock star. He grew his hair long, joined a band, attended a few dismal semesters at Georgia Southern University, and then dropped out to play fulltime with the Sons of Bach, known more familiarly as the "S.O.B.s."

Later Philip, now a grandfather himself, would recall, "My father's favorite saying was, 'I don't care if you're going to be a bricklayer, be the best one in the world.' I'd say to him, 'I don't care about laying bricks. If I'm going to be a bricklayer, I might just be a mediocre one. What's the big deal?'"

To Alaimo, who'd inherited Santa's seemliness along with her ferocious belief in the pursuit of higher education, this was unconscionable, beyond the pale. Yet, when the gales and tempests passed, Philip glimpsed another side of his father.

"He didn't want me to play music. He didn't want me to have long hair, but he never said I couldn't. His point was, 'You can do what you want to do, but don't expect my approval.' That kind of snuck up on me.... He realized he didn't have the moral right to force me to do what he wanted even though he was my father and had the power. There was never an unfair decision with him. He is the fairest person I've ever known. Absolutely."

Philip saw such glimmers again and again, qualities that set his father apart from most other men. In those years, racism was as casual as it was pervasive. "All my peers were racists and I wasn't," Philip recalled in 2007. "I remember once when I was a kid, maybe ten years old, I was talking to a black guy, an older gentlemen. And I happened to say 'Yes, sir' to him. My friends shouted, 'You don't have to say that to him!'

"I understood what racism was. I knew if I ever used the 'n' word, I'd get whacked. There are racists everywhere, but the South is where it started. It was the law. My parents were not racists. My father told me he would never turn anyone away who needed help. I believe that to be true."

On New Years Eve, 1999, Philip Alaimo was still playing the guitar. His band was called the Trade Winds. He was the only white guy on the stage.

# Chapter 16

"I'll be watching you."
—Anthony Alaimo to Vernon Martin

In 1965, Alaimo helped create the region's most powerful economic engine, the Coastal Area Planning and Development Commission[1] (CAPDC). Over the years, the agency would attract tens of millions of dollars in public and private investment, generate thousands of jobs, and pump hundreds of millions of dollars into the economies of twenty-five municipalities scattered over a dozen South Georgia counties.

Alaimo would serve for more than a decade as CAPDC member, chairman, and finally, when the tidal pull of his commitments carried him elsewhere, *eminence grise.* He would apply the gale force of his personality, negotiating skills, jeweler's eye for detail, and occasional arm-twisting to the mundane but vital tasks of planning, zoning, grant-writing, and lobbying.

CAPDC differed from the alphabet stew of governmental and nonprofit agencies seeking funding to redress and repair intractable problems with the finesse and focus of a scattergun. It was as precisely focused as one of Alaimo's legal briefs. It gave the less populated, less developed, and underrepresented coast—which had always had the hind teat—the tools, talent, and ability to compete head to head with the Macons, Atlantas, and Jacksonvilles for resources. "We put together a pretty sophisticated group of people," Alaimo recalled, "on a par with the big cities."

---

[1] In 1989, CAPDC became the Coastal Georgia Regional Development Center (CGRDC).

One of those people was Vernon Martin, a twenty-six-year-old with a planning degree from the University of Oklahoma and what Alaimo deemed sufficient "fire in the belly" to become CAPDC's executive director. Thirty-six years later, Martin remembered Alaimo convincing a skeptical board of "seasoned political folk with strong characters to give the young man a try."

He remembered Alaimo's unerring ability to get to the heart of a problem, hammer out an agreement that made everyone happy. What Martin occasionally forgot was Alaimo's advice to "stay out of the direct line of politics."

With great clarity, Martin recalled the day of his new appointment. He desperately wanted to prove himself to his new mentor, but Alaimo, stern as the Old Testament prophet Malachi, waggled the fingers of those enormous hands and warned, "I'll be watching you."

His work with CAPDAC, resulted in Alaimo's being named to the US Department of Commerce's National Public Advisory Committee. He met Deputy Secretary of Commerce Robert A. Podesta at a conference held at the King & Prince Resort on St. Simons Island. The two developed a friendship rooted in their Italian-American heritage and their Republican credentials. The South was indeed becoming a more complex and curious place when two Italians raised in Jamestown and Chicago, only a decade or so removed from poverty themselves, could reach out and make a difference in the lives of shopkeepers, dockworkers, and shrimpers in Brunswick or St. Mary's. This is the way America was supposed to work, its vitality and values endlessly invigorated by new generations.

Alaimo's networking helped attract $3.2 million in federal funding to build what he modestly called a "railroad spur"; in fact, it was the catalyst for Brunswick's hugely successful Colonel's Island Terminal, a 345-acre deep water facility that would become one of the nation's top three busiest automobile debarkation points. Colonel's Island processes hundreds of thousands of BMWs,

Porsches, Mercedes and other imports each year. Decades later, the Glynn County Commission would name a section of US Highway 17 near the port in Alaimo's honor.

A mile or so from the Anthony Alaimo Parkway, just south of Brunswick's Newcastle Street and the shrimp boats sheltered in Oglethorpe Bay, is a bustling facility operated by the Rich-SeaPak Corporation, purveyors of flash-frozen breaded shrimp, extruded onion rings, hush puppies, and clam strips that grace the menus of America's fast-food giants.

By the mid-1960s SeaPak, with annual sales in excess of $25 million, had been swallowed up by W. R. Grace, an enterprise in the middle of an acquisition binge so extensive its products ranged from asbestos to tacos. Yet binge inevitably leads to purge. A decade later, CEO Peter Grace was shutting down SeaPak plants in Brunswick, Brownsville, Texas, and elsewhere, taking with them 1,200 jobs.

Vernon Martin and SeaPak CEO Jack Cofer came to believe that a new and unproven financing strategy, the Employee Stock Ownership Plan (ESOP), was the only way to keep SeaPak afloat. In simple terms an ESOP is an internal buyout, a practice that would become widespread in the subsequent decades.

Martin and Brunswick attorney Jim Bishop, another Alaimo protégé, spent the next eighteen months "all over the place" doing due diligence on what was turning into a delicate and extraordinarily complex deal. In San Francisco they called on Louis Orth Kelso,[2] a visionary lawyer and investment banker who invented the ESOP in hopes of "democratizing" access to capital credit. SeaPak would be Kelso's second test case.

The key to the deal was securing federal support. "We can't afford to lose this thing," Alaimo had cautioned Bishop and Martin. "Every time you have a meeting, make sure you let me know how things are going."

---

[2] Mortimer J. Adler and Louis O. Kelso, *The Capitalist Manifesto* (New York: Random House, 1958).

135

In Atlanta, Charles Oxley, the Federal Economic Development Office's regional administrator, decided to pass the ball to his boss, Assistant Secretary of Commerce Wilmer Mizell. The hook was that SeaPak might evolve into a "model EDA project." The task of convincing the skeptical Mizell, a former pitcher with the St. Louis Cardinals known as "Vinegar Bend," fell to Vinegar Tony Alaimo.

The critical encounter took place in Augusta, Georgia. As Vernon Martin remembered it, Charles Oxley picked up Mizell at the airport and delivered him, like a floating fastball, to Alaimo. They talked baseball for about fifteen minutes to warm Mizell up. Then Alaimo got around to SeaPak and swung for the fences.

"Give us the opportunity to work with this grant," he pleaded.

Mizell squinted, as if shaking off a catcher's sign. "You really think it can be done?"

"I have every confidence," Alaimo shot back.

They talked some more, Alaimo's arguments unwinding as smooth and well-timed as Stan Musial's swing.

Mizell chewed on it a moment then nodded, "You got yourself a deal."

The Economic Development Authority approved a $5-million grant to underwrite the buyout. The ESOP, through a series of increasingly complicated financial maneuvers, purchased 51 percent of the company.[3] The loan was eventually repaid with interest and the proceeds invested in a revolving fund that would later seed the development of nearly 700 new businesses along the coast.

Jimmy Carter was an early proponent of a regional approach to economic development. He saw it a way to slice through the conflicting bureaucracies and unenlightened self-interests of a state with 159 separate counties; California, by contrast, has only 58. Carter served with the Middle Flint Regional Development Center,

[3] In 1976 SeaPak was acquired by food-processing giant Rich Products Corp. of Buffalo, New York.

which included Sumter, his home county. He and Alaimo knew of each other through their work with these commissions.

In 1967, when Carter was gearing up for a second gubernatorial run, he visited Brunswick and stopped by Alaimo's office. Such meet-and-greet rituals are as familiar as pig-pickings in local politics. Alaimo introduced Carter to Jim Bishop, who was right across the hall. He mentioned that Bishop had been politically active at the University of Georgia. As a dutiful Republican, Alaimo couldn't openly support Carter. He did, however, write him a $1,500 check. "I'm sure this was kind of strange from his standpoint," Alaimo recalled.

"What can I do for you?" Carter flashed his toothy grin.

"Nothing," Alaimo said. "I've got a good practice."

"Not a thing?"

"Well, I want you to be the best governor we've ever had."

Alaimo promised the beaming Carter he'd encourage Bishop to work on his campaign. Carter, in turn, made a mental note to remember the Italian-American lawyer in Brunswick.

Bishop, who could collect friends and build networks better than anyone Alaimo would ever meet, became an early Peanut Brigade member. He stayed close to Carter for the next forty years.

A year earlier Bishop, enrolled at Mercer University's Walter F. George School of Law, had approached Alaimo about a job. His brother-in-law Thomas Stroud, then-pastor of St. Simons United Methodist Church, Alaimo's place of worship, had recommended him.

"The interview might have lasted thirty minutes," Bishop recalled. "After a while, I called Mr. Alaimo to see how things were going. He said, 'I'm thinking about leaving my firm [Cowart, Sapp, Alaimo & Gale] and beginning a practice. You'll be a part of that if you want.'"

Somehow, this assurance did not put Bishop at ease. He was the son of a funeral director and viewed the world as an uncertain, unpredictable place. He summoned his courage and called a third time, saying, "Mr. Alaimo, I would like to understand what to expect. I'm not going to take the bar exam until I graduate and I'd like to know what your thoughts would be in the event, the unlikely event of course, that I don't pass."

"Let me worry about that," Alaimo said. "Come on down. You'll do fine."

He came and ran headlong into Alaimo's work ethic. "In those days," Bishop recalled, "young lawyers tried as hard as they could to impress their bosses. They were committed to working longer than their bosses to make a favorable impression. Well, in the practice of law, Anthony Alaimo worked six and a half days a week. All day Saturday. The half-day was after church on Sunday.

"I recall first walking into his law office," Bishop continued. "I didn't even know what I was going to make. He told me he'd pay me $100 a week. He took that $100 out of his pocket as an advance." Bishop, uncertain as to what to expect next, stood there gaping. Preliminaries over with, Alaimo got down to business. "I want you to prepare a trial brief for this case I've got to try next week."

"Yes, sir," Bishop saluted. He walked out of the office, asking himself, "I wonder what a trial brief is." He turned to Blen Taylor, one of Alaimo's partners, and asked him. Taylor shrugged as if to say, "You're on your own, buddy."

Bishop prepared the brief. Alaimo glanced at it, shoved it into his briefcase, and went off to the courthouse. Bishop was never certain whether Alaimo used it. "The man was so well-prepared."

He'd passed some sort of unspoken initiation, an untested brave ordered by the fierce old chief to find his way among the thickets and groves of the law. "From that point on," Bishop recalled, "he always let me do everything…even some things I wanted to do."

Alaimo didn't lose many cases, but one particular contract dispute in state court remained in Bishop's mind. Alaimo and his client decided an appeal was in order. The appeal revolved around the court's authority to extend time limits regarding the filing of opposing and response affidavits, not exactly the kind of red meat Bishop could sink his teeth into.

"He asked me to prepare the appellate work, which I did. When I filed the appeal, I was not admitted to the bar. I subsequently was admitted after the case was on the calendar."

"Why don't you handle the appeal?" Alaimo then suggested.

"I haven't been a practicing lawyer a month!"

"The only way to swim is to get out in the middle of the lake."

Bishop jumped into the lake. One of the judges on the three-man panel was state court of appeals judge Braswell Dean,[4] who hailed from Alma, Bishop's hometown; this posed a potential source of embarrassment. Word travels quickly in small towns.

"I was scared to death," Bishop recalled.

"May I please the court, not only is this my first case...," he began with a squeak. He cleared his throat and continued. The rest, if not history, is certain memorable. Not only did Jim Bishop regain his stride as the day wore on, but he won the darn appeal. If anyone was happier than Bishop that day, it was Tony Alaimo.

Alaimo was not one to spend a workday chattering about baseball or the likelihood of thunderstorms over the coast. (There's only so much a person can do in fourteen hours.) "We didn't have a lot of dialogue," Bishop recalled. "It was always about work...and work."

Tony Alaimo was forever on the phone, drafting arguments, dictating to secretaries, or at the courthouse. Every now and then he'd look in on Bishop to see how he was getting along. He always knew the answer when he asked questions, the good lawyer's secret to success.

---

[4] Dean, a staunch creationist, is remembered for his alliterative ability: "This monkey mythology of Darwin is the cause of permissiveness, promiscuity, pills, prophylactics, perversions, pregnancies, abortions, pornotherapy, pollution, poisoning, and the proliferation of crime of all types."

One day Alaimo walked into Bishop's office. "Still renting from Dick Everett on Santa Maria Circle? You know, you and Mary really need to buy a house."

"Yes, sir. We'll do it. Mary is teaching school. We're looking around for houses right now. Yes sir."

"Hmmm." Tony's hands fluttered, then he caught himself, and walked away.

The truth of the matter was, Jim and Mary Bishop did not have the proverbial pot, nor the likelihood of a window of their own to toss it out. A few weeks passed and Alaimo reappeared in the doorway.

"How you two coming along?"

"Oh, we're still trying to find something." Desperate, Bishop added, "We found a house in Wimberly on the Marsh [a St. Simons subdivision]. The fourth house. Jerry Newton's building it."

"Hmmm." Alaimo nodded.

In fact, the house Jerry Newton was building was selling for $27,500, a hefty sum in 1967, particularly on a $100-a-week salary and no savings to speak of.

"Go talk to Don Battle at First Federal," Alaimo suggested the next time they talked.

First Federal Savings Bank was one of just two S&Ls in Brunswick. Battle, a bank executive, went over the numbers and informed Bishop he'd require $3,000 as a downpayment to finance the house.

"We didn't have $100 worth of equity," Bishop recalled. "So I just dropped the notion."

Soon enough, he had to tell his boss what had transpired, adding with an optimism he didn't feel, "We're still saving. We'll find something else."

A day later, Alaimo called Bishop into his office. Now he informed him he'd talked with Don Battle at the bank.

Bishop stood there staring.

"I'm going to provide the equity for you and Mary," Alaimo announced.

"You can't!" Bishop exclaimed. "Our budget won't allow it."

"Yes it will. I'm going to raise your salary enough to buy the house. You can pay me back at no interest."

"He drew up a promissory note," Bishop remembered. "Every payday he'd write me a check and I'd write him one back. Then he'd mark off the payment on a scrap of paper he kept in his credenza."

Decades had passed since Jim Bishop bought his house. His hair had turned snowy white. He'd done very well in life, prospered as a lawyer, built businesses, sat on corporate boards, been appointed to the Board of Regents of the University System of Georgia, and served two years as chairman of Mercer University's board of trustees.

Bishop's resume runs on and on. But when he tells this story, when he remembers that long-ago kindness, his voice quivers and he fights back tears.

"How I wish to God I still had that handwritten paper."

He'd come to Tony Alaimo hoping for employment. Like Vernon Martin and so many others whose lives and careers intersected with Alaimo's, he'd found a mentor, a partner, a father-figure, a friend—a relationship that would still be strong forty years later.

# Chapter 17

There's a marina, Brunswick Landing, on Newcastle Street, a short walk from the pick-ups and sedans parked outside the SeaPak plant. On Tuesdays, Thursdays, and Saturdays in the summer, farmers and their wives drive into town to sell vine-ripened tomatoes and fresh corn, boiled peanuts, and Mason jars filled with pickled okra and chow-chow in an open-air market near the marina.

If you were a sailor and kept your sailboat at the marina, you'd surely find yourself of a summer's day making your way south along the calm waters of Oglethorpe Bay. You'd pass under the soaring Sidney Lanier Bridge, its angles and curves a functional piece of abstract art. You'd tack east into the sun-flecked waters of St. Simons Sound, then north past the fishermen and seabirds lounging on St Simons' Mallory Street Pier, past the freshly whitewashed Light House.

Further north, Sea Island is the narrow finger of manicured lawn, palmetto, and pristine beach on your port side. The starburst of elegant line and sinuous curve is the Cloister. To starboard, the ocean runs all the way to the Canary Islands and Morocco.

If you were a working man living in Georgia in the 1950s, Sea Island would have seemed as astonishing a place as the floating island in *Gullliver's Travels*, as unexpected as La Mamounia was to a twenty-three-year-old pilot making his way to war.

A luxury resort a few miles from the pulp mills and dusty cotton fields? The scent of magnolia, ginger lily, and jasmine just a pelican's flight across the marshes from paper mills belching sulfur and chlorine? This would have seemed as unlikely as Swift's Laputa.

But there it was.

In the late nineteenth century Georgia's barrier islands, the shimmering necklace of sandy beaches, unspoiled marshes, and pristine woodlands running south from Tybee Island off Savannah to the Florida border, had drawn the attention of a new privileged class of industrialists. In 1890, Thomas Carnegie built a fifty-nine-room "Scottish Castle" on Cumberland Island, south of St. Simons Island.

In the 1920s Howard Coffin, founder of the Hudson Motor Company, envisioned a resort among "the live oaks, beautiful, braided and woven" on a pristine sliver of land abutting St. Simons. His cousin A. W. "Bill" Jones and his descendants turned Coffin's vision into reality. Over the next seventy-five years, The Cloister would become a place, fabled yet subdued, whose existence remained unremarked by most Americans—unknown, but not unheralded. In 2004, The Cloister hosted George W. Bush and the world's leaders at a G8 Summit on Sea Island.

In the 1960s, before land prices soared into the stratosphere, ordinary individuals, albeit successful and farsighted ones, could afford the residential lots that ran along the numbered streets off Sea Island Road. In 1967 Anthony Alaimo, then partnering with George Cowart, Bob Sapp, and Neil Gale—successful, well-regarded, socially adept, and politically astute men—bought a lot on Sea Island.

He built a house.

Jeanne planted a garden.

Tony worked on his tennis game. And worked some more.

"He's not someone who does anything at half-speed," said his former doubles partner, attorney David Hudson. "A lot of guys selected to be pilots may not be physically imposing, but they have great hand-eye coordination. He would challenge anyone. His favorite target was Albert Fendig.[1] 'Get who you want,' he'd shout. 'Get John McEnroe! We'll take you on!'"

If his knees ached, if his exertions left him occasionally breathless or winded, he ignored it. He'd soon be fifty. Alaimo was a master of the dink-and-drop shot, eschewing brute power for feints and

---

[1] Fendig, a Brunswick attorney, retired in 1999 to "paint and grow flowers" on St. Simons Island.

deception. "I guess I was tricky," he admitted with a laugh. "I used the cut a good bit. After all, isn't it a game of concentration?"

So it is—and of keeping one's eye always on the ball.

# Chapter 18

"The Republican Party was the only place I could
make any mark. Among the Democrats there were a
lot of competitors."
—Anthony Alaimo

Along with millions of Americans struggling through the
Depression, Sam and Santa Alaimo had voted the Democratic ticket.
(Had Methodists embraced the notion, FDR might have been
revered as a saint.) The more established Swedish-Americans of
Chautauqua County were Republicans.

The church played a significant role in guiding meandering
congregants along the path to both salvation and the polling booth.
"My parents didn't have strong political feelings," Anthony Alaimo
recalled. "Politics was off in the distance. They'd just do whatever the
church told them to do."

Alaimo himself had no real political leanings until law school,
and these were shifting. At Emory he'd befriended James Mackay, the
son of Edward George Mackay, pastor of Emory's Glenn Memorial
Methodist Church. Mackay was a Democrat, a civil rights advocate
and attorney who would later represent Martin Luther King Jr.
Alaimo had supported Truman in 1948, Stevenson in 1952,
Eisenhower in 1956, and, thereafter, had voted straight Republican,
his reasons the mix of conviction and self-interest that de Tocqueville
had identified among Americans a century before.

"I was interested in really creating a two-party system in
Georgia," Alaimo observed many years later. "It's amazing how many
things were not done by the Democratic Party that were advocated by
Republicans. Civil rights, for instance. There was no question black
people were being mistreated by the local government here, as they

were everywhere. Republicans were far more against racial discrimination. It has always been difficult for me to understand why black people remain loyal to the Democratic Party."

He'd already answered that question. Like his parents, "they did whatever the preachers told them to do."

## The Redeemers

When Alaimo arrived in 1946, the Republican Party[1] in Georgia had been dormant for nearly seventy-five years. Over the next fifty years it would rise, reinvent itself, and spread its wings over the South.

In Georgia, the transformation of Abe Lincoln's party into Ronald Reagan's GOP is as fascinating as it is unlikely. During Reconstruction the Republicans,[2] i.e., a coalition of blacks and rural whites from North Georgia, a pro-Union enclave long before the Civil War, controlled an unpopular and impotent state government. In 1868, the Ku Klux Klan made its first appearance in Georgia, an avatar of the inevitable suppression of the GOP and its members.

In 1870, Georgia was readmitted to the Union. In 1871, the federal troops that had intermittently occupied the state since the Civil War departed. Democrats, labeling themselves "Redeemers," quickly won control of the state legislature. Rufus Bulloch, the state's first Republican governor, fled to avoid impeachment; his successor, Benjamin Conley, lasted seventy-two days. His replacement, Democrat James Milton Smith, was elected at a special session of the legislature.

Like the mountain towns flooded during the construction of Lake Lanier a century later, the Republican Party vanished.

---

[1] See the GAGOP web site (www.gagop.org ) for a concise history of the party's reemergence as a political force in Georgia.

[2] See http://www.georgiaencyclopedia.org/nge/Article.jsp?id=h-2533.

In 1948, Strom Thurmond, the segregationist governor of South Carolina, ran for president as a "Dixiecrat," trailing in his wake millions of "yellow dog Democrats."[3] Democrat Adlai Stevenson (who garnered Anthony Alaimo's vote) nevertheless carried Georgia in 1952 and 1956.

The Dixiecrats faded, replaced by an evolving Republican ideology more in keeping with the traditional, conservative, pro-military, big government-resenting, churchgoing South. At mid-century, neither party would distinguish itself in its advocacy of civil rights.

In the late 1950s, Alaimo felt the first stirrings of political activism. The wolf no longer at his heels, it was natural for an ambitious lawyer to move, albeit cautiously, into politics. He lacked the network of family and social connection as fine and far-reaching as the human circulatory system that seemed to nourish every politician, legislator, lawyer, and judge in the state. "The Republican Party was the only place I could make any mark," he recalled with a laugh. "Among the Democrats there were a lot of competitors."

His was the era of "post office Republicans," party apparatchiks who distributed patronage—typically post office jobs—trickling down from the Eisenhower administration. Alaimo was proactive, working GOP district and state conventions, making speeches, and connecting with party luminaries like Elbert Tuttle, later named chief judge of the US Court of Appeals for the Fifth Circuit.

In 1960, Alaimo was awarded a delegate's spot at the Republican National Convention in Chicago. According to Georgia Republican Party records, no Republicans held statewide office that year; there were no Republican congressmen and just three GOP members of the state legislature. In fact, John F. Kennedy carried Georgia by a larger plurality than he carried Massachusetts.

---

[3] The term referred to Southerners who supposedly would prefer to vote for a yellow dog than a Republican.

In 1962 Carl Sanders was elected governor, defeating Marvin Griffith, a former governor. That race didn't even include a Republican. One outcome of the voting rights initiatives then underway was the dismantling of the old "county unit system" in favor of districts based on population. As a result, Republicans in the state legislature inched up to 9 out of a possible 149 seats.

In 1964, Alaimo sat on the rules committee of the Republican National Convention at the Cow Place in San Francisco. He watched Senator Barry Goldwater of Arizona oust New York's Nelson Rockefeller for the presidential nomination.

Lyndon Johnson defeated Goldwater in a landslide, but Goldwater carried Georgia with 54 percent of the vote. Howard "Bo" Callaway became the state's first Republican congressman in a century.

In 1964, Alaimo created his own GOP upset. After squeezing onto the ballot with a petition signed by 5 percent of the registered voters, he was elected to the Glynn County Board of Commissioners, another "first since Reconstruction" victory, albeit a small one. The following year he was elected Commission chairman.

Later, Alaimo would joke that this brief venture into local politics was the worst mistake of his career. "Every time I voted on something, I had to vote against somebody. They never forgot. I'd go down and try a case and there would be somebody's brother-in-law sitting on the jury. I'd lose the case and wonder what in the world had happened. My poor clients suffered and I accumulated enemies. I didn't have any enemies that I knew about until after I'd served on that damn commission."

Actually, he had one enemy, a "dour Scot," to use Judge Griffin Bell's memorable phrase, "who saw the world darkly." This man, hidden and unsuspected, would soon drag Alaimo through hell.

In 1966, Callaway out-polled Lester Maddox in the governor's race. Neither man received a majority because a write-in candidate, former governor Ellis Arnall, served as a spoiler. It was no surprise that the Democratic majority in the statehouse picked Maddox .

Alaimo ran for the Georgia House of Representatives that year. He lost to Richard Scarlett, son of US District Court judge Francis "Frank" Muir Scarlett, by 110 votes. The elder Scarlett, whose obstructionist approach to desegregation in the aftermath of Topeka's *Brown v. Board of Education* and other civil rights rulings would define his legacy, was no fan of Alaimo's.

Alaimo had first appeared before Scarlett years earlier in Dublin, Georgia, representing a Florida woman suing the Laurens County sheriff. She claimed she'd been roughed up—and there were seemingly grounds for her claim—by the lawman in the course of an unruly probate hearing.

The lawsuit qualified as a "diversity of citizenship"[4] action handled by the federal courts. Alaimo sat among the spectators as Scarlett attended to other business. At one point the judge noticed him, grunted, and remarked for all to hear, "Who is this odd little fellow?"

Richard Nixon defeated Hubert Humphrey in the 1968 presidential campaign. In Georgia, Tony Alaimo was appointed general counsel to the state GOP, apparently a hands-on job. While tacking up Nixon posters out in the country, he remembered a farmer running him off with a pitchfork. "'Republican' was still a dirty word back then," he said. He was rewarded with a spot on the platform committee at the Republican National Convention in Miami Beach.

The year 1968 was seared into the nation's consciousness. In February, the Tet Offensive undermined any "light at the end of the tunnel" optimism about the war in Vietnam. In April, Dr. Martin Luther King Jr. was assassinated in Memphis. In June, Robert F. Kennedy was murdered in Los Angeles. Race riots broke out during

---

[4] Generally, district courts have original jurisdiction of all civil actions where the matter in controversy exceeds a specified sum or value and is between parties who are citizens or residents of different states.

the "long, hot summer. George Wallace, running as an independent, carried Georgia with 43 percent of the vote.

At the conventions, Alaimo rubbed elbows with the GOP's up-and-comers, has-beens, and never-to-bes, the ideologues, strategists, and architects spinning the webs, building the zeitgeist: Nixon, Goldwater, Reagan, Dirkson, Rockefeller, Javits, Charles Goodell (appointed by Governor Rockefeller to replace RFK), John Lindsay (the fair-haired liberal mayor of New York), and an unheralded but soon-to-be-heard-from history professor from West Georgia College named Newt Gingrich.

How far Alaimo had come. A generation earlier, his father might have lavished his attentions on a bushel of peaches, a cut of meat, or a Bible tract. Santa Alaimo's "unquenchable thirst" for her children's success had been sated.

In 1970, Jimmy Carter became Georgia's seventy-sixth governor. One of the Republicans in the gubernatorial primary was Judge Jeptha Tanksley, Alaimo's Emory Law classmate.

In 1972 Nixon was reelected, crushing George McGovern. He carried Georgia with 75 percent of the vote. On June 17, a second-rate burglary at the Watergate Hotel set the wheels in motion for Jimmy Carter's 1976 presidential run. In the wings, Ronald Reagan waited. In Georgia, future GOP standard-bearers Newt Gingrich, Mack Mattingly, Paul Coverdale, John Linder, and Johnny Isakson were on the march.

Anthony Alaimo, whose life had once been saved by a coin toss on a British airfield, whose existence was a gift of fate or Providence, flipped the coin again.

He quit his plummy law practice.

# Chapter 19

Puro e disposto a salire a le stelle.[1]
— Dante Alighieri, *Il Purgatorio*

In 1970, Congress authorized a new judgeship for the Southern District of Georgia, a sprawling, forty-three-county bailiwick that encompassed the cities of Augusta, Brunswick, Dublin, Savannah, Statesboro, and Waycross, extending all the way south to the Florida border. Frank M. Scarlett had taken senior status, and it fell to Judge Alexander Atkinson Lawrence Jr. of Savannah to handle the court's bulging calendar.

In Washington, Richard Nixon held sway. Democrats controlled the Senate, but neither Herman Talmadge nor Richard B. Russell Jr. would determine the new judicial appointee.[2] That responsibility would fall to Georiga's Republicans.

In Brunswick, the law firm of Alaimo, Taylor & Bishop was doing exceedingly well. Alaimo's personal income had surged to six figures. His closets were filled with fine suits. He and Jeanne traveled extensively. His sons were grown. He'd built a lovely house. He was fifty years old and his future seemed as regular and predictable as the tides washing ashore on Sea Island. His childhood, his Methodist upbringing, the POW camps, the struggle up, were beginning to blur into silvered images of a long-ago life, stories to be told at bar meetings and reunions—or passed on to children experiencing struggles and adventures of their own.

---

[1] "Pure and disposed to mount unto the stars." *La Divina Commedia* Canto XXXIII.

[2] The Senate Judiciary Committee, charged with confirming judicial nominees, grants additional weight to the votes of home-state senators.

Deeper currents were stirring. Wordworth's critical insight was proving an imperative. The child *is* father to the man. One can imagine Anthony Alaimo piloting his Cadillac over the F. J. Torras Causeway separating the drab bungalows of working-class Brunswick from the manicured lawns of Sea Island—dividing the salt of the earth from the elect—staring into his rear view mirror.

Imagine him slamming the brakes on his law practice, breaking the news to the imperturbable Jeanne, and driving in another direction.

In the stalags Alaimo had encountered the opposite of justice. He'd witnessed the subjugation of the rule of law—and its rebirth. Now fate had carried him to a place, at a moment, when ill-informed and arrogant men were setting themselves above the law. Certainly he was not alone in his outrage and fidelity.

He would not stand by as momentous events unfolded. Isaac Rosenfeld, a contemporary, had defined the forces driving men like Alaimo. "No man suffers injustice," Rosenfeld wrote, "without learning, vaguely but surely, what justice is."

*"If not you, then who? If not now, then when?"*
*—Rabbi Hillel, first century A.D.*

Alaimo wanted the new judgeship. "I'd always had this dream," he recalled many years later. "Every lawyer of my generation felt the same way. Yes, I'd been drawn to the logic and discipline of the law, but on a deeper level I wanted to participate in the administration of justice."

Seventy-five years had passed since the Supreme Court decided (in *Plessy v. Ferguson*) that "separate but equal" was not a violation of the Fourteenth Amendment's guarantee of "equal protection under the law." Sixteen years since *Brown v. Board of Education* of Topeka trumped *Plessy*, ordering the desegregation of the nation's schools.

"No, not one!" Ernest Vandiver had shouted during his 1958 gubernatorial campaign, a clear warning to those trying to integrate

Georgia's schools. Ralph McGill, editor of the *Atlanta Constitution*, countered, "When leadership in high places in any degree fails to support constituted authority, it opens the gates to all those who wish to take the law into their own hands."

In 1970, this dizzy clash of values and contrarian visions resonated powerfully; it energized Alaimo like nothing before. The prizefighter shed the unwieldy trappings of success. He pounded his fists together and stepped into the ring.

The process was deceptively simple. Georgia's National Republican Party chariman Howard "Bo" Callaway and his fellow committeemen would recommend their candidate to President Nixon and Attorney General John Mitchell, who would, in turn, submit the nomination to the Senate for approval.

"You really had to work to get it," Alaimo recalled. "It was about patronage. The IOUs you'd gained in supporting other people running for office, working for the party, things of that nature."

His credentials were impeccable. He'd served as the party's general counsel and had been a delegate to three national con-ventions, named to the platform committee, and elected, against the odds, to the Glynn County Commission. He'd been out on the hustings, given stem-winding speeches, attended innumerable meetings and party functions, and tacked-up more than his share of signs.

Alaimo resigned himself to the two-thirds salary cut his "elevation" to the bench would entail. He prepped his campaign with the attention to detail that characterized his legal work. He sounded out the committee about other candidates "to avoid the embarrassment of having my friends recommending an impossibility."

In fact, there was another man vying for the appointment, John B. Miller of Savannah, who'd served as president of law at the Central of Georgia Railway Company, chairman of the board of SunTrust Bank of Savannah, and chairman of the Georgia Board of Bar Examiners.

Alaimo soon had endorsements from forty-seven Georgia superior court judges. "Some of them were perfunctory," he acknowledged, "but some were great letters."

Ultimately, he got the nod. His name was forwarded to the Department of Justice. He filled out his paperwork and sent it off. All he awaited was the American Bar Association's investigation and approval.[3]

*Lasciate ogne speranza, voi ch'intrate.*[4]
—*Dante Alighieri, L'inferno*

The ABA imprimatur—"qualified" or "well-qualified"—should have been rubber-stamped. After all, Alaimo had been elected a decade earlier to the Georgia Bar Association's board of governors.

It was June 1970. On the Georgia coast, the magnolias and crepe myrtles were blossoming. The scent of jasmine and honeysuckle perfumed the air. Tourists were frolicking at the beaches of St. Simons. Word of Tony's nomination spread quickly. The legal grapevine functions as efficiently as its prison counterpart. He couldn't walk out of his office on Norwich Street (an exceedingly modest office) or escort Jeanne to their favorite restaurant, Bennie's Red Barn on Frederica Road in St. Simons, without a lawyer calling his name, pounding his shoulders, and offering congratulations and how-you-doings.

In due course, an ABA representative—another white-shoe attorney, this one from Jackson, Mississippi—came calling. He exchanged pleasantries, interviewed Alaimo, and shook hands. Undoubtedly, he strolled over to the courthouse, perhaps had lunch with a few of the town's prominent attorneys.

---

[3] Beginning in the early 1950s, the ABA's Standing Committee on the Federal Judiciary had formally rated the qualifications of candidates for federal judgeships. ABA approval had become *sine qua non.*

[4] "Abandon every hope, ye who enter here." *La Divina Commedia* Canto III.

In 1970, downtown Brunswick—its commercial district, courthouses, law offices, and jail—would have fit comfortably into a single block of midtown Manhattan. The ABA's man would have certainly visited Reese Bennet & Gilbert, the oldest law firm in the city.

If anything seemed curious about the interview, it was the fact that the ABA man had never brought up Alaimo's judicial recommendations. Nor did he mention any of the attorneys in Atlanta and Savannah who'd known Tony over the years.

Seasons changed. The tourists departed. The honeysuckle withered and the winds coming off the Atlantic Ocean grew cold. Alaimo checked his mailbox more closely as if it contained some secret crevice into which a letter might disappear. He tensed, despite himself, every time the telephone rang. This was not the way he'd lived his life.

On the street, "How you doing?" became "Have you heard anything?"

A year went by.

"Nothing happened with the appointment," Alaimo recalled. "Not a word."

He tried to focus on his cases, stay busy, but he couldn't. He understood what déjà vu really meant: helplessness, not knowing when things would end, how things would end, or even why—the same malaise had plagued him in Stalag Luft III.

"I'd walk down the street," he remembered. "And for the thousandth time, they'd say, 'Have you heard anything?'"

Fifteen months passed. Summer came and went, the bright blossoms of approbation withering in his mind, into infamy. "This absolutely demoralized me," he said. "I knew there had to be something. They were going to disapprove me for some reason. But I couldn't think of any reason. I didn't know of any damn thing I'd done. I felt the ABA had betrayed me.[5] I thought, 'I'm a better lawyer

---

[5] State Bar of Georgia president Irwin "Yutch" Stolz Jr. supported Alaimo and would soon rally the bar on his behalf.

than this,' but I kept still. It was a terrible thing in my life. You can imagine what it did to my practice. Had I realized this, I would have never entered the picture.'"

Griffin Bell, then a US Circuit Judge on the Fifth Circuit Court of Appeals, remembered, "The American Bar Association had already turned him down." Bell had known Alaimo from his own days as a practicing attorney in Savannah. "I'd heard about it."

Alaimo's Republican colleagues, so supportive of his nomination, began backpedaling. In such cases, a nominee is expected to "fall on his sword," withdraw his or her name from consideration. Calloway suggested that the time had come.

"I told him I couldn't do it," Alaimo remembered. "If I had, there would always be a stain on my reputation."

What happened next has been pieced together from a number of interviews, the *Journal of Southern Legal History,*[6] and other sources.

Sometime during this period, Alaimo got a call from Jimmy Carter, the Democratic governor he'd supported with a hefty campaign contribution three years earlier. Jim Bishop, Alaimo's junior partner, was very close to the Carter crowd in Atlanta.

"What can I do to help?" Carter asked.

Alaimo was at such a loss he couldn't think of anything that would help his cause. Then it struck him. E. Smythe Gambrell, Rube Garland's old adversary, was a former president of the American Bar Association.

"I called Governor Carter back and said, 'See if you can't get Mr. Gambrell to talk to the chairman of the ABA's judiciary committee.' This was a guy, Judge [Lawrence E.] Walsh, from New York City."[7]

---

[6] 2004; Volume XII, Numbers 1 & 2.

[7] Walsh, a former judge and deputy attorney general, would serve as a negotiator during the Paris Peace talks with North Vietnam. He would later be named by the Office of the Independent Counsel to investigate the Iran-Contra Affair.

Carter was as good as his word. Smythe Gambrell,[8] Alaimo recalled, quickly scheduled a meeting with Lawrence Walsh. "Smythe called me and said, 'I've just talked to Walsh and he'd like to see you.'"

Griffin Bell picked up the story.

"One day a lawyer from Chicago named Burt Jenner shows up at my office. I knew him pretty well already." (Jenner had made an appearance in Bell's office during the Johnson administration when the ABA had dispatched him to investigate another federal judicial candidate, Alexander Lawrence, who'd run into confirmation problems.) Jenner told Bell he'd been appointed to do a "special investigation" of Anthony A. Alaimo in Brunswick.

"I thought ya'll had already investigated him?" Bell said.

"We did, but we're going to do it over. There have been complaints about our first investigation."

Jenner told Bell he needed the names of some lawyers who were of Alaimo's generation so he'd start out, in effect, with an untainted pool of witnesses.

"Well, give me the names of the lawyers the committee interviewed before," Bell suggested.

The first name Jenner provided was John Gilbert.

As Jenner continued down the list, it struck Bell that other than Gilbert, there were no other attorneys from Savannah or Brunswick, a significant omission since Alaimo had spent much of his career and built many of his peer relationships practicing law on the coast.

"Let me give you some others, just as prominent or more so than these lawyers," offered Bell.

Judge Bell, who'd spent four years practicing at the firm Lawton and Cunningham in Savannah, knew the legal landscape of the coast intimately. He gave Jenner a list that included former Savannah mayor Malcolm Maclean, an attorney with a strong civil rights

---

[8] Smythe's son David Gambrell was appointed US senator after the death of Senator Richard Russell. David Gambrell served the remainder of Russell's term.

record; highly regarded Savannah attorney Anthony Solms, who'd worked with Bell on John F. Kennedy's presidential election campaign; and Cullen M. Ward, a former president of the Georgia Trial Lawyers Association. Bell also offered Jenner a vacant clerk's office in his Atlanta suite to use as a base of operations.

"I was a federal judge and I shouldn't have been dealing in things like this," Bell recalled many years later. "But when it finally came to my attention, it was clear Alaimo hadn't been treated fairly. I resented the fact that somebody[9] had manipulated the process. One lawyer was orchestrating the whole thing. All he had to do was tell some people and make a few phone calls."

In Brunswick, Jim Bishop was equally determined to unravel the intrigue against Alaimo. "Our local bar supported him," Bishop recalled. "At least, we thought everyone did. We fashioned a petition to see if we could flush out where the trouble was, if the opposition was here. And we did. We got everybody's name on the petition with one exception."

Neither Bell nor Bishop could provide absolute confirmation, and Alaimo, though sorely tested, never allowed himself to pursue what he deemed inappropriate and potentially prejudicial information, the evidence points to the influential lawyer John Gilbert, of Gilbert, Harrell, Summerford & Martin.[10]

A dozen years earlier, Alaimo and Way Highsmith had out-lawyered John Gilbert in a highly publicized breach-of-contract action (see pp. 120-21). The jury awarded the plaintiff, real estate broker Hadley Brown, $167,000 based on the testimony of just one witness, Brown himself. Gilbert,[11] the defendants' attorney, was further humiliated when he squandered the opportunity to appeal because of a procedural error.

---

[9] "Later on, when I was Attorney General," Bell added ruefully, "I saw that happen all the time. It was a normal thing, almost."

[10] At the time, Reese Bennet & Gilbert.

[11] Since deceased.

"John Gilbert just didn't like Anthony Alaimo," Griffin Bell suggested many years later. "He would have seen him as an outsider. He was an Italian. We didn't have a lot of foreigners in Georgia. Wasn't like it is now. Most of us never got out of our state until we got into the military. The fact that Alaimo was a Republican would have had something to do with it too. It meant he was against the Establishment. Anybody who'd be a Republican was thought of as disturbing the peace."

Bell paused, laughing before continuing. "And the Republicans now were the Democrats then."

Burt Jenner, armed with Bell's updated list of attorneys, made his way to Brunswick. He and Alaimo had dinner at the Yacht Club. James Gilbert (John Gilbert's brother) and Julian Bennet, also attorneys at Harrell, Summerford & Martin, gave Alaimo favorable ratings, as did other men Jenner interviewed. John Gilbert acknowledged he was supporting his friend, John B. Miller, of Savannah for the judgeship.

In any event, the logjam was broken. Jenner wound up his investigation and the Georgia Bar Association kicked into high gear its support for a man, suddenly a favorite son. "After the ABA rechecked him, they graded Alaimo 'well-qualified,'" Bell recalled. "And that about wound it up."

Alaimo received his long-awaited telephone call. A Justice Department official advised him that President Nixon had officially designated him the new US District Judge for the Southern District of Georgia. Accompanied by Jim Bishop, Alaimo flew to Washington, DC, where Representative Fletcher Thompson, a Republican representing Georgia's Fifth Congressional District, escorted him into the senate chamber. Alaimo remembered the confirmation proceeding as "uneventful."

Like Dante's Pilgrim, Alaimo emerged from "a dark wood, pure and disposed to mount unto the stars." Along the way, men very like himself, rose to assist him, to lend a hand, to point the way forward when he faltered.

Albert Jenner Jr. grew up near the Chicago stockyards in an Irish neighborhood christened Canaryville. To pay his college tuition he moonlighted as a professional boxer, bloody but triumphant. Jenner's career was long and impossibly distinguished: president of the American College of Trial Lawyers; chairman of the US Supreme Court Advisory Committee on the Rules of Evidence for the United States Courts; member of the ABA's Board of Governors; senior counsel to the Warren Commission. In 1973, his fellow Republicans appointed him chief minority counsel to the House judiciary committee investigating Richard Nixon. It was a thankless job. Jenner was forced to resign when he recommended impeachment.

This is the man who walked into Judge Griffin Bell's suite to set the record straight on Tony Alaimo. At Jenner's 1988 memorial service, Illinois governor James Thompson remarked, "When the wounds were deep and grievous for all Americans, when some impoverished soul was threatened, when some unpopular cause would have been extinguished but for the bravery and perseverance of that man, they all reached out for Bert Jenner."

Griffin Bell's father had been a farmer in South Georgia, a place not so far removed from the fields and family-oriented culture of Sicily. A. C. and Thelma Bell were poor and they invested their dreams in a precocious son. A.C. Bell was a compassionate man; Griffin Bell would spend his life and career "trying to be as kind as my father was."

Griffin Bell said he didn't have "a whole lot to get started in life." Alaimo worked at a Detroit foundry, Bell sold tires. Both answered the call during World War II and returned changed men. Bell attended Mercer University on the GI Bill, worked part time at a law firm, and was smart enough not to seek a job in Atlanta.

In Savannah, Judge David Atkinson, whose only son had been killed in World War II, noticed Bell's outstanding work. "You keep trying cases like that and you'll end up at the Coca-Cola law firm in Atlanta." Bell had no idea what firm that might be; sure enough he wound up as managing partner of King & Spalding *and* attorney general of the United States.

Eighteen months after his name had been submitted, Anthony Alaimo, with angels such as these at his side, was confirmed as US District Judge for the Southern District of Georgia.

# Part III

"The view from that Chair is so different from what it was when I practiced law."
—US District Court Judge Anthony Alaimo

# Chapter 20

"I, Anthony A. Alaimo do solemnly swear that I will
administer justice without respect to persons, and do
equal right to the poor and to the rich, and that I will
faithfully and impartially discharge and perform all
the duties incumbent upon me as US District Judge
under the Constitution and laws of the United States.
So help me God."

On December 20, 1971, a crowd of family members and well
wishers gathered in Brunswick's federal courthouse to witness
Anthony Alaimo's swearing in as a US district judge. His great friend
and colleague, John Sammons Bell, chief justice of the Court of
Appeals of Georgia, administered the oath. The two had been
classmates at Emory; both had survived harrowing combat in World
War II. Bell, whose Southern ancestry extended generations before
the Civil War, stood alongside the immigrant son. He praised Alaimo
as a scholarly, industrious, honorable, and conscientious man and
then probed more deeply into his friend's soul.

"Tony Alaimo is a kind man," Bell said. "He is a good man. He's
a compassionate man. I predict those attributes will make him a great
judge."

In a photograph taken while the oath was administered, Alaimo
stands ramrod straight, right arm raised, left hand clenched at his
side, as if willing the storms of memory and feeling swirling inside
him, calm. A newspaper reporter in the courtroom at the time noted,
with some understatement, "Alaimo refrained from making a public
statement because of the solemn, emotional nature of the ceremony."

Standing next to Judge Bell is Judge Alexander Lawrence, chief judge of the Southern District of Georgia. Lawrence is about to invest Alaimo with the black robes of his office. "It is with no small amount of relief and pleasure," he said, "to be receiving assistance from an able and experienced lawyer in handling the heavy case load of the circuit."

At the time, Alaimo was too exhilarated to notice that Lawrence had already prepared an order assigning him an escalating series of actions brought by African-American prisoners at the Georgia State Prison in Reidsville. "It was right there on the bench ready for me to sign," Alaimo remembered with a laugh. "I was so eager to get involved, I would have signed anything that day. I had no idea of the immensity of it."

After the Christmas holidays, he spent two weeks in Washington, DC, attending the Federal Judicial Center's orientation program of lectures on civil and criminal procedures, sentencing, ethics, and perhaps a session or two on judicial-congressional relations, always a sticking point. Jeanne Alaimo immediately christened the program an "obedience school for judges."

When Alaimo returned, Reidsville awaited him—a Gordian knot of a magnitude[1] and complexity Alexander[2] himself might have hesitated. It loomed, ever larger and more urgent, among the civil rights disputes, damage suits, contract actions, and criminal cases that would fill his calendars over the next twenty-five years.

Seen from the outside, the prison, an unexpected neoclassical pile rising among the cotton fields of southeast Georgia, projects the

---

[1] The files on the case (*Guthrie v. Evans*), now housed at the University of Georgia's Richard B. Russell Library for Political Research and Studies, fill forty-seven boxes.

[2] Alexander the Great fulfilled a prophecy that the one to untie the legendary knot would become king. Cutting to the heart of a problem is considered the "Alexandrine Solution."

monumental weight the state can bring down upon violent and incorrigible men. In 1936 it was built to accommodate 1,000 juvenile offenders, strictly segregated, in open dorms. Lacking adequate funding, safeguards, or staff, it was nonetheless converted into a maximum-security facility. Reidsville quickly devolved into a violent snake pit. By 1972, 3,300 inmates were crammed into dorms and cellblocks overflowing with filth and vermin.

"Rehabilitation," a frieze on the front of the main building, depicts trades industrious inmates might pursue, but Reidsville's best-known architectural element was "Old Sparky," its electric chair. Never intended to be a reformatory, Reidsville was a penitentiary, a purgatory against which the stalags appeared models of humane treatment.

Prisoners outnumbered correction officers twelve to one. Racial gangs moved freely through a complex that lacked even the basic access and control points vital in operating a maximum-security facility. Assault, rape, and murder were commonplace. The all-white staff was underpaid and ill-trained. At the top of this unfortunate pyramid were a series of wardens[3] who ruled independent of Department of Correction supervision, like feudal lords.

Fearful of their lives, guards relied on violence and intimidation to control their charges, some of whom were incorrigible sociopaths who would plunge a shiv into another human being's heart over a disrespectful word in the Yard. There were no policies, procedures, or rules, no guidelines at Reidsville. One did not plan or manage Reidsville; one reacted, or more likely overreacted. Medical care was virtually nonexistent, as were inmates' access to law books, legal counsel, educational materials, even exercise equipment. The list was endless.

In a state already segregated by law, black inmates endured the worst of these abuses.

---

[3] Six wardens passed through the prison between 1972 and 1982.

Such conditions were hardly unique. At the time Alaimo turned his attention to Reidsville, abuse and ill-treatment were a given in thousands of county jails and state prisons around the country. Elected officials are precisely attuned to the moods of their constituents, and given the law-and-order mood of the American voter in the 1970s, what politician would be willing to divert resources to improve the lot of men considered the dregs of society?

Nonetheless, the US Constitution vouchsafes certain rights to prisoners; most significantly, the Eighth Amendment protections against "cruel and unusual punishment" and Fifth Amendment guarantees that individuals not be deprived of life, liberty, or property without "due process of law."

The common vehicle for prisoner lawsuits is federal statute 42 U.S.C. § 1983, which permits inmates to sue in federal court for alleged violations of their rights by individuals acting under the authority of state law (e.g., a warden, supervisor, guard, corrections official, or governor).

Inmates' letters—many hand-scrawled and barely literate, others well-argued and eloquent—piled up by the dozens and then hundreds in the federal courthouses in Brunswick and Augusta. Over the years, the number of these communications would soar into the thousands. Among them were a number of formal legal complaints—lawsuits—that compelled a response from defendants named. The newly minted Alaimo read every one, even those scrawled on toilet paper. He found that most were frivolous, while others were profoundly troubling. "Ninety-nine percent were garbage," he recalled. "One percent had some merit. It was my function as a judge to ferret that one percent out. If I don't, then the system fails."

Inevitably, the day came when the former POW arrived at the forbidding walls and locked gates of the prison. "I had a marshal with me on my first trip to Reidsville," Alaimo remembered, speaking slowly as the sights, sounds, and smells of that visit returned from the iron vaults of memory to which he'd banished them. "As I walked along the cellblocks, I saw men who should have been in the insane asylum over in Milledgeville. Men lying on the floor in their cells covered in feces.... The guards used long poles to shove the food to them. It was just...you know, I could not look at this and consider myself a human being without doing something about it."

On September 29, 1972, Arthur S. Guthrie and fifty other black inmates of Reidsville signed a four-page *in forma pauperis*[4] complaint (*Guthrie v. Evans*[5]) seeking injunctive relief from the prison's cruel and inhumane conditions. In July 1973, Judge Alaimo certified the lawsuit[6] a class action.

On the bench, Alaimo would make his reputation as a peerless mediator, albeit one whose approach to fractious litigators and prevaricating bureaucrats was stick rather than carrot. In October 1973, he brought in Department of Justice mediator Robert Greenwald, hoping that what appeared to be a pattern of "systematic and compelling" abuse could be resolved without further litigation. (Legal terminology does not capture the vileness of the condition at Reidsville.) A year later, a period in which the US Civil Rights Commission documented the under-funding and unspeakable conditions of Georgia's prisons, Greenwald departed with no progress to report.

Over the years, the baleful stare and roseate effulgence of complexion would become precise indicators of Judge Alaimo's frustration. He next appointed Brunswick attorney Marvin Pipkin as special master to prepare the case for trial. Alaimo hovered over the proceedings for five years, a brooding thunderhead on a summer afternoon, as Pipkin dealt with pretrial motions, conducted endless

---

[4] "In form of a pauper or poor man," the term used by a judge to allow someone who has no money to file a legal action.

[5] David Evans, was commissioner of the Georgia Department of Offender Rehabilitation.

[6] Over the years this was variously titled *Guthrie vs. MacDougall*, *Guthrie v. Caldwell*, and *Guthrie v. Ault*.

inspections and fact-finding sessions, and took reams of depositions from inmates, guards, corrections officials, and experts, amassing more than 200 witnesses and 100 exhibits.

"Marvin spent substantial time and was paid well," Alaimo remembered. "He did a pretty good job mediating which committees were appointed among the inmates and assuring they represented a group that was authorized to speak for the population."

Pipkin's findings—endorsed in their entirety by Alaimo—demonstrated beyond doubt the defendants' liability. The state Department of Offender Rehabilitation (DOR) gave assurances—halfhearted as it turned out—that the prison would be brought into compliance.

*Guthrie v. Evans* was never tried in a courtroom. Judge Alaimo's remedies emerged as a stream of detailed orders and consent decrees addressing inmate health, safety, legal rights, educational opportunities, and a hundred other concerns issued over the next decade.

The real challenge was seeing the decrees implemented by a state bureaucracy immobilized by crushing inertia, budgetary constraints, and virulent, yet often subtle, resistance.

In April 1974, Alaimo ordered Reidsville integrated—a first step, he hoped, in ameliorating the overcrowded conditions. Along with other ills, segregation actually provided white inmates, a minority of the population, more spacious living conditions. The ruling triggered new rounds of violence, along with the oft-heard complaint that a federal judge was meddling in affairs beyond his ken and exacerbating an already explosive situation.

In November 1974 Alaimo, now embroiled in a number of highly charged civil rights cases unfolding in Augusta and its environs, was forced to issue an order for the protection of Reidsville's inmates. Five prisoners were killed and fifty seriously injured in racial confrontations over the next two years.[7] In spring 1978, a corrections officer was murdered in a riot the newspapers described as a "reign of terror."

That summer, violence increased to the point that Special Master Pipkin persuaded Alaimo to issue a controversial order temporarily re-segregating black and white prisoners "checkerboard" fashion in alternating dormitories. Reidsville's cellblocks, dining halls, and work and recreation areas remained integrated.

The move, which on the surface ran counter to a decade of prison reform legislation,[8] triggered an outcry from prison reform advocates and the NAACP Legal Defense Fund but, given the realities on the ground, Alaimo's action served to tamp down the worst of the violence. Originally issued for sixty days, the order was extended an additional six months without challenge.

"There were so many rumors and so much tension," Pipkin said at the time, "that I felt that if we separated the prisoners…and let things cool off, it would help the situation."

Alaimo was growing increasingly frustrated. He prepared to dismiss the case, short of some significant breakthrough.

In the mid-1970s, Robert Cullen was a young Massachusetts transplant working for Georgia Legal Services (GLS) in Augusta. GLS was familiarly known as a "poverty law center" that provided legal representation and other services to the indigent or those without the wherewithal to press their grievances in a court of law. The organization was sporadically funded by the federal government, the state of Georgia, and, when things got tough, the kindness of the liberal establishment.

---

[7] Between 1972 and 1982, there were thirty-four murders and innumerable assaults at Reidsville.

[8] In *Lee v. Washington*, the Supreme Court found the Alabama law enforcing segregation in jails and prisons unconstitutional under the Fourteenth Amendment.

A Boston College Law School graduate, Cullen also held a master's degree from Harvard in what would later be considered "alternative dispute resolution." He was a mediator, a gifted one, as well as an idealist, one of hundreds of young attorneys—Northern and Southern both—caught up in the romance, drama, and righteousness of the civil rights movement. Easygoing with a droll sense of humor, Cullen got along with most folks, a skill that would serve him well in the circumstances ahead.

After law school, Cullen had two firm job offers with legal aid offices in New York and Philadelphia. His decision to travel to Augusta to interview with Georgia Legal Services was almost an afterthought. If anything, his heart was in Boston, where an order by US District Court judge Arthur Garrity Jr. to desegregate Boston's public schools via busing had triggered massive and violent opposition.

"When I showed up in Augusta for my interview," Cullen recalled many years later, "Bill Cobb[9] decided to take me to meet some folks at the Department of Welfare. Bill had to stop at the District Court to file something and we ran into Judge Alaimo in the hall. I remember he had on his classic fedora."

The three men chatted for about fifteen minutes. Cullen recalled Alaimo as a "bundle of energy." Like St. Elmo's Fire, the shimmering electrical disturbance appearing on the masts of ships in storm-tossed seas, Alaimo's energy could jump and spark to those around him.

Cullen remembers being blown away by the brief encounter.

"I went back to Massachusetts," he recalled in a 2007 interview. "Everybody at Boston College was telling me, 'You've got these two great jobs! And you want to go to Augusta, Georgia? Are you a fool?'

"You don't understand, I told them. This guy is amazing! Judge Alaimo was incredibly bright, top-notch. He seemed to be a man who was, ultimately, practical and pragmatic. He wasn't interested in

---

[9] Georgia Legal Services attorney William J. Cobb.

some high-falutin' idea of what the world should be. He was interested in fundamental fairness. I'd been told the litany of problems in the Augusta area. It was a place where I might actually do some good. I could bring some of these issues in front of this man and see what happened.

"He never faltered. I'd met Judge Garrity and thought he was impressive. After meeting Judge Alaimo, I understood what impressive was." Cullen happily went to work in Augusta. Over the next eighteen months, Alaimo would be equally impressed with the attorney's grit and what seemed to be a remarkable ability to wrest agreements from warring parties.

The judge would never discuss the details of particular cases, but he was willing on occasion to chat, as Cullen put it, about issues that concerned him. "If you could read him at all well," Cullen added, "you sure walked out of those conversations knowing which way to jump."

In Reidsville, the situation continued to deteriorate. Inevitably the day came when the phone jangled in the Georgia Legal Services' Augusta office. Cullen recounted the incident:

"Judge Alaimo called and said, 'Bob, get over here.'"
Knowing which way to jump, Cullen rushed over to the courthouse.
"You've got to take over the Reidsville thing."
"What?"
Though buried in a blizzard of cases, Cullen quickly felt his resistance begin to wither under Alaimo's incandescent gaze.
"Judge I can't! …John Cromartie[10] won't let me. It would mean a huge commitment of our resources. We can't possibly do this!"
"Tell John to be in my chambers at 11:00 A.M. tomorrow."

---

[10] Attorney John Cromartie, later Georgia Legal Services' executive director.

The next morning when Cromartie strolled into the office, Cullen was already there, pacing.

"Judge Alaimo wants to see you."

"Okay?"

Cullen explained what the judge wanted.

"No way!" Cromartie exclaimed. "Don't worry about this, Bob, I'll take care of it."

The two attorneys hurried over to the courthouse. Alaimo was waiting for them. He waggled his fingers.

"Have a seat, Bob. John, you come with me."

"Cromartie goes into the judge's office for about seven minutes," Cullen recalled. "Out he comes, announcing, 'Oh Bob, Judge Alaimo has this great idea! Your new assignment is Reidsville!"

"I don't know what went on in that room," Cullen added. "But Judge Alaimo said, 'Do it,' and we did it. At the time, we were almost completely federally funded and had to do a whole dog and pony show to conform to all their bright ideas and priorities. Here we are throwing them over completely.

"That very day I was on my way to Reidsville prison."

Alaimo also remembered the encounter. "Well, I did [pressure them]," he recalled. "If a ruling were involved, I wouldn't have indicated my leaning one way or another. But it was a real shambles up there. I needed somebody to control it, someone who could represent the prisoners. Cullen was good and he improved immensely along the way."[11]

Alaimo paused then added with a chuckle, "Of course, you understand I had no power to *make* him do it."

That night, Cullen drove the two hours from Augusta to Reidsville along deserted, unlit country roads, feeling perhaps like another ill-starred young attorney sallying forth into unknown

---

[11] Cullen and his colleagues would develop an extensive network of corrections experts, academics and researchers, and even sympathetic journalists to provide the expertise and insight that guided Alaimo in his handling of the case.

territory—Jonathan Harker on his first trip to Count Dracula's castle in Transylvania.

"I walk in there and meet Marvin Pipkin, the first special master," he recalled. "He says there are these inmate committees, a white committee and a black committee, and they're threatening to have serious racial problems. I say 'Wonderful!' We go to a meeting in the warden's dining room. The white guys are at one end of the table and the black guys are down here. I could cut the tension with a knife. Marvin is right. They're not getting along.

"At one point, I need to use the restroom. Marvin says, 'You're better off holding it, man.' But I've got to go. My clients say they'll escort me. We walk into the hall and every one of them produces a shiv. These black guys form a protective wall around me. We walk past a guard in a little niche carved into the wall. He's in there with his billy-club and isn't coming out for nothing! There are roving bands of white guys everywhere. As we're walking back, a group of them pull out their shivs. The place is totally out of control."[12]

"I start working on it and it's a disaster. The place is unbelievably filthy. L and M buildings are the worst. There's raw sewage spilling all over the floors. The plumbing doesn't work. There are parts of M building where it's so dangerous the staff won't even go down there."

"For years, Reidsville was the most violent maximum-security unit in the country, incredibly overcrowded and really, really dangerous," Cullen said later. "But no matter how bad things got, the word somehow never got to the Department of Corrections[13] in Atlanta."

---

[12] Cullen eventually persuades the white inmates that it is in their interest to join the class action.

[13] Georgia's Department of Offender Rehabilitation was later renamed the Department of Corrections.

By all accounts, David Evans,[14] the Georgia Department of Offender Rehabilitation commissioner named as the defendant in *Guthrie*, was forward-looking and sympathetic, a civil servant rendered impotent by a system in which absolute power and authority had disseminated into the hands of the wardens.

The lines spoken by Warden Ranken to his prisoners in the 1985 prison film, *Runaway Train*, captures precisely the chain of authority Evans and the Reidsville special masters were struggling with:

First, there's God...
Then the warden...
Then my guards...
Then the dogs out there in the kennel...
And finally you:
Pieces of human waste—
No good to yourselves or anybody else.

In summer 1979, Alaimo appointed a second special master, Vincent M. Nathan, a criminal justice professor at the University of Toledo in Ohio. Nathan had extensive correctional reform experience. Alaimo assigned him broad powers to mediate, implement, and monitor the court's decrees. Over the next four years, Nathan, a hardnosed taskmaster cut from the same cloth as Alaimo, issued a series of scathing reports documenting the state's continuing noncompliance. Nonviolent and mentally ill prisoners, he reported, were being clubbed, kicked, pushed down staircases, and sprayed with chemical mace for seemingly minor infractions. Medical care was practically non-existent. At the time, more than 300 inmates were awaiting surgery. Talmadge Memorial Hospital in Augusta had stopped treating them because of security concerns.

---

[14] Alaimo remembered Evans's annual salary as $40,000—to him, clear evidence that the General Assembly had other priorities besides prison reform.

Nathan's assessments were particularly galling to the Georgia legislature because Alaimo had ordered Nathan's fees and expenses reimbursed by the state. "Here's this guy from Toledo, Ohio, who's getting paid more than the governor,"[15] Alaimo recalled. "You can bet I caught hell from the legislators about it."[16]

Officially, the state attorneys took the position that Special Master Nathan was imposing tighter standards and tougher remedies than even Alaimo had ordered. Therefore, real improvements in conditions at Reidsville were going unreported.

Behind the scenes, it was becoming exceedingly clear to Governor George Busbee and Attorney General Michael Bowers that they were in a no-win situation. "Prisoners' rights" was an issue that could reduce their careers and political capital to dust. There was Alaimo, who never had to worry about being reelected, breathing down their necks. In the statehouse, no bastion of progressive ideas, legislators were up in arms about this federal judge, this Yankee outsider,[17] ordering them to pour money into a murderous sinkhole. Reporters like the *Atlanta Journal-Constitution* journalist Marcia Kunstel were generating a drumbeat of stories documenting the violence and barbarous conditions at the prison.

*"The limits of judicial patience are at hand." —Judge Alaimo to Georgia corrections officials*

One evening, Busbee secretly flew down to Brunswick hoping to hammer out an agreement with Nathan and Alaimo. They met in the judge's conference room where, in the course of a long evening,

---

[15] The governor was George Busbee, whose term in office (1975–1983) paralleled the worst of the Reidsville unrest.

[16] The state of Georgia would later peg the cost of improvements to its prisons incurred as a result of the Guthrie litigation at more than $400 million.

[17] According to a 2007 interview with Alaimo, "They never quite came out and said it, but I was a foreigner."

Busbee agreed to Robert Cullen's suggestion that they import a federal warden, Charles Montgomery,[18] from Arizona to temporarily take control of the prison. When the dust and the political posturing subsided, Alaimo recalled, "Busbee continued spending money upgrading services at Reidsville."

Vincent Nathan stepped down as special master in December 1983. Hardnosed to the end, Nathan recommended that the court impose on the state even stricter punitive measures (e.g., forcing the prison into receivership). Alaimo next appointed Charles Bell, a Georgia Department of Corrections administrator, as independent monitor. Now it was the plaintiff's attorneys who expressed outrage. Bell was much less confrontational than Nathan. He was willing to work with the defendants. He gave them advance notice of deficiencies and opportunities to make corrections before presenting his findings to Alaimo. Over time, both sides came to view Bell as fair and equitable.

> *"Our state faced a challenge unlike any in its history*
> *when the Guthrie Case was filed. Out of the entire*
> *process, we've developed a correctional system which has*
> *become a model for the nation."*
> —*Georgia Governor Joe Frank Harris*

Bell issued a final report in June 1985.[19] That month, Alaimo made a surprise visit to Reidsville. He remembered being pleased with the improvements and upgrades he witnessed. When he'd conducted an inspection four years earlier, inmates had greeted Alaimo with death threats and a homemade bomb. After still another onsite visit James Henderson, a Leavenworth, Kansas, corrections consultant, reported that "Reidsville is literally a changed institution.... The

---

[18] After two years Montgomery resigned in frustration.

[19] Bell indicated that there was still much to be done. A newly constructed wing of the facility was barely at "minimum compliance."

atmosphere, the morale of the staff, and the mood of the inmate population have all changed in an impressive manner."

Georgia State Prison would become the first corrections facility in the country to be accredited by the American Medical Association for its healthcare services. Its mental health program has been adapted by a number of federal prisons around the country. The institution would become the first prison to receive accreditation by the American Correctional Association for meeting or surpassing its standards.

In summer 1985, Alaimo enjoined defendants from failing or refusing to comply with his prior orders and consent decrees. He warned them of further sanctions. He held them liable for plaintiff's legal fees. Then, satisfied, he returned the operation of Reidsville to the state of Georgia.

"We're free now to operate Georgia State Prison without federal court intervention," said Busbee's successor Governor Joe Frank Harris, "although we are bound forever to the requirements agreed upon under Guthrie."

At the time, the larger impact of the lawsuit was not yet clear. Over time, Judge Alaimo's actions in *Guthrie v. Evans* would trigger dramatic, even revolutionary, changes, not only in Georgia's wretched prisons but in the nation's penal system as a whole. In small, carefully considered steps, Alaimo had synthesized a critical relationship among the federal courts, state corrections departments, and penal reform advocacies. Slowly and painfully, Reidsville[20] had become that rarest thing, "a Constitutional prison."

The great irony, though politicians are rarely attuned to irony, is that the very legislators and executives who had vehemently protested the courts' meddling in state affairs would later sing the praises of a prison that had become the absolute gold standard for the rest of the nation's penal institutions.

---

[20] Reidsville was accredited by the American Correctional Association in August 1987.

Dismantling a system that, ungoverned and unaccountable, had descended to the depths of inhumanity Alaimo had witnessed under the Nazis had always been a subtext of the Reidsville litigation.

"I'd talked to Judge Alaimo at length about the wider issues," Cullen recalled many years later. "When he wrote the first consent order, it was phrased as a Standing Operating Procedure that would be effective system-wide. With Commissioner Evans's help, Georgia started moving away from individual fiefdoms where unspeakable cruelties were everyday occurrences."

In July 1997,[21] Alaimo formally terminated *Guthrie v. Evans.* He'd signed more than 1,200 orders mandating improvements in sanitation, nutrition, climate control, health, and safety. Reidsville was desegregated; its inmate population had dropped from more than 3,300 in 1972 to fewer than 1,000. Racial tensions had eased dramatically.

"The thing the wardens finally learned," Alaimo later remarked, "was that the best friend they had was a federal judge, because he made the state spend the money to make these improvements."

The dormitories—former breeding grounds for murder and abuse—had been replaced by individual cells. New standards were in place regarding inmate classification, disciplinary and grievance procedures, religious freedoms, visitation rights, and exercise privileges. There were adequate medical, dental, and mental health programs, educational and career training opportunities, and a law library.

No detail was too small to escape Alaimo's notice. He ordered prisoners' polyurethane palettes replaced by fire-retardant mattresses. Then he went after prison administrators when they delayed implementing the change. He knew the minimum standards for a prisoner's cell ("not less than 60 sq. ft.") and even what rights prisoners had in terms of requesting a special diet.

---

[21] Alaimo had observed sufficient improvement in conditions at Reidsville to end the role of the special monitor with an injunctive order in June 1985.

"Most judges would just sign a consent order for anything you put in front of them," Cullen recalled. "Judge Alaimo would carefully review the policies and point out things he didn't think were workable. He had a really active role."

In a 2007 interview, Judge Alaimo was careful to note that it was Dorothy Toth Beasley, the Georgia assistant attorney general assigned to the case, who first proposed that he certify *Guthrie* as a class action. "I relied heavily on the integrity of the lawyers[22] on both sides of the case," he said. "If there was a villain, it was the state legislature that refused for decades to implement any improvements."

On July 1, 1985, an *Atlanta Journal-Constitution* editorial would proclaim, "Judge Alaimo has freed the state only from the strict demands of federal supervision and not from its responsibility to maintain a well-run, safe and humane prison system. The lawsuit has ended but the job has not changed." The editorial would prove prophetic in ways Alaimo could never have imagined. Unlike Stalag VIIA, Reidsville was a prison he would never escape. Twenty-five years later he was still considering complaints from individual inmates.

---

[22] Robert Cullen's associate, NAACP Legal Defense Fund attorney Steven L. Winter, played a significant role in these discussions.

# Chapter 21

"I was running trials from 8:00 A.M. in the morning
until 6:00 to 6:30 P.M. at night with just one hour for
lunch. I'd start up again next morning. This was
pretty hard stuff on the lawyers. They thought I was a
first-class son of a bitch."
—Judge Anthony Alaimo

If Reidsville was the Gordian knot, the remainder of Anthony
Alaimo's docket resembled the Augean stables. The Southern District
of Georgia encompasses six statutory divisions: Augusta, Brunswick,
Dublin, Savannah, Statesboro and Waycross. At the time of his
appointment, the sprawling territory was handled by Judge Alexander
Lawrence,[1] who came to the bench after Frank M. Scarlett's death in
1971. Reidsville was a lagniappe. Judge Lawrence next served Alaimo
the main courses: jurisdiction over Augusta, Brunswick, and
Waycross.

In a sense, Frank Scarlett's memento mori to Alaimo was as
unsettling as his first salutation had been a decade earlier ("Who is
this odd little fellow?"). He left behind hundreds of backlogged
cases—damage suits, breach of contract actions, injunctions, prisoner
complaints, and voting rights grievances, along with criminal cases of
every stripe.

The coast that comprised the eastern border of the district, with
its marshes and hidden coves, sea lanes, and secluded highways,
retained much of its seventeenth-century pirate sensibility. US 17, for
example, then the main north-south artery between New York and

---

[1] Today the district is overseen by seven judges, including four who have taken
senior status.

Miami, was a breeding ground for corruption and plunder, a good bit of it under the auspices of a sheriff who ran McIntosh County like a feudal fiefdom. Further inland, Waycross would become a node in a network of violent narcotics operations moving up out of Florida.

A parade of alleged Mann Act violations, bootlegging, prostitution, interstate transportation of stolen goods, car theft, hijacking, and soon drug smuggling conspiracies marched across Judge Alaimo's desk.

"It was there," he said simply, "and had to be dealt with."

His approach was reminiscent of the Great Escape. He took stock of an intolerable situation, grabbed his tools and started to dig his way out.

### "It's my lawsuit"

Alaimo began overhauling the court's administrative procedures, which he found to be "a shambles." He focused on pretrial hearings—in simple terms, conferences between the bench and attorneys on both sides of a case to determine, for example, the parameters of a pending trial. "They'd never had pretrial practices," Alaimo recalled. "Sure enough, during a trial, a guy would press an objection to something that could have been decided pretrial. And I'd have to run the jury out. It confused things, sometimes willfully. My intent was to get a case to a jury as cleanly as possible, so they could decide, rather than running them back and forth while I heard objections.

"Attorneys would get argumentative over nothing, particularly in the discovery phase over depositions and that kind of stuff," Alaimo continued. "Or they'd make completely artless pleadings trying to magnify trivial things. I wouldn't tolerate it. I enforced rules and didn't grant continuances except for providential cause. How terrible it was to watch a lawyer representing a client walk into court with a single sheet of paper in a file. I enforced rigid time limits. Sure, they grumbled, but I impressed upon them that once you file a lawsuit, it's my lawsuit. I control how it's going to be handled."

Thirty-five years later, still a sitting judge, Alaimo found no reason to alter his approach. "My theory is to decide all pretrial problems in advance. The truth is lawyers don't talk to each other in the course of litigation, so I'd get them together in a status conference. I'd require the principals to be there and begin talking about settlement. I'd impress on them that going to trial was expensive."

In civil cases, particularly those involving corporations, Alaimo's absolute focus on *settling* rather than *trying* would define his tenure on the bench. He asked rhetorically, "Why would they want twelve strangers or six strangers, as the case might be, deciding these big, complex disputes? And why would they think they'd be better served than in a settlement? I've always preached that settlement is the best form of justice.

"Oh boy, in the beginning it was bad. The lawyers thought I was a first-class son of a bitch. After a while, they realized the value of the system. They were able to dispose of a case, get their money, and move on to the next case. I don't know of any case that improved with time."

David Hudson, then a newly minted attorney with Hull, Towill, Norman, Barrett & Salley in Augusta, remembered trying his first case before Alaimo. "He was very demanding," Hudson recalled in a 2007 interview. "Whether you'd practiced for thirty years or two years, he wanted you prepared. He wanted written materials on time. And succinct arguments. If you had a pretrial motion, he'd say, 'Okay, I'll see you gentlemen at 7:00 A.M. because the jury will be arriving at 9:00 A.M.' If it went to trial, he made sure you moved along. It was superb training for someone like me to have to perform to the level of expectation he demanded of any lawyer in his court."

Hudson laughed, then added, "We had a saying: 'We just finished a six-week trial with Judge Alaimo. It started Monday and ended on Friday.'"

Alaimo's calendar was so clogged that he was forced to schedule hearings every thirty minutes. Many days he had to prepare a dozen cases, not simply to be ready for the parade of querulous and procrastinating lawyers marching through his courtroom, but also "to impress people with the fact that they were going to get a fair shake. I'd never force a lawyer to try a case before me who felt I was going to be biased."

He described his workload in the early years as "continual," hardly an exaggeration. His courtroom soon resembled the all-night diners, strung like the forlorn outposts along US 17 he'd frequented as a young attorney: open for business seven days a week, every week. Court would start 8:00 A.M. sharp and run to 6:00 P.M., though midnight jury deliberations and Sunday sessions were commonplace.

If sequestered jury members wanted to attend church on Sunday, Alaimo ordered a marshal to accompany them. Pity the white-shoe attorney or Fortune 500 executive who, after flying into St. Simons' Malcolm McKinnon airport on the corporate jet for a hearing or trial, imagined Sundays would be reserved for a round of golf at the Sea Island Golf Club and a leisurely lunch at The Cloister. Alaimo boiled William Gladstone's maxim "Justice delayed is justice denied" to a modus operandi: "Dispose of business with dispatch."

Alaimo's ability to clear cases would become legendary. In later years, he would become a kind of judicial outrider—Have Robe, Will Travel—roaming the country hearing cases, some highly charged and controversial. In the aftermath of the assassination of district judge John Wood Jr. by a hit man linked to a drug conspiracy, he traveled to San Antonio, Texas, and took over Judge Wood's calendar. A chance encounter with District Court judge Hubert Teitelbaum led to a friendship and a two-week trip to Pittsburgh, where Alaimo plowed through a backlog of cases. He settled eight in his first week—including a three-day jury trial—and six the next.

All through the 1970s, Reidsville hung over him, a miasma that showed no signs of dissipating. He was spending six months a year in Augusta, where a series of complex criminal, discrimination, desegregation, and voter rights cases were unfolding. He and Jeanne purchased a condo there and would drive back and forth between Brunswick and Augusta every three months, with sessions at the courthouse in Waycross sandwiched between.

*Willful as a field of kudzu.*

When Alaimo arrived in Augusta, it's fair to say the local bar was as ingrown and enclosed as a Charleston garden, a *hortus conclusus.* The hope had been that one of its own worthies would be appointed district judge. Now, courtesy of a handful of Republican upstarts, came a Yankee wiry and willful as a field of kudzu. It's hardly a surprise that Georgia's "Garden City," home to azaleas, tasseled loafers, green jackets, and the sacrosanct traditions of the Masters, did not embrace its long-awaited federal judge with open arms.

"For many years, Georgia had been a one-party state and the people in power, the good old boy network, were all Democrats," David Hudson explained. "The leaders of the bar were all from the big defense firms. And here's a plaintiff's lawyer from outside the state. He'd worked with Reuben Garland up in Atlanta, who was a character."

Beneath its veneer of civility, Augusta was a deeply troubled city. Its Fourth Street Jail was as overcrowded and inhumane as Reidsville. Corruption was a fact of life. Arthur "Buck" Kent, the head of the city's vice squad, was a one-man crime wave. An extortionist, he prowled the city's clubs and juke joints competing with the criminals he was supposed to be pursuing. In the mid-1970s, Alaimo sent Kent to federal prison for income tax evasion. The Augusta Police Department, backed by the city's civil service commission, was resisting any real attempt at desegregation. In October 1973, after eleven black officers filed suit alleging discriminatory hiring and promotion practices, Alaimo issued an order to integrate the force. (The officers' lawyer, John Ruffin, begged Alaimo to put the whole department into receivership.) As he'd done with Reidsville, Alaimo wound up rewriting the department's policies and procedures manual to force a measure of minority advancement, a "dictatorial" move that won him the lasting ire of the *Augusta Chronicle* editorial board.

No one complained when Alaimo sent a country moonshiner like Palmer Flakes or a draft resister like Edward Tenney to prison, but when the heat got closer to the country clubs and the well-feathered law offices overlooking Broad Street, the city fathers could not have been happy. In 1975, the First Augusta State Bank collapsed. It took federal investigators two years to unravel the tangled web of unsecured insider loans and fraudulent scams spun by three of Augusta's leading citizens—former state senator R. Eugene Holley, G. Bertrand Hester,[2] and bank president John R. Adamson. Holley, an oil man considered one of the richest individuals in Georgia, was one of Augusta's biggest boosters, bringing in the world-renowned architect I. M. Pei to develop a downtown revitalization plan. In 1980, after a week-long trial, Alaimo sentenced Holley and Hester to ten years in prison; Adamson drew three years. Underscoring the existential loneliness of life on the bench, Alaimo later remarked, "These were all people I knew pretty well...a perfect picture of how greed can take over people's lives." At the time, he described the sentencing as "the saddest day of my life

*Chiusa Una Porta, Se Ne Aprirà Un'altra .[3]*

Of his early years in Augusta Alaimo recalled, "I was a stranger all over again. You know, still the immigrant outsider." The

---

[2] Both Holley and Bert Hester were law partners with former Georgia governor Carl Sanders.

[3] "One door closes, another will open."

difference was that he was now duty-bound to live up to the authority vested in him. He'd taken an unshakeable oath to "administer justice without respect to persons and do equal right to the poor and to the rich...." This was, after all, the same man who had sworn to resist his country's enemies by any means—and who had assumed that this included the obligation to stare unblinking into the muzzle of a German machinegun.

As David Hudson remembers: "When Judge Alaimo arrived, he perceived the older lawyers as having rejected him. We young lawyers[4] looked for things to include him in, playing tennis, going to lunch, and so forth. He came to realize that he could trust us, that he could speak to us in confidence and we weren't going to run around saying, 'This is what the judge thinks about such and such.'

"Alaimo didn't play favorites. He treated young lawyers with equal dignity and gravitas as the older, more seasoned lawyers who appeared before him. I recognized that he was an exceptional person. I wanted to be around him and know what he thought, and talk about things with him."

Those who know him say Alaimo could unerringly take the measure of a man's weight and worthiness, an ability that either rallied people or repulsed them. This perhaps reflected an unacknowledged benefit of unsheltered childhoods, barbershop revelations, and military experience: he'd lived in the real world. In private, there was an Old-World courtliness to Alaimo's speech and manner as well as an unexpected sense of humor that ran counter to his Old Testament countenance on the bench. He dressed fashionably and had impeccable manners.

Jeanne Alaimo was a woman so comfortable in her own skin that she'd make her way in any circumstance or situation. No mere satellite orbiting in her husband's shadow, Jeanne was a fully realized planet, complete with her own atmosphere and gravity.

---

[4] Other attorneys in Hudson's cohort included John B. Long, John C. Bell, and Thomas W. Tucker.

In short this was an interesting, even intriguing, couple.

To his wife, Tony's ascendancy to the bench hardly seemed different from his days as a plaintiff's attorney. He continued hauling bulging briefcases home each night, poring over paperwork seven days a week, scrawling endless notes, and dictating memos to himself, enduring Jeanne's worried or peeved looks. A cynic might have noted that Alaimo, now in his fifties, was laboring to the point of exhaustion for less than half the money he'd once earned in his law practice. A shrink might have said that the former POW had succeeded in creating his own prison from which there was no escape.

If Alaimo's workaholic ways drained him, if the cold shoulder pained him, if he flashed back to his own father's bitterness at being an outsider denied the fruits of his labor, he kept it all locked up deep inside himself.

In 1973, on the bench less than two years, Alaimo developed a persistent pain in his back. It radiated across his shoulders and down his left arm. It quickly became clear that this was well beyond the aches and pulls of middle-aged tennis players. Jeanne drove him to Brunswick-Glynn County Hospital, where cardiologist Dr. Hurley Jones diagnosed his distress as angina associated with atherosclerosis, a clogging of the small arteries that supply the heart muscle. Typically such blockages are the result of deposits of a fatty substance known as plaque. In short, Alaimo was well on his way to a myocardial infarction, a devastating heart attack. He was fifty-three years old. Freddy, his youngest brother, would suffer a fatal heart attack in his mid-fifties.

Released from the hospital after three days of tests, Alaimo was put on a regimen of the anticoagulants Heparin and Warfarin (Coumadin), so-called blood thinners that reduce the risk of a clot forming in these narrowed vessels. Alaimo took his medicine, modified his diet, and shrugged and waded his way back to a bench seemingly awash in stress.

The 1970s were years that heralded today's tremendous advances in cardiology. Three years after his first episode, Alaimo underwent an angiography and cardiac catheterization, diagnostic procedures that measured the volume of blood flowing through the intricate web of coronary arteries that supplied his heart with oxygen and nutrients. "The catheter showed I had two blockages," Alaimo remembered. Dr. Jones now recommended that Alaimo have double-bypass surgery at Emory University Hospital, then one of the region's leading cardiac care centers. At the time Alaimo was in no distress and understandably hesitant to undergo such an invasive procedure. "It was a mistake for me to agree to have it done," he said later.

"But anyhow, I did."

Emory University had transformed itself in the decades since Tony had attended law school in the late 1940s. Thanks to Robert W. Woodruff and the Woodruff Foundation's huge transfusions of Coca-Cola money, the leafy and bucolic Methodist institution in East Atlanta was now a bustling educational and research megalopolis.

Everywhere in the country, high-powered medical facilities were beginning to exhibit the doctor-patient divide—human connection sacrificed at the altar of technological advancement—that characterizes much of the healthcare system to this day. Emory was no exception. "I talked to my surgeon for maybe five minutes the whole time," Alaimo reflected in 2008. "I didn't much care for it. Cardiac surgery was a big money-maker and it was obvious they were running a production line."

In the operating theater, Alaimo's surgeon made an incision about 8 inches long, cutting through flesh and muscle down the center of his sternum. The electro-surgical tool he used to cauterize the incision filled the suite with the odor of burning flesh. His rib cage was cracked opened. The surgeon made the necessary shunts and placed him on a heart-lung bypass machine. The device removed carbon dioxide and other waste products from his blood, oxygenated it, and recirculated it throughout his body. His heart was stopped—

still and bloodless—for perhaps sixty minutes of the four-hour surgery. Veins previously removed from his leg were sewn from his aorta to the coronary artery below the site of the blockage. His heart was restarted, the equivalent of overhauling an engine with clogged fuel lines and a dead battery. Finally, the surgeon wired his chest together and sent him off to the recovery room trussed like a turkey.

Alaimo left the hospital feeling no better than when he had arrived. And he went right back to work without missing a proverbial beat. "How did I deal with it all?" he said later. "There was nothing to deal with! It really wasn't any more misfortune than becoming a POW. Didn't weigh on me at all."

By now, Tony Alaimo's body was becoming a detailed road map of his life: childhood scars, bullet wounds, broken nose and collarbone, surgical incisions, and now, unknown to him and his physicians, a jerry-rigged heart that was still ticking like a time bomb.

# Chapter 22

"I was the most unpopular person in this world in
Burke County"
—Judge Anthony Alaimo

In June 1976, tens of millions of Americans were preparing to celebrate the nation's bicentennial. A fleet of Tall Ships mustered from around the world was making its way to the Verrazano-Narrows Bridge at the mouth of New York Harbor. On July 4, a spectacular fireworks display, mirrored in the glass of the World Trade Center towers, would wreathe the Statue of Liberty in the red glare of rockets and starbursts.

A thousand miles south in Burke County, Georgia, a black Korean War veteran named Herman Lodge was feeling no such exuberance. Twelve years had run their course since Congress had passed the landmark Civil Rights Act outlawing segregation in schools and public places. Yet in Waynesboro, the county seat, "Colored" and "White" signs above the courthouse restrooms were still visible beneath a thin veneer of paint—symbolic, perhaps, of the deeply rooted and often virulent opposition to the changes sweeping the rest of the South. A segregated laundromat still operated in the shadow of the courthouse. Streets in the county's black neighborhoods remained unpaved and unlit. Of the homes occupied by African Americans, 75 percent lacked plumbing; for whites, the figure was 16 percent. In 1965, the Voting Rights Act abolished poll taxes and literacy tests, but voter registration among blacks remained dishearteningly low.

In 1976 Burke County, an area two-thirds the size of Rhode Island, had a population of 19,000. Blacks comprised 53.6 percent of the residents and 38 percent of the registered voters. Waynesboro, its largest city (population 5,800), is 25 miles south of Augusta. The county was governed by a five-member board of commissioners elected at-large. Despite holding a majority of the population, no black candidate had ever been elected to the board. No black had ever been a member of the county executive committee of the dominant Democratic Party.

Attorney Robert Cullen, who would be drafted by Alaimo into the Reidsville prison case, had barely unpacked his suitcase in Augusta when Herman Lodge burst into the Georgia Legal Services' office. "Everybody had left and they told me to baby-sit for two weeks," Cullen recalled. "I wasn't even admitted to the bar."

"Are you the new kid who's been assigned to Burke County?" Lodge demanded.

"Yes, sir," Cullen answered.

"We're going to do a lot of work together."

Lodge slapped a sheet of paper on Cullen's desk. "This is a list of lawsuits I want brought."

Lodge, who worked at a nearby VA Hospital, introduced himself as president of the Burke County Improvement Association. Among the "improvements" he was demanding for his constituents were political access, an equitable jury selection system, admission to public parks, and humane treatment of prisoners in the county jail (which at the time was "amazingly bad," Cullen remembered).

Preeminent among the blizzard of lawsuits that followed was an action on behalf of all black Burke County citizens filed in the United States District Court for the Southern District of Georgia. It alleged that the county's system of at-large elections of county commissioners violated the Constitutional rights guaranteed by the Fourteenth[1] and Fifteenth[2] amendments.

---

[1] The Equal Protection Clause of the Fourteenth Amendment of the US Constitution prohibits states from denying any person within its jurisdiction the equal protection of the law.

Historically such at-large schemes, though seemingly "neutral in origin," have been used to dilute voting strength by permitting a minority, in this case the white power structure, to control elections by bloc voting. Given the political powerlessness of what was actually a black majority population and the subsequent abuse rained down on its members, Burke County seemed a classic example of a system twisted to nefarious purpose.

In 1977, Alaimo certified the case (*Lodge v. J. F. Buxton*, later *Rogers v. Lodge*) a class-action suit. By agreement, it would be decided in a bench trial, i.e. without a jury. Beneath the mountains of evidence marshaled before him over the next years, *Rogers v. Lodge* was much more nuanced than it appeared. And it did not play out in a vacuum. The case was argued in tandem with a virtually identical class action, *Wiley L. Bolden v. City of Mobile*, making its way onto the Supreme Court's calendar.

In 1976, the Federal District Court for the Southern District of Alabama had found that Mobile's at-large method of electing its board of commissioners violated black residents' constitutional rights "by improperly restricting their access to the political process." The judge ordered that the commission be replaced by a mayor and nine-member city council elected from single-member districts.

The Alabama decision left a fundamental question unanswered: does discriminatory *result* necessarily prove discriminatory *intent?* Four years later, in April 1980, Justices Potter Stewart, Harry Blackmun, Warren Burger, Lewis Powell, William Rehnquist, and John Paul Stevens overturned the Alabama district court decision and with it one of the pillars of the civil rights era. In an opinion that triggered a firestorm of protest, Justice Stewart wrote that "Past discrimination cannot, in the manner of original sin, condemn government action that is not itself unlawful.... Disproportionate

---

[2] "The right of citizens of the United States to vote shall not be denied or abridged by the United States or by any State on account of race, color, or previous condition of servitude."

impact alone cannot be decisive and courts must look to other evidence to support a finding of discriminatory purpose.

"...While multimember districts are not unconstitutional per se, they violate 14th Amendment if they are conceived or operated as purposeful devices to further racial discrimination by minimizing, canceling out, or diluting the voting strength of racial elements in the voting population. Only if there is purposeful discrimination, can there be a violation of the equal protection clause of the Fourteenth Amendment."

The Court found that the evidence in the Mobile ruling "fell far short" of this smoking gun. Supreme Court Justice Stewart added, "The 15th Amendment prohibits only direct purposefully discriminatory interference with the freedom of Negroes to vote. Having found that Negroes in Mobile register and vote without hindrance, the District Court and Court of Appeals were in error...in the present case."

*Rogers v. Lodge* would also wind its way to the Supreme Court, though with none of the *Sturm und Drang* that would mark the Alabama case. Alaimo would both anticipate and move beyond the high court's reasoning. In a prescient analysis, he came up with a remedy that fused both the letter of the law and its spirit.

Robert Cullen, who was on the team that argued *Rogers v. Lodge* before the Supreme Court, recalled, "The Mobile case said you could only prove vote dilution with direct evidence, a smoking gun...an incredibly explicit smoking gun. Judge Alaimo said, 'Nonsense, you can to prove it all with circumstantial evidence. And this is how you do it.'"

Justice would be served, Alaimo seemed to be saying, but justice required diligence, honesty and hard work. Justice could not be rendered from the steps of the temples of law. There were times when you had to roll your sleeves up and plunge your hands into the throbbing heart of the American democracy.

How was such wisdom rewarded?

"I was close to being hung in effigy and all that kind of stuff," Alaimo remembered with a laugh.

He began his deliberations by attempting to assess the impact of past discrimination on Burke County's African-American residents. He found a long and sordid history. As far back as the 1880s, there had been lynchings in the county. In fall 1890 two black men, General Thomas and John Williams, were lynched in Waynesboro. Prior to 1965, the evidence suggested that literacy tests, poll taxes, whites-only primaries, and other methods of voter suppression had ensured that "black suffrage in Burke county was virtually non-existent." In the aftermath of the Voting Rights Act, registration among eligible black voters quickly climbed to 38 percent, evidence enough to infer the chilling effect of the county's haunted past.

In the late 1970s, Burke County remained an unsubtle place. "There were allegations that certain of the defendants, shall we say, panicked some of our plaintiffs," Robert Cullen recalled. "One of them just took off and fled the county. Others were threatened. There was a house-burning. We could never prove it, but it happened.

"I'm not ACLU," Cullen added, trying to convey the tenor of the times. "I'm not even particularly far-out there. Soon after I arrived, there was a dispute over access to a public park in Waynesboro. It seemed to me that this kind of stuff should have been resolved, but it wasn't. There were still essentially segregated white and black parks. The white park was a lot better than the black park. A community group got together. They didn't want to litigate, they wanted to march. I said, 'I'd rather litigate.' I went to a couple of the meetings and I was stopped on my way back and forth several times by police just for harassment. At one of those meetings, the police burst in and I happened to be to standing up talking and they shoved an M-16 or something into my gut and sat me down."

The county school system remained essentially segregated, with blacks generally lagging behind their white counterparts in graduation rates;[3] the schooling they did receive proved "qualitatively inferior to a marked degree." Burke County's depressed economy weighed far more heavily on black residents. They earned less money than whites for similar work and tended to be more often employed in menial jobs than their white counterparts. More than half were scraping by in jobs that kept them trapped fully 25 percent below the poverty level.

None of this was new or surprising. But Alaimo ruled it concrete, documented, admissible evidence, as were a corrupted grand jury system; property ownership requirements that made it difficult for blacks to serve as county registrars; and all-white appointments to the boards and committees that oversaw county government.

Burke County's white establishment met this attempt to thwart its grip on power head-on. "They came loaded for bear," Alaimo recalled in 2008. "These were real segregationists. They believed in the states' rights philosophy and were just absolutely confident they could win that case, not only in front of me but later on. I can recall the county lawyers talking to Robert Cullen and his cohorts saying, 'Why don't you dismiss this case? You're going to lose.'"

On September 29, 1978, with a county commission election fast approaching, Alaimo rendered his decision. He found that there had been bloc voting along racial lines, that past discrimination had restricted Burke County's blacks' participation in the political process. He ruled the appellees, Lodge et al., were entitled to prevail and issued detailed findings that backed up his conclusions. Burke County's method of electing county commissioners, while "racially neutral when adopted," Alaimo wrote, "was being maintained for invidious purposes." He tossed out the at-large system and ordered the county divided into five, single-member electoral districts.

---

[3] A notable exception is Georgia Court of Appeals judge John "Jack" Ruffin, a Waynesboro native and former civil rights attorney actively involved in the Burke County litigation.

Rather than the smoking gun the Supreme Court seemed to be demanding in *Mobile v. Bolden*, Alaimo concluded that discriminatory purpose could be inferred not only from direct evidence, but also from circumstantial evidence (i.e., the totality of the relevant facts, including the fact that the law lay more heavily on one race than another).

It is the nature of things that Judge Alaimo wrote what is considered by some the most significant opinion of his long career not at his desk, with the chiming of the clock in his chambers for company, or beneath a portrait of his hero, the jurist and sublime legal craftsman Benjamin N. Cardozo, but while sitting next to Jeanne on a crowded airliner. The two inveterate travelers were en route to the newly opened Peoples' Republic of China, courtesy of a nonprofit outreach called Friends of China.[4]

"Well, I pondered it plenty, but you know my wife and I were going overseas," Alaimo recalled. "I'd made up my mind as to what I was going to do, but I hadn't had time to write the opinion. So I called the lawyer on the other side and told them, 'Hold up on the election.'[5] Then I wrote a good bit of that opinion flying to Los Angeles. I had a legal pad with me. After I wrote it up, I sent it back in a pouch to my secretary, Sue Wiggins, to type."

The ruling hit Burke County like a bombshell. With the election looming, Alaimo refused to stay his order pending an appeal. Commission Chairman Quentin Rogers and his attorneys went to the Eleventh Circuit Court of Appeals, where failing to get a stay, moved on to the Supreme Court. Justice Powell granted their motion pending an appeals court's decision. Circuit Court Judges Peter Fay

---

[4] Two friends, US Circuit Court judge James Hill and attorney Hamilton Lokey, had made the trip a year earlier. Primitive accommodations on a trip organized by what Alaimo later called "a very liberal group" did much to cure his Asian wanderlust.

[5] November 8, 1978.

and Warren Jones then affirmed Alaimo's ruling two to one. They held that Alaimo properly required proof that the at-large system was maintained for a discriminatory purpose, his findings were not "clearly erroneous," and his conclusion was "virtually mandated" by the overwhelming proof.

"In a voting dilution case in which the challenged system was created at a time when discrimination may or may not have been its purpose," the court elaborated, "it is unlikely that plaintiffs could ever uncover direct proof that such system was being maintained for the purpose of discrimination. Neither the Supreme Court nor this Court, however, has denied relief when the weight of the evidence proved a plan to intentionally discriminate, even when its true purpose was cleverly cloaked in the guise of propriety. The existence of a right to redress does not turn on the degree of subtlety with which a discriminatory plan is effectuated. Circumstantial evidence, of necessity, must suffice, so long as the inference of discriminatory intent is clear…The general election laws in many jurisdictions were originally adopted at a time when Blacks had not received their franchise. No one disputes that such laws were not adopted to achieve an end—the exclusion of Black voting—that was the status quo. Other states' election laws, though adopted shortly after the enactment of the Fifteenth Amendment are so old that whatever evidence of discriminatory intent may have existed, has long since disappeared. This case falls within that category. The focus then becomes the existence of a discriminatory purpose for the maintenance of such a system."

*Rogers v. Lodge* moved on to the Supreme Court. Given what the court had ruled in Mobile, Alaimo was convinced he would be overturned. "I said as much to Robert Cullen," he recalled. "He came back and said, 'No, Judge, you're wrong.' What happened is he had access to the law clerks up there. All a bunch of liberals! They told him 'They are going to affirm. And sure enough…"

On July 1, 1982, almost six years to the day after the Tall Ships had gathered in New York City, the high court upheld Judge Alaimo. In a ruling that mirrored its own bitterly divided opinion in *Mobile v. Bolden* two years earlier, the court did not strike down at-large voting schemes as unconstitutional per se; however, it now affirmed that historical data showing that minorities had been denied effective participation in the electoral process could be employed as evidence.[6]

In 1982, Herman Lodge was one of two African Americans elected to the Burke County Board of Commissioners. "Two years later," Alaimo recalled, "Mr. Lodge was elected Chairman. He had to run for that seat at-large and had to garner white votes. Apparently, he did a good job."

The battle over *Mobile v. Bolden* and the Supreme Court's alleged retreat from the civil rights reforms of the previous decade is said to have been a factor in Congress's 1982 vote to extend the 1965 Voting Rights Act. The revised legislation now allowed the use of an "effects" standard if—in accord with Alaimo's ruling—discrimination could be proved based on a totality of the evidence.

In *Mobile*, Justice Potter Stewart argued that past discrimination was not original sin. It could not condemn future government action that was not, in itself, unlawful. In the Lodge case, Alaimo, ever the good Methodist, proved that the stain on the soul of Burke County was a sin of commission, active and intentional

---

[6] For further information, see http://law.jrank.org/pages/13412/Rogers-v-Lodge.html.

# Chapter 23

"The value of plaintiff's mark will be eroded; a little
now, more later, until the magic of the Masters will
be mortally dissipated if not completely dispelled."—
Judge Anthony Alaimo

In 1975, the Northwestern Mutual Life Insurance Company of
Milwaukee announced plans to host an LPGA event on a former
hunting preserve—Hog Bluff Plantation—it was developing into a
resort near Hilton Head Island. The resort was suitably renamed
Moss Creek and the golf tournament dubbed the "Ladies Masters."

The Ladies Masters was to be held a few weeks after the Augusta
National's famed Masters Tournament—a blatant and piratical
attempt, in the mind of Chairman Clifford Roberts, to legitimize the
distaff contest by linking it to his world-renowned brand.

This was not the first time such a thing had happened. Over the
years, the club had beaten back a tire company's attempt to market a
"Dunlop Masters," Colgate-Palmolive's "Ladies Masters," and even a
"Black Masters." Augusta National, Inc., not only claimed rights to
"the Masters," "Masters tournament," and "Augusta," but it had also
branded "Amen Corner."

In 1976, Augusta National filed suit in federal court to prevent
the Northwestern Mutual Life Insurance Company from sponsoring
the "Ladies Masters." The giant insurance company was not some
easily cowed giftshop owner on Broad Street selling trinkets to
tourists. The trademark case landed on Alaimo's docket. It was
adjudicated as a bench trial—too late, as it turned out, to enjoin the

first LPGA Masters, which was won by South African Sally Little on Sunday, May 9, 1976 and still appears in LPGA records.

On the golf course, Little won the tournament; on the witness stand, Clifford Roberts and the Augusta Masters swept everything else. Arnold Palmer, whose career exploded after his 1958 Masters victory, gave a highly emotional and effective defense of the hallowed traditions in danger of being trampled like so much azalea.

Roberts was his irascible self, at one point refusing to answer what he called a "dumb question" posed by one of the Northwestern Mutual lawyers. The attorney objected and Alaimo sustained the objection, instructing the witness to answer. Roberts said he would answer, legend has it, "but only because you asked me to, Judge."

"I ruled in favor of Augusta National," Alaimo reflected in 2007. "As I recall, Northwestern Mutual didn't even bother to appeal."

Alaimo also recalled that he'd researched and written his own opinion. "I did it all myself," he said with a grin. "My law clerks had nothing to do with it, which is not true with most cases you see now. That's why I remember it."

In fact, Alaimo's writing, published in the United States *Patents Quarterly*, was not only persuasive but elegantly crafted and later cited in a number of other cases. He was talking about the dry business of trademark infringement and a corporation's right to control its "business reputation," but in his steady hands the opinion took flight. If the term "Masters" in "Ladies' Masters at Moss Creek Plantation" is used, he wrote, "there is reasonable certainty that the value of plaintiff's mark will be eroded; a little now, more later, until the magic of the Masters will be mortally dissipated if not completely dispelled."

He then permanently enjoined Northwestern Mutual from using the term.

Alaimo's ruling in this, his first trademark case, has stood the test of time. If anything, it has been strengthened. In 1997, Charles A. Moye Jr., senior US District Judge for the Northern District of

Georgia, enjoined a California company from producing golf towels bearing the word "Augusta." Moye held that even the word could be deemed an Augusta National trademark if linked to golf paraphernalia. In another case, Senior US District Judge for the District of South Carolina, Sol Blatt Jr. (who rivals Alaimo in years on the bench) wrote, "The Masters' mark, in the context of golf, is one of the strongest, if not the very strongest, golf-related marks in existence in this country."

If Alaimo's stout assessment of the rights and privileges associated with the Augusta National trademark won him the approbation of the city and its standoffish bar, things soon soured.

*"The dispensation of justice is not a popularity contest."*
*—Anthony Alaimo*

It's no exaggeration to suggest Alaimo views the courtroom as the cradle of liberty. Jury service is a citizen's highest calling. "One of the rare times," he likes to say, "when the average person participates in what this government is all about, in what a democracy is all about."

Woe betide anyone Judge Alaimo feels disrespects this sacrosanct place or process. His decades on the bench resound with stories of the "correction" of white-collar lawbreakers, heedless lawyers, overstepping prosecutors, and prospective jurors who consider themselves too busy or important to heed the summons.

The story still reverberates through the ladies' luncheon circles about the Wayne County doyenne who declined to answer a jury call because her bridge foursome took precedence. Unfortunately, a fifth player showed up at her home that day to play a hand: an ill-disposed US marshal who'd had to drive 40 miles to Jesup, round her up, and haul her back to Brunswick like a sack of potatoes. Alaimo remembers the story well. "They called the roll that morning and she wasn't here. She hadn't called, so I asked the marshal to go look in on her. Sometimes, jurors' cars break down on the drive in. I didn't know what the hell she was doing."

When the lady arrived, Alaimo had her escorted to a cell where she spent the remainder of the day. "We had enough numbers to select the jury," Alaimo recalled. "Maybe in state practice they'd say nothing about this kind of stuff, but she was a very prominent person and I was trying to send a message out."

The message was mixed at best. "Let me tell you, I got a bad reaction from the Jesup newspaper," he added with a chuckle. "They were indignant that this judge would take a nice young lady and put her in the common jail…. In any event, we don't have many people who don't show up."

Alaimo has jailed parties of bird hunters (among them, at least one group of medical doctors) for dove hunting on a baited field, a violation of Title 50 Code of Federal Regulations Part 20.21(i).

"I put them in jail for at least twenty-four hours," he said. "They're outraged when it happens, but hell, we've got statutes here that they've violated with impunity. Unless I do something about it, the statute doesn't mean a damn thing!"

Alaimo has famously been accused of incarcerating a construction worker for making too much noise while he presided over a trial. The story is only half-true. "At the time I was presiding in Augusta," Alaimo recalled. "He was doing some work down on the first floor. We were up on the third. I was doing final arguments and I hear this big clatter. So I instruct the marshal to tell him if he didn't stop it, I was going to put him in jail. And he would have stopped.

"Well, the marshal went down but he didn't follow my instructions. He put the guy in jail—without my authority. Of course, the *Augusta Chronicle* got ahold of it and did a big story. All of this was on the record, but the newspaper just got his version of it. I just let it roll off my back."

"Whereas, it is inconceivable that a federal judge would not respect the deliberation of the General Assembly of Georgia; and Whereas, federal judges can prevent legislators from attending to their duties, the right of the States to govern themselves is in serious jeopardy…"
—State Senate Resolution condemning Anthony A. Alaimo

Perhaps Alaimo's most memorable clash took place in Augusta on Monday, February 6, 1978. It was a conflict that went far beyond scorching the sensitivities of smalltown socialites. An attorney named Thomas F. Allgood was scheduled to appear in front of Alaimo representing a client, an alleged bookie named Flavious J. Cullpepper who was about to be retried as part of a federal gambling conspiracy.

"Allgood[1] initially wanted a severance," Alaimo recalled many years later. "He wanted his guy tried all by himself, so whatever the other guys did wouldn't be washing over him. Well, I don't grant those motions. I try them all together."

Allgood, vice president of the Georgia Trial Lawyers Association, wore another hat. He was a well-regarded state senator who represented Augusta's Twenty-second District.

"He said, 'Judge, you know the legislature is going to be in session,'" Alaimo continued. "I knew they had a two-week hiatus during the session and I said I'd set the trial for that two-week period, the first Monday of the recess. Well, the legislature changed the dates of the recess. When the time came, I had already scheduled the trial, which brought jurors in from as far away as 100 miles."

That Monday morning, Allgood never showed up. In his stead, he sent his law partner, T. Allen Childs, to seek a continuance. Childs hoped to convince Alaimo that Allgood's health prevented him from making an appearance. The attorney had suffered a heart attack in

---

[1] Thomas Allgood, his wife Thelma, and pilot Stephen Patterson were killed in the crash of a private plane in August 2000.

the course of Cullpepper's first trial and claimed his doctor ordered him to stay out of the courtroom for a few more months.

In fact, Allgood was in Atlanta attending a session of the General Assembly. He now claimed to have notified the court in writing that the legislature was scheduled to be in session. In any event, the fact that Childs handed the judge an unsigned affidavit regarding the state of Allgood's health did not help the senator's case. (Allgood's doctor was "not available and could not be contacted to reaffirm his advice."[2])

That afternoon, Allgood telephoned Alaimo from Atlanta and, after some discussion, agreed to appear in court on Tuesday morning. Things did not go well, particularly after Allgood admitted that he'd known of the hearing at least a week in advance.

"You mean you made a conscious and deliberate choice not to be here for the calendar call?" Alaimo demanded.

"Yes, sir," Allgood replied

"That's when I got a little mad," Alaimo confessed. He pointed his long finger at Allgood and ruled that this failure showed "a flagrant disregard for the court" and "set a bad example to lawyers."

A moment later, Allgood was cited for contempt. When he told Alaimo he would refuse to pay the $250 fine "as a matter of principle," the judge had the marshals haul the startled politician off to a detention cell—suit, tie, vest and all. Twenty minutes later, Allgood was a free man pending an appeal to the Fifth District Circuit Court.

"It was dumb for me to put him jail," Alaimo remembered with a laugh. "He went in there, but he had cohorts outside. They bonded him out. He really outwitted me and created a great public outcry about a federal judge interfering with a legislator during the session."

In fact, from the ensuing hullabaloo in the Georgia Senate, you'd think Anthony had murdered Cicero all over again. It was pure

---

[2] *Augusta Chronicle*, February 8, 1978.

political theater, a states' rights advocate crushed by the oppressive hand of the federal government—the same hand, it should be noted, that was outraging the legislature by forcing them to spend scores of millions of dollars improving conditions at Reidsville prison.

Allgood played his part to the hilt, later claiming, "when they slammed that door on me, I cried." Both the *Augusta Chronicle* and *Atlanta Constitution* gave the story dramatic, multicolumn coverage. The *Augusta Herald* ran a banner headline and photos of Allgood, looking forthright and determined, staring across the front page at the brooding, hawk-nosed judge, who, in keeping with the times, would be branded "Ayatollah Alaimo."

State senator Roy Barnes, who'd later be elected Georgia's governor, declared himself "infuriated," claiming that Alaimo had set a "very dangerous precedent." Senator Pierre Howard, a future lieutenant governor, decried Alaimo's decision an "act of absolute arrogance." And those were the moderates. Others shouted for Alaimo's impeachment.

On February 8, 1978, the Georgia State Senate issued Senate Resolution 310, "Condemning and urging the reprimand of Judge Anthony A. Alaimo." The document contains no fewer than ten separate "WHEREAS" paragraphs commending Allgood and denouncing Alaimo's behavior on the bench, among them "Whereas, it is inconceivable that a federal judge would not respect the deliberations of the General Assembly of Georgia; and Whereas, if federal judges can prevent legislators from attending to their duties, the right of the states to govern themselves is in serious jeopardy...."

Zell Miller, another future governor and US Senator, signed the resolution, as did secretary of the senate Hamilton McWhorter Jr., who sent it along to a list of notables that included President Jimmy Carter, Attorney General Griffin Bell, Chief Judge John Brown (Chairman of the Executive Committee of the Judicial Conference of the United States), and Senators Sam Nunn and Herman Talmadge.

Ironically, many of these men would later consider Alaimo the absolute standard of both courage and decorum on the federal bench. Not one of them paid any attention to the legistlature's caterwauling. Like the resolution, Thomas Allgood's appeal to the circuit court petered out. "He realized I'd passed a pretty good order and supported it by findings," Alaimo recalled. "He figured he wasn't going to come out too good, and dismissed his appeal. Then the son of a gun came up to my office with two other lawyers representing him saying that he'd agree the thing ought to be dropped!"

"Oh yes," Alaimo recalled with a twinkle in his eye. "He paid the fine."

The great irony may be that thirty years later, a visitor to Alaimo's chambers cannot distinguish the damning resolution— replete with the bright gold foil "State of Georgia" seal in the left hand corner—from the dozens of awards, citations and plaques honoring the life and career of the Honorable Anthony Alaimo.

# Chapter 24

Jacksonville, Florida lies 60 miles south of Brunswick, Georgia, on I-95, the main north-south artery linking the cities of the northeast and Canada with the balmy climes of South Florida. Jacksonville is the closest major city to Brunswick. With a population of nearly 800,000 souls, it is home to the Jacksonville Jaguars, the annual Georgia Bulldog-Florida Gators football classic, a bustling deepwater port, and a thriving healthcare center that includes Saint Vincent's and a branch of Mayo Clinic. The US Court of Appeals for the Eleventh Judicial Circuit, the busiest federal appellate court in the country, maintains a presence in a gleaming highrise on North Hogan Street, the John Milton Bryan Simpson US Courthouse.

For more than thirty years, US Circuit Court Judge Gerald Bard Tjoflat has kept a watchful eye on Tony Alaimo—mostly in amazement, partially in bemusement at his colleague's workaholic antics, but never because of the quality of Alaimo's work.[1] Like John Sammons Bell,[2] the former Chief Justice of the Georgia Court of Appeals, Tjoflat (affectionately nicknamed "Tojo" by the young prosecutors who appeared before him during his tenure as a district judge) is a close as a brother to Alaimo. Though born of a generation and a calling rigorously self-contained and stoic, the two jurists are sensitive, even passionate men, registering the joys and tragedies that inevitably accompany long and eventful lives. When Tjoflat's wife Sarah passed away in 1997, for instance, Jeanne and Tony Alaimo were there to offer support and consolation.

On first encounter, Tjoflat is as gregarious and expansive as Alaimo seems reserved. If Alaimo's humor is understated and ironic,

---

[1] Alaimo has consistently been one of the least-reversed district court judges in the country, an achievement once cited in *Time* magazine.

[2] Bell passed away on December 8, 2006.

Tjoflat's is as overpowering and effusive as a geyser. Nearly a decade younger than Alaimo, he has become a self-proclaimed repository of Alaimo lore, though Alaimo swears that Tjoflat has buffed and polished and annotated him to the point that he feels like a museum artifact, an ancient suit of armor restored and embellished a few too many times.

"If I make a mistake when I'm retelling a POW story," Alaimo says with amusement, "he'll actually jump up and correct me."

Tjoflat keeps a judicious eye on his friend's health, particularly given that, at eighty-eight, Alaimo occasionally acts as if he were still in training for the Golden Gloves. "Hell, he once went over to Alabama when he was damn near dying of pneumonia or some blooming thing," Tjoflat recalled. "He'd made a commitment to go try a case for two weeks and you couldn't stop him. You bet I chewed him out!"

The tale inevitably takes him back to the year 1981 and his favorite Alaimo story:

> "This one Wednesday afternoon," Tjoflat begins with the dreamy cadence of a storyteller embarking on a fairy tale, "my secretary, Dot Bradley, comes into my chambers."
>
> "I need a hotel room and I can't find one anywhere," she says.
>
> "What the hell for?"
>
> "I...I can't say."
>
> "So I wrangle it out of her. Old Alaimo had been holding court someplace. He'd called and told Dot he was coming down to Jacksonville Thursday night, but not to tell me. It turns out he's going to check in at Saint Vincent's with Angel De La Torre."

The Chartrand Heart and Vascular Center at St. Vincent's Medical Center (now St. Vincent's Healthcare) is one of the foremost cardiovascular facilities in the country. At the time, the aptly named Dr. De La Torre ("Angel of the Tower") was the center's most prominent cardiologist. Tjoflat knew this visit did not bode well. Alaimo, then sixty-one, had already undergone double-bypass surgery at Emory University Hospital in the mid-1970s.

"Dot makes some calls and I finally get a hold of Tony and say 'What the hell are you doing coming to Jacksonville for something like this and you don't even tell me?'"

"Oh, I didn't want to bother you."

"Hmm."

" I call Angel De La Torre and tell him, 'My brother Tony Alaimo is going to be in your shop Friday and you've got to take good care of him.'"

"It's my day off," De La Torre announces.

This is not the response Tjoflat is looking for.

"Angel, I'm telling you you've got to handle Tony."

The doctor sighs, visions of golf games or boating excursions no doubt exiting his head.

"Yes, sir."

"So anyway," Tjoflat continues, " I've got to go to Savannah for an ABA committee meeting of some sort that Friday. When it's over, I drive back to Jacksonville and get to my office around 3:30 or 4:00 P.M. to pick up messages and that kind of stuff. When I get there Dot Bradley is frantic.

"Angel De La Torre has been calling you every ten minutes!'"

"So I call Angel."

"Judge, you've got to get over here!" Angel stammers in his thick Cuban accent.

"What's wrong?"

"Judge Alaimo, he need five bypass! Five bypass!"

"Okay. Let's...."

"...and I can't keep him in the hospital!"

"Well, I race over to Saint Vincent's. Angel's got Tony ensconced in a VIP room overlooking the river. I walk in and he's getting DRESSED!"

"Where do you think you're going?"

"I've stuff to do. I've got a tennis match tomorrow and then we're having a court picnic for the whole Southern District. Monday, I've got to go to Waycross to accept a guilty plea in a highly sensitive case."

"'Whoa!' Meanwhile, he's showing me a hand-drawn diagram of his heart. Angel had written in all the arteries that needed to be fixed. It looks like a construction site."

"When the hell are you going to get around to the five bypasses?"

"Well, it's going to be a sealed courtroom in Waycross. There's a contract out on the guy who is going to plead."

"Jeez, Tony, Angel just said...."

"It was a bad, bad criminal case," Tjoflat says, breaking his narrative. "Nothing tension-free if you know what I mean."

"Angel's downstairs. Let's call down and ask him."

"Meanwhile, Tony's still getting dressed!"

"Angel, I'm up here with Tony. He says he wants to play tennis. What do you think...?

"He won't get through the first set!"[3]

"Tony, get back in that damned bed!"

"Sometimes you just have to order Tony around like that. Well, he's hemming and hawing...I make a deal with him. I tell him I'll handle the Monday pleading. Then I tell the nurse to go get a couple of decks of cards. We wind up playing gin rummy until way in the evening. Yup, he had five bypasses Monday morning. And I'm up in Waycross taking the guilty plea."

---

[3] Alaimo comments in 2007: "I planned to play the tennis match. You know, what the hell. Besides, I had these other commitments." He admitted he was concerned that the defendant in the Waycross case would change his mind and withdraw his plea. Justice would not have been served.

As in any fairy tale, there is a magical ending. Alaimo was playing tennis just five weeks after the surgery. In fact, he kept on playing until he was seventy-five years old.

In the late 1990s, Alaimo had another cardiac event. At the time Judge Tjoflat, recently remarried, had driven up to Brunswick to introduce his new wife, Marsha, to the Alaimos and a group of friends at a luncheon at the Sea Island Beach Club. He showed up at Alaimo's chambers in the Frank M. Scarlett Federal Building on Gloucester Street.

"His secretary says, 'He's at the doctor,'" Tjoflat recalls. "'He'll meet you over there.' Well, we head over to Sea Island. And we're having lunch and no Tony. Next thing you know, he's in the hospital. Soon enough, they've got to haul him by ambulance back to Saint Vincent's in Jacksonville.

"I head over there and they've got him all wired up. Dr. [Walter] Smithwick is pacing up and down the hallway. 'We can't do any more bypasses,' he tells me. 'We just can't.'

"Just then, the damn bell[4] starts ringing!

"They rush him into the operating theater. He's in there four or five hours. They wind up doing a couple of stents. It's a real touch-and-go proposition. Around 11:00 P.M., Marsha, Jeanne, and I are with Dr. Smithwick. He's showing us what he's done on the screen.

"Anyhow, I leave for Atlanta. I've got court the next morning. Around 2:30 P.M., when I get off the bench, my secretary calls. She says, 'Judge Alaimo is getting out of bed!'"

Tjoflat begins to laugh hysterically. "This time I can't stop him! He goes back to Brunswick. About four days later, Tony is back in the courthouse. Can you imagine this man?!"

In May 2008, Alaimo, eighty-eight, was operating with the same patched-up heart plus a new hip and two knee replacements. That month, he attended a reunion of former Stalag Luft III POWs in

---

[4] This would have been the Code Red or Code Blue alerts hospitals use to designate a cardiopulmonary arrest.

Cincinnati, Ohio, made appearances at judicial functions in Savannah and Augusta, and then developed a severe chest infection. He was hospitalized with walking pneumonia, released a few days later, and was back in his chambers the following Monday, still somewhat under the weather. When asked why he didn't take a little more time to recover, he grumbled, "What the hell am I going to do at home?"

# Chapter 25

Like the currents rhythmically pulsing in the coastal estuaries, Anthony Alaimo's life and work flowed across the decades of the 1970s, 1980s and 1990s, spilling over the millennial divide and into a new century. Like the tides, many of the issues that rose before the bar evidenced a powerful gravitational pull—the moods, indulgences, and distractions of a nation desperately trying to define itself in an increasingly uncertain world. Other cases reflected darker impulses: greed, violence, and discord; and some nobler. Like the estu-aries, Judge Alaimo's world teemed with *vita abbondante* (abundant life) both mundane and exotic: predators and preyed upon, innocent and corrupt, brilliant and benighted. The cases, the places, and the people passing before him were ever-changing and innumerable. He labored mightily to remain constant and true to his oath, though even granite mountains and glacial valleys are slowly subject to erosion.

His years on the bench also spanned the great deluge that burst across the South, an amniotic flood that would birth the Sunbelt.

This was the world Anthony Alaimo was born to inhabit—an exhausting and vital place.

This clash of light and dark, civil versus primal, Apollonian versus Dionysian impulses is obvious in Alaimo's landmark cases like Reidsville and Burke County, but also in his day-to-day challenges and decisions, seemingly *sub rosa* legal minutiae unless you happened to be an individual or entity seeking justice, mercy, or redress of grievances. Like the tides, these cases passed before the bench in an immeasurable and seemingly inexhaustible flow.

## The Vietnam Era

In spring 1972 Alaimo, newly arrived on the bench, had to weigh the case of a Paine College philosophy professor who protested the Vietnam War by claiming Vietnam, Laos, and Cambodia as exemptions on his tax return—and then, moving from the momentous to mundane, he had to mete out justice to two grocery clerks whose offense was accepting food stamps for illegal food purchases. As coincidence would have it, a newspaper article on the food stamp case was laid out next to another story that suggested that the racial divide—the backdrop of so many of Alaimo's upcoming cases—was deep and perhaps impossibly wide.

The story's headline, unconscious or intentional, incorporated the minstrel-show mockery black men have had to endure: "Negro Eyes U.S. Senate Seat."

The Vietnam War ended with the fall of Saigon on April 30, 1975, but the prosecutions against alleged draft dodgers dragged on. ("Failure to report for an Armed Forces physical examination"[1] was typically grounds for prosecution.) In 1968, a law student named Henry Samuel Atkins Jr., who felt he was entitled to a hardship deferment as head of a family, had begun bombarding his draft board (and later the criminal justice system) with letters, motions, and legal demurrers that slowed but did not avoid his being indicted. By 1974 Atkins, now a lawyer, was arguing that his indictment should be dismissed because his Sixth Amendment right to a speedy trial had been violated.

The case wound up on Alaimo's docket. Alaimo ruled that the delay was the result of Atkins's own motions. The defendant then accused the judge of prejudice. Alaimo, who'd already afforded Atkins an opportunity to participate in a newly established clemency program, disqualified himself, handing the case to Judge Alexander Lawrence in Savannah.

---

[1] 50 U.S.C. App. § 462.

Atkins was convicted in 1975. He turned to the Fifth Circuit Court of Appeals where in March 1976 his appeal was denied, though he'd outlasted the war he was determined to avoid.

*Augusta Agonistes*

In 1977, the Augusta Police Department and the city's Civil Service Commission had still not implemented Alaimo's 1973 order to integrate the force. Now the argument was that the department's affirmative action program was being hamstrung by the budget cuts and hiring freezes associated with inflation and a slumping economy. One could feel Alaimo's impatience growing, his hands fluttering in agitation, when commission chairman Eugene Long whined that Augusta did not practice discrimination and that he was tired of "constantly being called before you for something we've done."

In response Judge Alaimo growled, "You'd think that men as intelligent as the Civil Service Commission would have done a better job!"

Alaimo brought his jeweler's eye to bear. He made nuanced changes to the department's five-part rating system, hoping to jumpstart minority advancement. On May 13, 1977, the *Augusta Chronicle* editorial board denounced his efforts:

> As we said more than a year ago, the control over almost every phase of human activity in the Nation [*sic*] that the federal judiciary has arrogated to itself is a phenomenon that ought to be modified immediately. This phenomenon is again underscored by federal District Judge Anthony Alaimo's desire to see the Augusta Police Department increase the number of blacks to 40 percent of the force and his order that hiring of blacks over whites will be on a four-to-one ratio.... What is the purpose of a candidate for promotion taking a test when a federal judge dictatorially says they should have

those members of the department whose test scores might be expected to be lower than normal?

Later that spring, five black residents of Thomson, Georgia, in McDuffie County west of Augusta, filed a class action suit essentially identical to the Burke County litigation. It was intended to offset the voter dilution created by at-large elections for city, county, and school officials. Meanwhile, Alaimo was pulled back into the bitter Burke County desegregation dispute, now issuing a restraining order against the county jury commission temporarily enjoining the clerk from furnishing jury lists to the criminal courts. (He determined that juries in Burke County were not representative of the population.) This earned Alaimo another editorial attack in the *Augusta Chronicle*, one of a long series essentially accusing him of *obstructing* justice: "His actions effectively put a temporary hold on any criminal indictments and other actions taken by a grand jury and bars any trials."

A few months later, the wheels of justice gained some traction. McDuffie County agreed to a redistricting plan that abandoned at-large elections in favor of a ward system, opening the door to the election of black commissioners.

In November 1977 Alaimo left the law's ephemeral plane, as all judges inevitably must, and plunged into lights and shadows of the real world. He ruled against a black nurse who was suing a Veterans Administration hospital administrator in Augusta for illegally discharging her after twenty years on the job. Alaimo found "nothing improper or unconstitutional" in the defendant's actions, but at the same time he kept alive the woman's complaint of "harassment and long-standing, invidious racial discrimination."

In March 1978, Alaimo unhesitatingly sent a real estate broker and the broker's wife to prison for soliciting kickbacks from contractors responsible for repairing and maintaining public housing sponsored by the Department of Housing and Urban Development (HUD), a federal agency notorious for incompetence and corruption.

A few months later, Alaimo reviewed the conviction of self-made millionaire and recording executive Charles A. Schafer on three counts of willful income tax evasion. After first exhausting an appeal to the Fifth Circuit, Schafer tearfully threw himself on the mercy of the court. "I can say nothing except to beg for mercy," Schafer pleaded with Alaimo. "I'd like to devote the rest of my life to service of God and my family."

Though moved, Alaimo was reminded of his higher obligation. Sentencing in such a case, he says, "…is one of the most difficult things a judge has to do. The Court must not only keep faith with the defendant and his family, but with those twelve people on the jury who agonized over their verdict. Another consideration is that many thousands and millions of people out there pay their taxes. They like to feel that the government keeps faith with them too."

He reduced Schafer's prison time to three years.

An "artistic" bank robber named Alton Benjamin Garrett received no such consideration. Garrett's attorney described him as a "talented artist whose life has just taken some wrong turns."

"It really has," Alaimo replied. "He looks quite distinguished and is quite intelligent. He's just robbed too many banks."

Garrett drew a twenty-year sentence.

*The Drug Epidemic*

In the twilight of the 1970s, the social activism of the previous decade had given way to a self-centered and destructive hedonism. Traditional values and institutions—the family, the church, and the federal government—were awash in cynicism. The "Me Generation" was on the march, and in lockstep with it, AIDS—an epidemic, accelerated by casual sex and IV-drug abuse that would kill millions around the globe. The whirling dancers at New York City's Studio

54, oblivious to everything but their own desires, had become avatars of the popular culture.

The casual drug use of the 1960s had accelerated into a hunger for harder drugs—heroin, cocaine, amphetamines, angel dust, and later crack. This in turn gave rise to a multibillion-dollar industry overseen by brutal drug lords, international smugglers, and a supply chain that extended from the urban ghettoes, small towns, and middle-class suburbs of America to Medellin in Columbia or the poppy fields of Afghanistan.

No corner of the nation was free of the plague. It was only a matter of time before smugglers working their way north up I-95 from South Florida spread their poison across the small towns and rural counties of South Georgia. Only a matter of time before they began offloading bales of marijuana and uncounted kilos of cocaine into the hidden coves and estuaries of the coast. Only a matter of time before their airplanes, range extended by extra fuel cells, began touching down like dragonflies in the cotton fields of rural Georgia.

"Shrimp boats would come in with tons of marijuana and elude detection," Judge Alaimo recalled. "Maybe five percent, not over ten percent were caught, but they really flooded the courts. We had trials going most all the time."

The cash that changed hands in these transactions was as inconceivable as the mayhem and corruption the trade set in motion. It wasn't long before some down-on-his-luck shrimper from McIntosh or Liberty County would agree to offload "product" from a mother ship newly arrived from the Caribbean or Central America and then deliver the load to Harris Neck or some hidden inlet a few miles east of I-95. Or some sheriff would accept a bribe *not* to be anywhere near a certain rural airstrip on a particular night.

From the bench, Alaimo sensed it happening. "This is one of the vicious and unrecognized aspects of the drug trade," he reflected in a 2008 interview. "It makes criminals out of people who otherwise might have led decent lives.... I've had cases I almost cried over. The drug smugglers would often hire kids to unload their boats. One time, they hired a bunch of medical students. Dumb kids, honest-to-goodness. They were told, 'Don't worry about it. The worst you could get is probation.' Well, they got caught and I put them in jail. It ruined their lives."

In the winter of 1978, Alaimo sentenced five men who'd been arrested on a dock in Valonia in McIntosh County with 14 tons of marijuana. He gave them up to ten years in prison. A defense attorney called the sentencing "the toughest I'd ever heard of," but if Alaimo was trying to send a message, it fell on deaf ears.

"We convicted seven sheriffs[2] and deputies from the counties surrounding Augusta," Alaimo recalled. "Of course, these guys were poorly paid. You take a deputy making $15,000 a year and he gets $50,000 to turn his head when a plane comes in. It's ridiculous...."

One of the sheriffs Alaimo encountered was the John David Davis of Dawson County in north Georgia, a convicted moonshiner who was granted a presidential pardon by President Nixon and then went on to become a law enforcement officer. Unfortunately, moonshiners in the Georgia mountains have a history of moving into the marijuana trade, either growing or importing the weed. Davis soon slipped back into his old ways.

In 1984 Davis was convicted, along with a state revenue agent and two other men, of conspiring with one of the state's largest drug smuggling rings, the Larry Douglas "Red" Evans Gang. Sheriff Davis and his cohorts were importing massive quantities of marijuana into South Georgia, a scheme sophisticated enough to include intelligence-gathering and the construction of air strips in isolated parts of the state. Davis implicated another sheriff, Charles Starrett of Elbert County. Convicted on every count in the indictment, Davis then attempted to use the fact that Judge Alaimo had deemed his prior moonshine conviction admissible to overturn his conviction. In

---

[2] The Georgia Bureau of Investigation reports that sheriffs in nearly a dozen of the state's 159 counties have been implicated in drug smuggling.

simple terms, Davis and his lawyers, among them the redoubtable Bobby Lee Cook of Summerville Georgia, argued that the pardon had expunged his record; the mere mention of it was reversible error.

It wasn't. In 1986 the Eleventh Circuit Court denied the appeal. Alaimo later recalled, "Davis was a good sheriff, but nevertheless...." Hesitating, he added, "You know, if they'd come to me with a fairly decent motion to modify sentence, I might have granted it."

### Justice Tempered with Mercy

Time and again during sentencing, Alaimo's stern, unforgiving reputation was undercut by an instinctive desire to leaven justice with mercy, to somehow fuse penance and the possibility of reform in those who stood before him. Without this hope, the bench would be a cynical and poisonous calling. In part, this impulse was likely a reflection of his mother's love, his religious upbringing, and his claustrophobic experiences in the stalags. Alaimo knew full well the acid-drip of passing time, the ache of endless days spent locked away like an animal in a cage.

Against this forgiving impulse, Judge Alaimo's calling required fidelity to the law. "Sentencing remains the hardest thing I do," he said in an 2008 interview in his chambers. "Right from the beginning when I took the oath, it was onerous. You're God, as far as the person standing before you is concerned, and yet you don't have a lot of discretion. You really don't. The federal guidelines[3] determine what range I have in sentencing. Generally, it's very narrow."

Not until 2005, (*United States v. Booker*) did the US Supreme Court finally restore a measure of discretion to sentences imposed by district court judges. In *Booker*, the Court held that the sentencing guidelines were thereafter to be deemed "advisory only" but that the

---

[3] Rules setting out a uniform sentencing policy for defendants convicted in federal court. Created by the United States Sentencing Commission in the 1980s, the guidelines have been roundly criticized for taking away the court's discretion in weighing the pros and cons of individual cases.

district courts must still give them "respectful consideration." In 2007, (*Kimbrough v. United States*), the Supreme Court upheld the authority of district court judges to sentence defendants convicted of crack cocaine possession comparably to individuals convicted of possessing of powdered cocaine. Under the sentencing guidelines, crack cocaine possession was often subject to penalties many times more stringent than possession of "recreational" powdered cocaine, a bias considered racial in its impact.

In the course of an interview in 2008, Alaimo reached into a desk drawer and pulled out a file. "Not long ago," he continued, opening the file, "a Reidsville prisoner wrote me. He said, 'Judge, I've been in solitary confinement for seventeen years. I've had no intercourse with other human beings except the guards. I'm fifty-odd years of age and I'd like to be put in the general population so that I can talk to people before I die.' It was really a plaintive letter. I called the general counsel for the Georgia Department of Corrections. I said, 'How about seeing about this?' I knew the administration was opposed because the man had a horrendous record back in the day. He was put in solitary because he'd made numerous escape attempts and caused all kinds of disruption. They wanted to keep him there forever."

Unconsciously, Alaimo might have been describing his own experiences as a POW.

"Well, I finally got a letter back from the general counsel. In it, he says, 'We've agreed to let him out into the population.'"

Alaimo allowed himself the briefest smile before he stuck the file back in his desk. Among the tens of thousands of actions he's taken over his decades on the bench, this would not even register. To the man in solitary confinement, however, it was as if he had been touched by the hand of God.

"I don't know that the prisoner knows I did this for him," Alaimo added before moving on to another topic. "I didn't tell him. I didn't even respond to his letter."

### A Christmas Bombing: Walter Leroy Moody Jr.

In Alabama, December 16, 1989, dawned cold and overcast. That morning, a postman had delivered a shoe-box-sized parcel to the white-columned home of Judge Robert Vance in Mountain Brook, a leafy suburb outside of Birmingham. Vance, a member of the Eleventh Circuit Court of Appeals, walked back into the house. Sorting through the Christmas cards and junk mail, he dropped the brown-wrapped parcel on the kitchen table. Its return address indicated that it had been sent by an old friend, a judge named Lewis Morgan. Vance told his wife it was no doubt a collection of the "horse magazines" he enjoyed.

Helen Vance was standing next to her husband when he opened the box. It exploded, driving a spray of nails and red-hot shrapnel into Vance and his wife. The blast killed Vance instantly and grievously injured his wife.

The tragedy repeated itself two days later when a second mail bomb literally shredded black civil rights attorney and Savannah alderman Robert E. "Robbie" Robinson. A third pipe bomb arrived at the federal courthouse in Atlanta, and a fourth at the offices of the NAACP in Jacksonville, Florida. The latter two were intercepted and diffused.

The attacks were both a throwback to the past and a portent of the future. The bombings spread fear among civil rights activists and a federal judiciary that had implemented desegregation, busing, affirmative action, and a dozen other hot-button issues.

Still, the string of bombings that had punctuated the civil rights era had seemingly ended. A nascent, neo-Nazi movement, racist and virulently antigovernment, was on the rise. However, its locus was the Farm Belt and the Pacific Northwest, where organizations like the

Posse Comitatus and Aryan Nations bombed government agencies and terrorized minorities. Islamic terrorism would not visit American shores until the first World Trade Center bombing in 1993.

By coincidence, a Bureau of Alcohol, Tobacco, and Firearms (ATF) agent working on the bombings recognized a design characteristic of the device defused in the courthouse attack. Rather than the round, threaded end caps typical of pipe bombs, these were square and bolted to the ends of the device by long threaded rods—identical to a bomb that had been fabricated by a Georgia man named Walter Leroy "Roy" Moody seventeen years earlier.

In 1972, Moody, a brooding sociopath with a high IQ and a litigious streak, had been convicted of possessing a bomb allegedly intended for an auto dealer who'd repossessed his car. Instead it exploded in his wife's face, severely injuring her and sending Moody to federal prison for three years. Upon his release, Moody worked feverishly to have the conviction overturned. His reason, as Alaimo recalled it, seems as incomprehensible as his crime:

"He was trying to clear the air so he could be eligible to become a member of the bar. At the time, you didn't have to go to law school to become a lawyer. With a felony conviction, he was ineligible to proceed."

To that end, Moody had filed a coram nobis[4] petition with the US District Court for the Middle District of Georgia. In it Julie Linn-West, an acquaintance, swore that another person had planted the bomb that injured Hazel Moody. Additionally, Linn-West's mother Susan Ekstrom corroborated this version of events.

In 1988, Moody's *coram nobis* petition was denied in district court. In August 1989 the Eleventh Circuit—Judge Vance's circuit—affirmed the ruling. Robert Vance had a more direct connection to Moody. He'd sat on a panel that denied another of the actions

---

[4] The designation of a remedy for setting aside an erroneous judgment in a civil or criminal action that resulted from an error of fact in the proceeding.

Moody, a serial filer of lawsuits, had unsuccessfully appealed to the circuit court.

Four months later, Vance was dead. The FBI and special prosecutor Louis Freeh,[5] who handled the prosecution, came to believe that the murder of Robert Robinson and the bomb mailed to the Jacksonsville NAACP were red herrings, attempts to shade Moody's animus against the federal courts.

In early 1990, Moody knew federal investigators were closing in on him. He attempted to bribe Julie Linn-West to keep her and her mother from testifying against him. Unbeknownest to Moody, Linn-West was already cooperating with the government, eventually providing tape recordings of her meetings with Moody that would be later introduced as evidence.

On July 11, 1990, Moody and his second wife Susan were indicted on charges of federal perjury, bribery, obstruction of justice, and witness-tampering. That October, after chief judge Wilbur D. Owens of the Middle District of Georgia recused himself, the Eleventh Circuit's chief judge Gerald Tjoflat handed the delicate and potentially sensational trial to a man he knew to be fair and fearless in the pursuit of justice: Anthony Alaimo.

In effect, Alaimo's November 1990 trial was a run-up to the murder case against Moody that would later unfold. Moody filed flurries of motions, most of which Alaimo batted down as lacking merit. Moody mounted, then dropped an insanity defense, fired his attorneys, and attempted to have Alaimo recused. He even demanded that the judge grant him a haircut for the trial—Alaimo agreed—then changed his mind.

"He thought he was smarter than everybody else," Alaimo recalled, "mostly me."

A Brunswick jury convicted Moody, fifty-seven, on all thirteen counts. According to the sentencing guidelines, Alaimo sent Moody

---

[5] Freeh would later be named FBI director.

to prison for 125 months, dropping his judicious demeanor only once when Moody attempted to shield his wife from the consequences of his wrongdoing: "That's the first admirable thing I've heard you say," Alaimo snapped.

In fact, Susan McBride Moody, twenty-eight, had already testified against her husband. The testimony was part of a secret deal her attorney, Sandra Popson, had worked out that allowed her to plead guilty to one count in the obstruction of justice indictment. Popson had argued that she evidenced a "battered wife syndrome."

"She was pretty much overpowered by him and his influence," Alaimo later conceded, "though in the end, I did feel there was some responsibility on her part. She got a pretty good deal."[6] And she did, when Alaimo granted her attorney's plea for probation.

Moody fought his conviction all the way the US Supreme Court. By the time his appeals were exhausted, the wheels of justice had caught up with him. In June 1991, a St. Paul, Minnesota, jury convicted Moody on seventy-one criminal counts including first-degree murder in the deaths of Judge Vance and Robert Robinson. He was sentenced to 7 life terms plus 400 years with no possibility of parole. In November 1996, Moody was then tried on capital murder charges in Alabama. He was convicted and sentenced to die in the electric chair. Prosecutors in that case suggested that he'd planned to kill seventeen judges in letters in a war on the judicial system. In the summer of 2008, Moody was still awaiting execution.

*"A Cesspool of Malevolent Verbal Regurgitations"*

In the mid-1990s, Matthew Washington, a cop-killer serving a life sentence at Reidsville, sued Alaimo[7] for $5 million in damages. He claimed that the millions of dollars the judge had ordered the

---

[6] Susan, who had purchased bomb-making materials for her husband, pled guilty to one count of conspiracy and never served prison time.

[7] *Washington v. Alaimo* (1996).

state to spend to improve conditions at the prison were a waste of taxpayer money.

As it turned out, Washington was a serial litigator who'd filed non-stop complaints and torrents of frivolous but time-consuming motions against the state and federal judiciary, his lawyers, Sam Nunn, and even media mogul Ted Turner. One of the lawsuits, *Matthew Washington v. James T. Morris, et al.*, alone included seventy-five pleadings, each of which required "the considered attention" of Judge Alaimo or magistrate judge James E. Graham. Washington filed a slew of more colorful filings: "Motion to Behoove an Inquisition," "Motion to Impeach Judge Alaimo," "Motion for Restoration of Sanity," "Motion for Deinstitutionalization," "Motion for Catered Food Service," and the more generalized "Motion to Kiss My Ass."

Chief District Judge William T. Moore, Alaimo's colleague in Savannah, noted that Washington was clever enough to pay filing fees when he filed his lawsuits rather than proceeding in *forma pauperis*, which effectively allowed him to dodge the filter of a so-called frivolity review.[8] "It has come to the attention of this Court that Plaintiff's litigation practice is largely, if not entirely, underwritten by the Federal Treasury as he periodically receives a substantial check for veterans' disability benefits," Moore fumed. "As a result, patently frivolous lawsuits have languished in this district longer than would otherwise be warranted with other prisoner litigants."

Washington triggered a torrent of overheated prose from another of Alaimo's colleagues, district judge Dudley H. Bowen, who was also targeted by the endless litigation: "The courts continue to wade through a cesspool of deranged and malevolent verbal regurgitations from the twisted minds of misanthropic felons," Bowen wrote. "[This is] the frivolous, malicious, vindictive work of a paranoid megalomaniac."

---

[8] 28 U.S.C. § 1915(d).

In the late 1980s, when the Iran-Contra Affair was making headlines in Washington and the rest of the world, Alaimo tried a miniature version of the scandal involving an Augusta Army & Navy store owner arrested for attempting to ship spare Jeep parts to Iran. Alaimo also oversaw the trial of an East Central Health District administrator on bribery changes and was none too pleased with the jury's decision to acquit. "You ought to get down on your knees and thank God," Alaimo rumbled at the defendant.

In 1990, Judge Alaimo overturned a jury verdict in a complex Federal Tort Claims Act [9] malpractice suit brought by Mary Ann Newmann, the wife of a US Army Captain stationed at Fort Stewart outside Savannah. The woman had been treated with toxic amounts of the antibiotic Gentamiacin after developing a postpartum infection. Expert testimony established that the drug can damage the ear's vestibular function, the mechanism that controls balance, and the evidence indicated that the medical team did not monitor the amount of the drug administered into her bloodstream. In any event, the jury denied Newmann's claim that negligence on the part of doctors at the Winn Army Community Hospital had destroyed her ability to work—she was a CPA—take care of her child, and perform the ordinary functions of everyday life. Alaimo ignored the jury and awarded the woman $1.67 million in damages against the federal government. He sat back and waited for the storm he knew would follow. Sure enough, in August 1991 the United States appealed his ruling to the Eleventh Circuit Court of Appeals.

Sure enough, Alaimo was upheld.

*Corporate Polluters: The LCP Chemicals Trial*

"The father, who was the CEO, had induced his son,
a Harvard Business School graduate, to come on

---

[9] The FTCA provides a limited waiver of the federal government's sovereign immunity when its employees are negligent within the scope of their employment.

down to salvage the business. And the cost of it? They
got convicted. Both did." —Anthony Alaimo

For all its pristine beauty, coastal Georgia, South Carolina, and swaths of the Florida Panhandle are heavily industrialized. The rivers and marshes are dotted with paper mills, refineries, and chemical plants, many of them dating back to an era in which environmental concerns were not an issue, when laws and law enforcement were lax or nonexistent, and when the term "green" referred to the money associated with maximized profits, job creation, and development. Human nature, of course, is as fragile and subject to pollution as the environment. Imprudent, even reckless men, some at the helm of multibillion-dollar conglomerates, approved or turned their heads at what now seem unspeakable acts of environmental rape and pillage. With their privileged pedigrees and Ivy League credentials, their phalanxes of lawyers and country club memberships, these men seemed a world removed from the gaudy drug dealers and their "Rolex-wearing attorneys" whose cases clogged the federal courts in Florida, Georgia, Alabama, Mississippi, and Louisiana. Yet, like the drug dealers, they spread devastation and disease across the land; like the drug lords, a percentage found themselves facing juries of their peers in Anthony Alaimo's courtroom—juries, that for all the dazzling defenses and ingenuity of their lawyers, often remained unmoved.

Four of the fifteen Georgia locations designated by the Environmental Protection Agency as toxic Superfund[10] sites are in Glynn County, just miles from Alaimo's chambers. The first, a location formerly operated by LCP Chemicals Georgia, is now regarded as the worst case of corporate pollution in the Southeast and possibly the nation. Final costs to clean up the mercury and other

---

[10] Officially the Comprehensive Environmental Response, Compensation, and Liability Act 42 U.S.C. § 9601–9675.

poisons dumped on the site, which then leached into the surrounding waterways, have been estimated in the hundreds of millions of dollars.

The immensity of the environmental devastation wrought by LCP Chemicals Georgia emerged when EPA investigators began picking up traces of mercury poisoning in indigenous birds and wildlife as well as the abundant populations of oyster, blue crab, and shrimp that are the backbone of the coastal fishing industry. The case had a terrible precedent, a harbinger of what might well lie ahead. Forty years earlier in Japan, the owners of Chisso Corporation, a chemical company, had authorized the dumping of large amounts of mercury into Minamata Bay. Ironically local residents had originally welcomed the corporation, persuaded by the prospects of jobs and a better life.

Fishermen from a small fishing village of the same name plied the bay and their harvests were a mainstay of the local diet. Quickly, thousands of people from Minamata and the surrounding areas began to develop symptoms of mercury poisoning, among them terrible birth defects. Puzzled at first, the medical community declared that an "unclarified disease of the central nervous system" had broken out.

"...Almost all the town's cats went insane, throwing themselves into the ocean. Birds fell out of the sky. Panic gripped the city. In time, thousands of people would die from the poisoning."[11]

The American photographer William Eugene Smith captured a shattering image of a grieving mother bathing her horribly deformed sixteen-year-old daughter Tomoko Uemura, a photograph known around the world as the Minamata Pieta. Smith's photo is an unknowing reenactment of Michelangelo's sculpture of the Blessed Mother holding the lifeless body of the crucified Christ in her arms.

Less well-known but equally significant is another photograph Smith took during the trial of Chisso Corporation president Kenichi

---

[11] See http://redstarcafe.wordpress.com/2007/06/26/the-minamata-pieta/.

Shimada. In the picture, an aide mops Shimada's sweating brow after the executive has touched his forehead to the ground outside the courtroom, "a formal ritual of apology" for the devastation wrought.

On May 28, 1998, a ritual enactment of corporate shame began again: a federal grand jury in Savannah indicted four former LCP executives on forty-two counts of conspiring to violate the Clean Water Act, the Resource Conservation and Recovery Act, the Comprehensive Environmental Response, the Compensation and Liability Act, and the Endangered Species Act among other statutes, setting the stage for what would become a landmark environmental prosecution.

Among those charged were Christian A. Hansen, former chairman of the board of Hanlin Group, LCP's parent company; his son Randall W. Hansen, who held executive vice president and CEO titles; Alfred R. Taylor, former plant manager; and D. Brent Hanson, the former environmental manager for the facility.

In retrospect, the trial could have taken place decades earlier. LCP Georgia shut down its Brunswick operations in 1994, the result of a bankruptcy the parent company had filed three years earlier, but the 550-acre site had been a witches' brew of toxic waste for more than seventy-five years—polluted, in turn, by the Atlantic Refining Company (ARCO), Dixie Paints and Varnish Company, Allied Chemical (later Allied Signal), and Hanlin.

In 1979, LCP had begun manufacturing bleach, caustic soda, hydrogen, and hydrochloric acid at the facility. More than 150 employees, mostly unskilled laborers, worked at the plant. The chemicals were manufactured in what were known as "cell rooms," each the size of a football field. The process generated massive quantities of toxic wastewater, as it turned out, at levels beyond the plant's treatment capacities. This waste eventually overflowed the plant's storage sumps and made its way into the groundwater, much the way a malignancy travels through the human lymph system.

In the process, prosecutors alleged, the defendants knowingly exposed their employees to potentially fatal levels of mercury vapor and other hazards. Stop-gap measures had been taken: a system of boardwalks was built throughout the plant to keep employees from being burned or electrocuted as they sloshed through the deadly waters.

Upon the plant's closing, the state of Georgia asked the Environmental Protection Agency to take immediate action at the site to stem the release of chlorine gas and the flow of contamination into the adjacent saltwater tidal marsh containing endangered species.

Evidence presented by the EPA's Criminal Investigation Division and the US Fish and Wildlife Service suggested that LCP and Allied Signal together had already dumped 150 tons of mercury, a neurotoxin, and polychlorinated biphenyls (PCBs), a known cancer-causing agent used in the manufacture of chlorine, into Purvis Creek (a tributary of the Turtle River) and the surrounding marshes. (In Japan, the Chisso Company had dumped 27 tons of mercury into Minamata Bay with devastating consequences.) The creek, along with a mile of the Turtle River, were found to be contaminated with lead and other toxic compounds that had made their way up the food chain in levels sufficiently elevated to support a ban on commercial fishing in the area.

Four of the seven men charged in the case pleaded guilty before the trial got underway in January 1999. After a two week trial, the jury convicted Christian Hansen, the Hanlin chairman, and plant manager Alfred Taylor on forty-one counts. Randall Hansen, the chairman's son who'd been brought in by his father to run the operation during the bankruptcy proceedings, was found guilty on thirty-four counts of conspiracy and violations of environmental pollution laws.

"The father, who had been the CEO, had induced his son, a Harvard Business School graduate, to come on down to salvage the business," Alaimo remembered. "And the cost of it? They got convicted. Both did."

On June 3, 1999, Alaimo sentenced the elder Hansen to nine years in federal prison; Alfred Taylor drew six years. Together these were among the longest sentences ever imposed in a case involving criminal violations of environmental law. The judge clearly struggled with the fate of Randall Hansen, the chairman's son who'd been convicted on thirty-four counts including "knowingly" exposing his workers to environmental hazards. Alaimo delayed Randall's sentencing, announcing, "I'm going to think about it for a while." In a public apology to the community, the senior Hansen confessed, "I have many regrets," reminiscent of the apology made by his Japanese counterpart. "I am particularly concerned about my son," he added.

Here again, the federal sentencing guidelines limited Alaimo's ability to be more nuanced in his sentencing. The trial transcript suggests that, though sympathetic, Alaimo could find no compelling reason to justify a "downward departure" from the guidelines. ("I simply cannot make such a finding.") Twenty years later, the case still troubled him. "It was really heartrending for me to sentence him," Alaimo recalled. "This guy had an impeccable background. Talk about looking after his children. He was the ideal kind of parent. Always with his kids. And his wife made one of the most impassioned speeches I'd ever heard. I had to send him up for four years. Nothing could be accomplished by incarcerating this man, but nevertheless, it was the law."

On August 23, 2001, the United States Court of Appeals for the Eleventh Circuit upheld the convictions.

Nearly a decade after the trial, the government did extend mercy, but it did so for Christian Hansen, the father whose sins had been visited upon his son. "I never heard from the young man again," Alaimo reflected in 2008. "The old man we let out early. He was in his late seventies by then and in horrible physical condition. It cost more in terms of medical treatment to keep him incarcerated. We felt his family could take better care of him."

The case didn't end there. In January 1995, a team of lawyers from Brunswick and Augusta—Joel Wooten, Robert Killian, John Bell, and Pam James—filed a civil suit against Hanlin and Allied Chemical (now Honeywell) on behalf of Glynn County and more than 200 property owners for knowingly polluting Purvis Creek and the Turtle River. The proceedings dragged for twelve years before being settled in November 2006 for $50 million, the largest successful environmental litigation in Georgia history.

# Chapter 26

It little profits that an idle king,
By this still hearth, among these barren crags,
Match'd with an aged wife, I mete and dole
Unequal laws unto a savage race,
That hoard, and sleep, and feed, and know not me.
—*Ulysses*, Alfred Lord Tennyson

Anthony Alaimo turned seventy on March 29, 1990. As the law requires, he relinquished his duties as chief judge of the Southern District of Georgia, a position he'd held for fourteen years, and took senior status. As tradition has it, he was presented with a portrait of himself that now hangs near the painting of Sir Thomas More, the martyr and unbending moralist, in the Anthony A. Alaimo Courtroom in Brunswick, Georgia.

Alaimo's painting, done by a self-taught artist named Dean Pauls, is remarkable in that it captures the inner Alaimo, what Judge Dudley Bowen described at the unveiling ceremony as his "iron will, shrewd intellect, experience, and inner strength." What may have gone unnoticed among the tributes and affectionate jokes of his peers on that August afternoon in 1990 was that these flames burned as fiercely and as brightly in the septuagenarian jurist as they had in the fearless young boxer, the dedicated pilot, the determined escape artist and fierce patriot.

Alaimo's friend Judge John Sammons Bell, who had administered Judge Alaimo's oath of office nineteen years earlier, recognized his old comrade's devotion to duty for what it was. He referred to it as "the totality of his personality," a fire so intense and pure it threatened to consume the clay vessel that contained it.

Ever the clever schoolboy, Alaimo deflected the praise and scrutiny that afternoon by joking that he felt "like Tom Sawyer" who'd eavesdropped on his own funeral. "I'm tempted to plead guilty," he said, "but I'm afraid the plea would not stand.... Instead, I plead *nolo contendre.*"

Eighteen years later, Anthony Alaimo is still active on the bench, still curious and engaged, by turns stern and compassionate. What propels his frail, failing body is the purest will—an unintentional beacon, but a beacon just the same, of how a life might be lived.

His health had shadowed him all those years. His brothers Philip and Freddy, his sisters Sandy and Irene, had all passed away of heart related illnesses. Tony improved his diet, quit smoking, kept exercising, and dismissed any intimations of mortality. The various shunts, bypasses, and stitches that kept his heart patched together like an old inner tube held.

Alaimo outlasted the controversies and upheavals that marked a career spanning seven presidencies and waves of cultural upheaval. The brickbats, to his amusement, had become blossoms strewn in his path. On Saint Simons and Sea Island, doors fly open at his arrival; friends and well-wishers crowd around to greet him and Jeanne like celebrities at the Red Barn, his favorite restaurant, or during his lunches at The Cloister's Oak Room.[1] He jokes that had he been a district judge in New York City, "no one would have ever known my name."

On November 13, 1997, the Reidsville prison case came full circle. With pomp and circumstance, the state of Georgia officially dedicated the "Judge Anthony A. Alaimo Courthouse" inside the walls of the state prison. One after another, representatives from the Georgia attorney general's office, the state Department of Corrections, and the state legislature (the same body of worthies that had so roundly condemned Alaimo's meddling) now praised the

---

[1] For decades, the Alaimos' favorite breakfast spot was the much more modest Huddle House on Saint Simons.

judge's courage and steadfastness in pressing the reforms that grew out of *Guthrie v. Evans*.

"You have been the heart and soul and conscience of prison reform in this country," Corrections Commissioner Wayne Garner said of Alaimo.

The courthouse was built to speed the flow and reduce the red tape associated with hearing the myriad *habeas corpus* suits and other legal actions that seem to be the main product (despite the license plate stereotype) produced in the American penal system.

That November day, Alaimo as usual wasted no time getting to work. Before the last encomium had stopped ringing in his ears, he had hopped on the bench and begun hearing arguments in yet another class action suit; this one involved access to prison law libraries and the use of taxpayer funds to underwrite inmates' legal actions.

Even the prisoners got into the spirit of things. An inmate named Bill Noll declared, "We all have a right to change. Thank you for allowing me to be more than when I first came to be here." The same inmate had painted an inaugural portrait of the seventy-seven-year-old Alaimo's craggy, hawk-nosed countenance, which, with the passage of time, had begun to resemble Caesar's depiction on a Roman denarius.

"What do I know about running a prison?" Alaimo later remarked of the Reidsville case. "And yet, I had a duty to do it. What was always uppermost in my mind was the obligation to uphold the rule of law. If you don't, our whole society crumbles. Where I saw injustices against these inmates, I had the power to do something about it. That's one of the glories of this job. And I'd never hesitate to do it for fear of being not liked or fear of being highly criticized. No, I called them like I saw them."

In the spring of 1997, Judge Tjoflat, Georgia attorney general Michael Bowers, mayor Homer Wilson, Sea Island Company CEO A. W. "Bill" Jones III, District Court Judges Dudley H. Bowen and

William T. Moore Jr., and a dozen other notables were on hand at Brunswick's Mary Ross Park as Alaimo was granted the American equivalent of knighthood: a section of US Highway 17 was dubbed the "US District Judge Anthony A. Alaimo Parkway."

A year earlier, Judge Alaimo, clad in white shorts and tennis shoes, basked in another signal honor. Designated an Olympic torchbearer, he delivered the flame, despite his "inflexible bones," to a relay point in front of the Glynn County courthouse in Brunswick while a Baptist choir sang the "Battle Hymn of the Republic." Jeanne and their son Philip cheered him on. Later, the aluminum and brass Olympic torch Alaimo carried would find its place among the memorabilia, the medals and awards,[2] and the scale model of the B-26 bomber crowding his chamber walls.

In 1995 he had attended the fifty-year reunion of former Stalag Luft III POWs at the Air Force Academy in Colorado Springs, finding himself among a thousand of his old comrades. At another POW gathering, he was startled to bump into an unexpected guest, Sergeant Major Hermann Glemnitz, the Luftwaffe guard Alaimo had foolishly ordered to step aside on the camp's snowy exercise track. Glemnitz, the chief of the ferrets, had marched him into the commandant's office. "I was not too happy," Alaimo recalled. "This was the guy who had poked me pretty hard in the ribs with his rifle butt. And here we are paying his expenses to fly to the United States!" Later, Alaimo came to realize that his resentment of the German's presence was wrongheaded.

At a reunion in Kansas City, only fifty former airmen showed up. Alaimo recognized two of them. At the last reunion he attended, at Cincinnati in spring 2008, there were twenty-three veterans in

---

[2] Among the awards was an Emory University medal for career accomplishment and a scholarship endowed in his name at Ohio Northern University's School of Law.

attendance. He didn't know any of the men. "So you begin to see," he said softly, "that it's gone."

# Chapter 27

"I've never quite gotten over it…the pure injustice of
justice."—Anthony Alaimo, 2007

The Howard Miller clock adjacent to the Robing Room in
Anthony Alaimo's chambers mournfully chimes the hour. The
eighty-seven-year-old judge has chosen this moment after months of
interviews to recall a trial, out of the thousands that have passed
before him, that shook his core beliefs—a case that fifteen years later
brings him to the verge of tears.

The case was not a matter of great Constitutional import, nor
the subject of arcane legal debate. It never appeared in the West
Publishing Company journals or online in *Westlaw*. It was a systemic
injustice that swept a man into a meat grinder, a man who but for
family, faith, and *bella fortuna*[1] was not so different from young
Alaimo or a thousand other disadvantaged young men yearning to be
a part of things and not knowing how.

The young man's name is Lester Bell. He lives in Waycross,[2] a
bleak southeast Georgia crossroads that has hemorrhaged jobs and
residents for decades, a city with a majority black population and a
median income less than half that of the rest of the state. It is not an
easy place, as the Reverend Jesse Jackson liked to say, "to keep hope
alive."

In the 1980s, Waycross became a caravanserai for crack cocaine
distributors wending their way north from Florida. Among the
miseries the drug dealers delivered to Waycross were spiraling

---

[1] Fortuna is the goddess of fortune and good luck.
[2] Waycross drew national attention in 2008 when a group of third graders were
apprehended for plotting to murder their teacher. Among the evidence: steak
knives, duct tape, and handcuffs.

violence, crime, and AIDS, which spread heterosexually in the frenzied atmosphere of the city's crack houses.

Macon criminal defense attorney Sandra Popson remembered Waycross as "a little town of huge problems."

In the early 1990s, a petty drug dealer named Eugene Edmunds put together an enterprise to peddle cocaine to the growing ranks of desperate and diseased "crackheads" who roamed the inner city like locusts. Unlike heroin abusers, whose single injection takes them through the day, crack addicts need to get high a dozen times; they will rob, steal, and peddle their bodies to feed that hunger.

Perhaps patterning himself after the drug-dealing icon portrayed by Al Pacino in the movie *Scarface*, Edmunds bragged that every day he drank a bottle of Dom Perignon champagne. As Popson described him, "Edmunds was the typical smalltown kingpin type who'd recruit poor black kids off the street who had little or no education, little or no home life, and get them to sell for him."

Lester Bell was one of his recruits. Bell was an uneducated black male with nothing to recommend him in life but an innocent face and, according to those who knew him, "the most charming smile in the world."

"Bell was a gofer in a gang of maybe fifteen or twenty people," Judge Alaimo remembered. "He knew nothing. All he did was run errands."

In Washington, President George H. W. Bush and Attorney General Richard Thornburgh were escalating the "War on Drugs" President Ronald Reagan had declared during his second term, targeting the epidemic of crack cocaine devastating the nation's inner cities. "Major drug cases were referred to the feds," Popson recalled. "If you were found to be a member of a criminal conspiracy, the consequences of conviction were draconian."

Sentencing guidelines reflected the Justice Department's focus on crack cocaine. Critics argued that they disproportionately punished poor blacks (the majority of crack abusers) while scaling back the incarceration and punishment of "recreational" powder cocaine abusers and dealers who tended to be white and middleclass, a reality still reflected in today's prison populations. "The disparity between sentences for powder cocaine and crack was enormous," Popson remarked. "It could be 100 times more severe."[3]

Eugene Edmund's pipe dream of building a drug empire quickly came crashing down. Unlike Al Pacino's Tony Montana, who went out in a blaze of automatic weapons fire, Edmunds moved to cut a deal with federal prosecutors. He agreed to testify against his fellow conspirators, individuals known in Waycross by names like "Humpy," "Lady Red," and "Boo-Boo."

Sandra Popson, who had first encountered Alaimo when she defended Susan Moody in the obstruction case involving Walter Leroy Moody, was now appointed to represent Lester Bell. Popson was a criminal lawyer. Among the other attorneys appointed by the court to represent the defendants—Southern District of Georgia rules require that attorneys who have been admitted to practice in the district may be appointed to defend any client any time—was a bankruptcy attorney so over his head that his indigent client would later insist on giving his own closing argument.

The case was tried in Alaimo's Brunswick courtroom. Given the weight of evidence, its outcome was hardly in doubt. "'Guilty' was a foregone conclusion," Popson admitted. On April 16, 1993, a jury convicted Lester Bell and eight other defendants of conspiring to distribute controlled substances in violation of 21 U.S.C. § 846.[4]

---

[3] Under the federal sentencing guidelines, crack cocaine offenders have typically been sentenced to 50 percent more jail time than powder cocaine offenders. A gram of crack cocaine is, in effect, equated to 100 grams of powder cocaine. The Supreme Court moved to end this disparity in 2007, ruling that the sentencing guidelines were purely "advisory."

[4] Title 21 US Code Controlled Substances Act. Attempt and Conspiracy. "Any person who attempts or conspires to commit…shall be subject to the same penalties as those prescribed for the offense."

It was in the sentencing phase that Alaimo, always steady and certain, faltered. The guidelines to which he'd adhered over the years as precisely as a chemist mixing his compounds, failed, rendering him—there could be no argument—an instrument of injustice, at odds with his absolute fealty to the law and the counsel of Alexander Solzhenitsyn he'd held so dear: "...a society with no other scale but the legal one is not quite worthy of man either. A society which is based on the letter of the law and never reaches any higher is taking very scarce advantage of the high level of human possibilities. The letter of the law is too cold and formal to have a beneficial influence on society."

The probation officer had prepared a pre-sentence report (PSR) for Alaimo on each of the defendants. The report included a determination of the amount of cocaine attributable to each defendant under the sentencing guidelines, a questionable calculation at best. The officer essentially concluded that Eugene Edmunds and his gang distributed a kilogram of crack cocaine per month. He then multiplied this figure by the number of months each defendant was involved in the conspiracy. The source of that bit of information was Eugene Edmunds. In other words, Lester Bell was sentenced as though he had sold a kilo a month when in fact that was the amount sold by fifteen to twenty individuals, many of them much more involved.

Such was the math that forced Anthony Alaimo to sentence nineteen-year-old Lester Bell, errand boy and gofer, to 360 months in prison—30 years, most of it to serve.

"Lester was just a little kid," Popson remembered. "He had one prior conviction, a very tiny, little minute nothing. A probation case. And here he gets thirty years."

Popson teared up at the sentencing, making her plea for leniency while struggling unsuccessfully to contain her emotions. The image embedded itself in Alaimo as deeply as the shrapnel wounds he carried home from the war.

Ironically, ringleader Eugene Edmunds, who never faced a jury of his peers, drew 200 months. "What generally happens, and it's kind of disturbing," Alaimo later commented, "is that the government makes deals with the guys at the top for giving them information, and the poor guy at the bottom can't offer anything. He doesn't know anything and he gets the bigger sentence."

Did Alaimo's own experiences in the POW camps haunt him over the long years Bell spent incarcerated? Did he, stern-faced and rigid of demeanor, ache for the young man as his youth and promise slipped away? Did the ring of steel cell doors clang in his ears?

"Under these damn guidelines, I had to do it," Alamo recalled, still seemingly at war with himself. "I almost cried at the...pure injustice of justice. But you know, I'd sworn to uphold the law. I had no choice. And I did it."

In fact, Alaimo was already having serious doubts about the efficacy of the so-called "War on Drugs." The Bell case may have driven him to take a completely different approach. "For many years, I'd been opposed to the legalization of drugs," he remarked during a 2008 interview. "I believed prosecuting to the fullest extent of the law was the way to go. But after spending billions of dollars, it hasn't worked."

Alaimo had seen the corrupting influence that the enormous sums associated with the drug trade had on ordinary individuals, particularly underpaid local police officers, so many of whom he'd sent to prison over the years. He'd watched the rise of self-perpetuating federal bureaucracies like the DEA with increasing dismay. "It's become an industry just like the drug dealers," he grumbled. "These guys don't want it solved. They're stationed in nice places around the world with good per diem and that kind of stuff. This is one of the curses of a bureaucracy."

Today Alaimo favors decriminalization, in effect, taking the money of out the drug trade. "Illicit profit is what's driving these farmers down in Columbia and Venezuela and Afghanistan," he argues. He has spoken publicly about legalizing drugs and setting up trial programs in key cities to treat addiction as a public health problem—to little effect. "I don't see any effort or any person taking the lead to do it," Alaimo admits.

Attorney Popson was part of an appeal to the Eleventh Circuit that won a modest sentence reduction for Bell and three of the other defendants based on the flawed calculus of drug distribution. Popson later wrote to President Bill Clinton's Attorney General Janet Reno, hoping for redress. Popson was a faithful steward. Over the years she stayed in touch with Lester Bell and his family via letters and Christmas cards. She and her husband were waiting in the anteroom in the spring of 2008 when Bell—now in his thirties—was released from the Federal Correctional Institution in Jesup, Georgia.

Due to a long-overdue amendment to the guidelines, Bell had become eligible for immediate release in March 2008—three and a half years earlier than he expected. Judge Alaimo signed his release order. Altogether, Bell served sixteen and a half years.

"I've always remembered you," Bell told Popson that day. "You were the last person who ever cried for me."

Neither Popson nor Bell knew it, but the last person who cried for Bell was Anthony Alaimo. Alone in his chambers, inconsolable in his grief and uncertainty as the clock chimed the interminable hours.

# PART IV

...Old age hath yet his honor and his toil.
Death closes all; but something ere the end,
Some work of noble note, may yet be done,
Not unbecoming men that strove with Gods.
The lights begin to twinkle from the rocks;
The long day wanes; the slow moon climbs; the deep
Moans round with many voices. Come, my friends.
'Tis not too late to seek a newer world...
...Tho' much is taken, much abides; and tho'
We are not now that strength which in old days
Moved earth and heaven, that which we are, we are,—
One equal temper of heroic hearts,
Made weak by time and fate, but strong in will
To strive, to seek, to find, and not to yield.
—*Ulysses*, Alfred Lord Tennyson

# Chapter 28

"The most politically explosive trial in Atlanta history opened today as a former city councilman and two of the city's most well-connected businessmen face charges of engaging in a multimillion-dollar conspiracy at Hartsfield International Airport to bribe elected officials and defraud Atlanta's citizens. But much more is at stake than the fate of three men. City Hall itself will be on trial."—*Atlanta Journal-Constitution*, January 3, 1994

In 1957, Anthony Alaimo departed Atlanta after nearly a decade struggling to make his way as an attorney. When he returned in 1994 to preside over the most sensitive conspiracy and corruption trial in the city's history, Atlanta was a dramatically different place from the days when he and Reuben Garland[1] had hustled for business out of the Candler Building.

Atlanta's population had exploded, thanks to a flood of in-migration from the Northern rustbelts and an exodus out of the withered small towns of the South to the big city. Atlanta had become a regional headquarters for dozens of Fortune 500 and international companies, Porsche and Siemens among them. Atlanta was still true to its roots, a "go-go" city, overbuilt, overextended, entrepreneurial, and, not surprisingly, subject to cycles of boom and bust, birth and rebirth, rise and fall, as regular as the seasons.

One thing had changed over the years. Beginning with the election of Maynard Jackson as mayor in 1973, political power in the city of Atlanta shifted to its majority black population. The

---

[1] Garland died in 1983.

transformation—Atlanta was the first major Southern city to elect an African-American mayor—was overdue. It burnished the city's bustling, "too busy to hate" image, but with the trappings and perquisites of power came corruption, a vice that is completely colorblind.

One of Atlanta's crown jewels is the city-owned Hartsfield-Jackson International Airport, statistically the "world's busiest passenger airport" but more importantly an economic engine that pumps a staggering $5.6 billion into the local and regional economies each year. Revenue derived from airport concessions, rentals, parking fees, taxes, and other sources now approaches $300 million annually, a temptation that in the mid-1980s spun a tangled web of bribes, kickbacks, and corruption that continued to expand until it finally drew the attention of Joe Whitley, US attorney for the Northern District of Georgia.

A two-year investigation led to the indictment of three of the city's more prominent figures: Ira Jackson, a high-profile city councilman and former aviation commissioner; Daniel Paradies, owner of the Paradies Shops, a chain of airport gift stores with more than $100 million in annual revenue; and entrepreneur McKinley "Mack" Wilbourn, who allegedly conspired with Paradies and Jackson to seize control of the percentage of the airport's gift-shop concessions set aside for minority ownership.

Greed is commonplace, but there was a particular odiousness to the airport scandal because it undermined the city's attempts—those of Hartsfield's Minority Business Enterprise Program in particular—to ensure that women and blacks, excluded in the past, received a fair share of government contracts let by the airport authority. In fact, Hartsfield's affirmative action program had become the capstone of Mayor Maynard Jackson's legacy, a national model that over the years had supposedly generated millions of dollars for minority-owned companies.

To Alaimo, it might have seemed like the Burke County case all over again. This time, however, the conspiracy was more cynical and sophisticated and the alleged perpetrators were both black and white.

Ultimately, the investigation, run by razor-sharp Assistant US Attorney Sally Yates, laid bare a trail of sweetheart deals, political favors, and systematic corruption. It would culminate in the trial and conviction of former Atlanta mayor Bill Campbell for income tax evasion twelve years later.

In 1992, Ira Jackson was indicted on eighty-three counts of mail fraud, forty-three counts of bribery, and five counts of income tax evasion, all tied to more than $1 million in illegal payments he allegedly received between 1985 and 1992. Paradies was charged with eighty-three counts of mail fraud as well as conspiracy to bribe Jackson and other members of the Atlanta City Council. Wilbourn, the largest minority participant in Paradies's enterprise and an alleged front man for Jackson, stood accused of mail fraud and witness tampering.

Jackson and Wilbourn are African American; Paradies is white. But race was not the issue that drove Judge Gerald Tjoflat to appoint seventy-three-year-old Anthony Alaimo to handle a trial that would draw immense local coverage as well as the scrutiny of the national media. Certainly Judge Alaimo's vast experience and rigorous deportment were factors, as was his unerring ability to reassure and even inspire jurors over the course of what would be a long and complex trial. Yet there was something more, something that led Orinda Evans, chief judge for the Northern District of Georgia, to recuse herself and her fellow judges.

Dan Paradies's sister Janice was the wife of District Court Judge Marvin Shoob. Every day of the three-week trial, the close-knit Paradies family—Shoob included—would pack Courtroom 2308 on the top floor of the Richard B. Russell Federal Building to show their support.

"In my little world," Tjoflat recalled, "Alaimo is probably the only guy in Georgia who could try this case and not let it affect him. Everything was going on. You had the whole city government and the mayor and this one and that one. And all these things have tentacles."

The three defendants, all men of means, surrounded themselves with a cavalcade of top-flight lawyers. At any given moment during the trial, as many as ten attorneys crowded the defense tables. Among them were Bobby Lee Cook (Paradies) of Summerville, Georgia, a legal magician in the histrionic mold of Reuben Garland; Harvard-trained Emmet J. Bondurant II (Paradies), later recognized by the National Law Journal as one of the top ten trial lawyers in the country; former federal prosecutor Jerome J. Froelich (Wilbourn), and veteran criminal trial lawyers P. Bruce Kirwan (Jackson) and Anthony Axam (Jackson).

On the first day of the trial, Alaimo sequestered the twelve-member (plus four alternates) jury. They, in turn, requested that court be in session seven days a week. Never deviating from his Southern District standards, Alaimo ruled that court would be in session from 8:30 A.M. until 6:30 P.M. (it often ran until 7:30 P.M.), a move that quickly exhausted defense attorneys Cook, Froelich, and Bondurant and started them howling.

"No one should be able to work a jury seven days a week, from 8:30 in the morning until 6:30 at night," Froelich later protested to Ann Woolner, editor of the *Fulton County Daily Report*. "It's the most unfair situation I have ever been in."

As the trial unfolded, the defense focused on undermining the government's chief witness, Harold Echols, another airport concessionaire. Echols had already cut a deal with prosecutors, pleading guilty to one count of conspiring to bribe Ira Jackson and other Atlanta city councilmen. Echol's get-out-of-jail card: a series of incriminating conversations he'd secretly taped with Atlanta officials.

The point man in the defense's attack was Bobby Lee Cook, who lambasted the hapless Echols as "not just a liar, but a pathological liar...a common thief and a rogue." An excerpt from a January 12, 1994 *Atlanta Journal-Constitution* story reads like a transcript from an announcer covering a prize fight:

"...The Summerville, Ga., attorney paced, his hands gesturing wildly, his voice booming as if from Sinai. Echols seemed confused, twisted, uncertain how to respond. His confidence on the wane, Echols slumped in his witness chair and once nearly disappeared from sight. Cook induced Echols to admit to lies in sworn testimony before a grand jury in 1992. Echols couldn't remember many details from that testimony.

"Your memory is still good, isn't it?" Cook said. "No, sir," Echols said. "Not the best in the world."

Later Cook barked: "Do you know when you are lying and telling the truth?"

"Yes, sir," Echols said.

"How can anyone else tell?"

The prosecution counterpunched, presenting a mountain of damning evidence including videotapes of a number of Atlanta's top elected officials seemingly caught in the act of accepting bribes. Among the more telling blows was then-city councilman Jackson's 1985 purchase (in his wife's name) of Mack Wilbourn's interest in Paradies's Atlanta operation, a violation of a board of ethics ruling that deemed such a transaction improper. Yates insisted Paradies knew that while Wilbourn continued to act as an owner in the business, Jackson claimed the profits—more than $1 million from 1985 to 1992, income never disclosed to the IRS. In return, Yates said, Jackson actively influenced and voted on legislation that saved millions of dollars for Paradies.[2]

---

[2] Among others, Atlanta city councilman, D.L. ("Buddy") Fowlkes would later be tried and convicted on bribery charges associated with the case.)

From the bench Alaimo spotted Janice Shoob (sitting next to Judge Shoob) and her sister, Billie Paradies, wincing at every damning piece of testimony directed at Dan Paradies. "They'd make faces during the trial," Alaimo recalled. "It didn't affect me. It's hard for the public and many people to understand, but you can be impersonal with respect to things like this. If there's any validity to our system of justice, you have to be that way."

Certainly, Judge Shoob's unexpected appearance raised eyebrows in the legal community. But as Gerald Tjoflat explained, "it didn't have anything to do with the jury. It didn't bug Alaimo in the least. He's the last guy it would have any effect on. Those who thought about it concluded you had an extremely distraught person who is so entangled because of his wife's family. His brother-in-law is the defendant. He's probably under enormous pressure. You can see the family's all over him, not knowing what is proper or not proper. And he caves into it."

Another highlight of an otherwise grim and exhausting business were the clever exchanges between Judge Alaimo and sixty-four-year-old Bobby Lee Cook, who eyed each other like two bull moose in the rutting season. Cook had a hearing problem, and one of his appeals to the jury was his claim of being old and feeble—a tactic lifted right out of the Reuben Garland handbook. Alaimo, seventy-four at the time, wore a hearing aid, which he "offered" to Cook.

In the course of Cook's grilling of Harold Echols, Alaimo asked a telling question from the bench: did Echols give bribes or kickbacks to Bill Campbell, the new Atlanta mayor who'd been sworn in just days before the trial got under way? Echols testified that he had bribed the mayor. Campbell, at the time still a darling of the media and the white business establishment, declared the accusation "false and baseless."

"The powers that be in the town were for him [Campbell]," Alaimo recalled in a 2007 interview. "They thought he was okay [laughs] and were trying to protect him. They criticized me!"

If there was a climax to the trial, it was the meltdown of defendant Ira Jackson on January 13, the tenth straight day of testimony. Jackson suddenly began railing against his lawyer P. Bruce Kirwan, the prosecutors, and the media. In chambers, Kirwan advised Judge Alaimo of Jackson's prediction that if he were not allowed to testify the next morning, a "race riot" would ensue. The fact that the next morning was the middle of the prosecution's case did not faze Jackson, whom Alaimo quickly dispatched for a psychiatric evaluation.

There, Jackson accused psychiatrist David Davis of planning to inject him with "truth serum," apparently something he felt was not in his best interest. Jackson's wife reportedly called the police on Davis. The next day Jackson, accompanied by his new lawyer Tony Axam, agreed to the evaluation by Davis but insisted that the doctor be frisked by a black US marshal to be sure the psychiatrist was not carrying a concealed syringe. Davis told Kirwan that Jackson might be having a psychotic episode, but another court-ordered psychiatric evaluation found him competent to stand trial.

A week later, Jackson took the witness stand and by all accounts proceeded to bury himself and Paradies under Sally Yates's tough cross-examination.

On January 22, a Saturday, the jury found Ira Jackson and Daniel Paradies guilty of bribery, conspiracy, mail fraud, and tax evasion. Mack Wilbourn was acquitted on all counts. The panel deliberated for just six hours in a trial that had included dozens of witnesses, thousands of documents, and the best defense money could buy. The sixty-three-year-old Jackson was convicted on all eighty-three counts of mail fraud and forty-three counts of accepting bribes. He was cleared on one of the tax evasion charges. As his sister Janice Shoob sobbed, the foreman announced that Paradies, seventy-two, was found guilty of all eighty-three mail fraud counts plus one count of conspiracy. His businesses, Paradies Midfield Corporation and the Paradies Shops, were convicted of the same charges.

The trial that had been estimated to run six weeks ended in three, no doubt thanks to Judge Alaimo's grueling ten-hour days and six-and-a-half-day weeks, including a session on Martin Luther King Jr. day. (Alaimo did allow a weekend recess when one of the defense attorneys suffered a family emergency.)

Emmet Bondurant later complained in the *Fulton County Daily Report* that "A trial ought to be a trial; it ought not to be a physical ordeal." He added, "Speed is not necessarily a virtue." However, the pace of the proceeding was never part of the extensive appeals process that followed.

Prosecutor Yates was similarly exhausted but suggested that the grueling schedule made it easier for jurors to stay focused. "It was the same for everybody," she told the *Daily Report*. "I don't think it was appropriate for me to whine."

"It was pretty hard stuff on the lawyers, Alaimo later allowed, "and very stressful running trials from 8:00 in the morning until 6:00 to 6:30 at night, with just one hour for lunch, and starting the next morning. From that standpoint, I may have been a little too harsh."

If there is such a thing as a *positive* chilling effect, it would certainly apply to the damper the verdicts almost certainly put on the nefarious activities of the half-dozen or so city officials whose names or videotaped images surfaced during the course of the trial. Mayor Bill Campbell may have been the glaring exception. In summer 2008, he was serving a thirty-month sentence for tax evasion in a federal prison outside Miami.

In April 1994, Alaimo sentenced Paradies to thirty-three months in prison. His company was fined $1.5 million. Jackson drew forty-two months in prison.[3] The case did not end there. Two years later both men were still free on bond. In January 1996, Jackson, now sixty-five, and Paradies, seventy-five, appealed their conviction to the

---

[3] For a more detailed account of the Hartsfield Corruption Case and its aftermath, see http://www.law.emory.edu/11circuit/sept96/94-8485.opa.html.

Eleventh Circuit Court of Appeals. They contended that Alaimo had committed reversible errors when he refused to let defense attorneys see responses by potential jurors before the trial and excused potential jurors without any discussion. During his instructions the judge, according to the appeal, also neglected to tell the jury the defense's theory of the case. Paradies brought yet another big gun to bear in his defense: former US Attorney Larry Thompson.

On September 24, 1996, a three-judge panel of the Eleventh Circuit Court of Appeals unanimously affirmed the convictions and sentences of Jackson and Paradies (Jackson began serving his sentence a year later). At the time Yates concluded, "Hopefully this will serve as a reminder that corrupt public officials and private citizens who participate in their corruption will be prosecuted and will go to jail."

Yes, but not necessarily right away.

Following this decision, Paradies filed a petition for "rehearing and suggestion of rehearing en banc" (by all the judges in the circuit), which, on December 26, 1996, the Eleventh Circuit unanimously denied. On February 21, 1997, Paradies filed a petition for *certiorari*.[4] On December 8, 1997, the United States Supreme Court declined to hear Paradies's appeal. Paradies next filed an emergency motion with the Eleventh Circuit for leave to file a second petition for rehearing and a motion for stay, contending that there had been an intervening change in the law since the circuit court affirmed his conviction. The Eleventh Circuit denied that motion as well.

In January 1998, four years after his conviction, a tearful Paradies, now seventy-six, appeared before Judge Alaimo in Brunswick. He now filed a motion for resentencing, claiming his debilitated physical and emotional condition guaranteed that jail time was equivalent to a death sentence. He further claimed that his

---

[4] A petition for certiorari is a document a losing party files with the Supreme Court asking the court to review the decision of a lower court. It includes a list of the parties, a statement of the facts of the case, the legal questions presented for review, and arguments as to why the court should grant the writ.

relationship with Judge Marvin Shoob would put him at risk for abuse if incarcerated, and that his financial losses constituted sufficient punishment for his crimes. In short, Paradies wanted his thirty-three-month sentence commuted.

According to an account of the hearing published in the *Atlanta Journal-Constitution*, Paradies pleaded with Alaimo, "I take Prozac, medicine for my prostate, cortisone shots for my arthritis and shoulder, and pain medicine for my knees from time to time.... The depression began shortly after the trial. I used to play tennis frequently. I can't do that anymore. I used to play golf. I can't do that anymore...."

Alaimo had been forced to give up his own beloved tennis matches in his seventies because of failing knees and a deteriorating hip.

As always, Paradies came armed with a battery of lawyers and experts. According to the *Journal-Constitution* account, career corrections official Patrick McManus warned Alaimo, "The likelihood of Mr. Paradies emerging from prison alive is not good at all." Dr. William Reid, a surgeon, testified that it would be "an extreme risk" to incarcerate Paradies: "Any further anxiety could lead to myocardial infarction and death."

Reid referred Paradies to an Atlanta cardiologist named John Hurst Jr. Hurst, however, testified that tests on Paradies were inconclusive, having shown "nothing particularly dangerous." A US Bureau of Prisons health administrator testified that prison healthcare professionals could treat all of Paradies' health needs, and, in fact, there were many other inmates with similar conditions.

Alaimo ruled that Paradies's allegations of vulnerability to prison abuse and his economic setbacks did not support a departure from the sentencing guidelines. Nor did his age, physical, or mental condition justify the divergence.

Over the years, however, Dan Paradies's had done considerable charitable work and community service. He had served as a US Army

Air Corps officer in World War II. Like young Second Lieutenant Alaimo, Paradies had flown B-25 Marauders. Ironically, he had also been the sole survivor of a military aircraft crash. Would these shared experiences have weighted Alaimo's calculus as he pondered the desperate man's fate?

In any event, Anthony Alaimo did grant Daniel Paradies's motion for a downward departure from the Sentencing Guidelines. In February 1998, US District Court for the Northern District of Georgia agreed, reducing his thirty-three-month sentence to eighteen months.

Ten years later, Daniel Paradies still counted himself among the living.

Alaimo was still on the bench.

# Chapter 29

"He lives his life the way we all wish we had the
courage to live ours."
—US District Court judge
Lisa Godbey Wood

In May 1999, the Eleventh Circuit held its biennial judicial conference on Marco Island, a Gulf Coast resort north of the Florida Everglades. According to the statute,[1] "The chief judge of each circuit may summon…the circuit, district, and bankruptcy judges of the circuit…at a time and place that he designates, for the purpose of considering the business of the courts and advising means of improving the administration of justice within such circuit."

In the circumscribed world of the federal courts, invitations[2] to these conferences—venues for presentations and debates on timely legal issues—are hot tickets. They provid rare opportunities for a select group of lawyers to interact with judges outside the constraints of trial and courtroom.

That spring, US District Court judge Lisa Godbey Wood was part of a private practice with Gilbert, Harrell, Sumerford & Martin located in Brunswick on Gloucester Street, next door to the federal courthouse. An honors graduate of the University of Georgia School of Law, Judge Wood had been Alaimo's law clerk from 1990 to 1991. Both were extraordinary achievers; both had a living, breathing connection to the law. In many ways, Alaimo and Wood would become closer than most fathers and daughters. In 1997, Alaimo

---

[1] 28 USC, Sec. 333.

[2] The conferences are now open to any attorney who is a member of the bar of a federal court in Alabama, Florida, or Georgia.

would officiate at Wood's wedding to FBI Special Agent Richard Wood.

After one of the conference sessions, a group of Southern District of Georgia judges, attorneys and their spouses—among them, Judge and Jeanne Alaimo, Judge Dudley Bowen and his wife Madeline, Judge William and Jane Moore, Lisa and Richard Wood and Savannah attorney John M. Tatum—went to dinner at an elegant Italian restaurant, a place Richard Wood had carefully investigated and determined would meet Alaimo's approval.

A decade earlier, Alaimo had scrutinized Agent Wood with the intensity of a Sicilian father about to give away his only daughter. At Lisa's engagement party, he had issued a warning that Wood "had better not hurt her," a threat that unsettled the broad-shouldered agent.

Richard Wood's selection proved exemplary. After dinner, dessert, coffee, wine, and conversation extending many hours, the group made its way outside.

Judge Wood describes the events that night:

> There were about ten of us.… We'd had this great dinner and everyone was feeling great and we were walking out into the night to get cabs back to the Marriott hotel. When we exited through the restaurant's door, there were a few steps.
>
> There was an elderly woman who was by herself. Judge Alaimo at this point would have been seventy-six or seventy-seven. This woman was a good deal older, late eighties, but dressed just wonderfully. Really sharp looking, perfectly coiffed, good makeup, a handsome woman. She had a cane and she was having difficulty with the heavy door.
>
> The rest of us were just taking in the scene. Before we even realized she needed help, Judge Alaimo was there. Stomach in, chest out, arm out, in the escort posture. She

takes his arm and he escorts her down the three stairs. She had a limousine waiting, and she gets into the back seat.

The car starts to pull away and then stops. The rear window rolls down. The woman looks out at us and says, "Which one of you is his wife?"

"I am," Mrs. Alaimo says.

"Oh you lucky woman!" she says and drives off.

Judge Wood had graduated from UGA's law school at the top of her class and had worked as editor of the law review and as chief judge of the honor court. She'd spent her summers interning at blue-chip firms like Alston & Bird, Kilpatrick & Cody, Troutman Sanders, and King & Spalding, the "Coca-Cola law firm" that had intrigued Griffin Bell so many years before—"and loved it."

After college, Wood had taken two years off before enrolling in law school. She was acutely aware that her contemporaries were practicing law while she was still at her studies.

Clerking was not in her game plan.

"I had this thing that I wanted to be a great attorney as quickly as I could," she recalled. "This sitting around with a judge for a year...."

In the summer of 1989, King & Spalding offered Wood a permanent job. "I thought, that's where I'm heading and this is my future," she remembered. That spring, however, at the urging of her law school mentors, Wood had taken a small detour, agreeing to head down to Brunswick to interview with Judge Alaimo for a clerk's position. The job was set to begin in summer 1990.

I thought, "Alright, I'm going down there and if I can get this [clerkship] with Judge Alaimo, maybe I might be interested." What an incredibly inappropriately, cocky attitude to have!... So I enter his chambers and he's at his desk at the far end of the room. We sit for just two minutes.

It's "Hi, how are you? Who are you?" And then he takes me through the side door into the courtroom. It's empty and dark, just those sort of emergency lights are on.

And he says, "This is my courtroom and it's the most special room because in it people can lose their freedom; they can be made to tell secrets they wouldn't even tell their spouse; they can lose all the money they've ever made and, in really rare cases, they can lose their life.

"And you as my law clerk would be the guardian of all that." And I thought, if I don't get this job, I don't know what I'll do!

When Alaimo offered Wood the position a few minutes later, she accepted it on the spot.

"In hindsight, I'd had a kind of strangled view of what the law could offer and what you could do as a lawyer," she later said. "In that moment, it just opened—wide open—to all it could be. And I've kept that with me all my life."

Wood never did go to work for King & Spalding. She fell in love with the coast. At the end of her year-long clerkship, she moved one door down to work at Gilbert Harrell, where she spent thirteen years as a litigator. Her most senior partner was none other than John Gilbert. She knew him as a meticulous lawyer, unassuming philanthropist, and humanitarian far removed from the "dour Scot" who'd opposed Alaimo's judicial appointment nearly two decades earlier.

Lisa Godbey Wood began to receive her own appointments. In 2004, President George W. Bush named her US Attorney for the Southern District of Georgia. In January 2007, the Senate confirmed her nomination as US District Judge for the Southern District of Georgia, to replace the retiring Dudley Bowen.

Judge Alaimo administered Wood's oath of office.

As Wood stood surrounded by family, colleagues, and friends at her swearing-in ceremony, Alaimo said, "I couldn't be more proud if you were my own child."

In a 2008 interview Wood recalled, "Of all the things that happened at that ceremony, that's the thing I'll hold on to...to have made him so proud."

Lives as long and full as Anthony and Jeanne Alaimo's will inevitably experience their portion of tragedy and disappointment, pain that can seem as unexpected and intense as their blessings.

On June 14, 2006, Robert "Bobby" Bischoff, Jeanne's son from her first marriage, was driving home after working late at Smokey Mountain Romance, a gift shop he operated in Gatlinburg, Tennessee. One of the thousands of black bears that populate the Smokey Mountains wandered out of the forest directly into the path of Bischoff's scooter. In the resulting crash, Bischoff, sixty-one, suffered grievous injuries—including a collapsed lung—and had to be airlifted to the University of Tennessee's medical center in Knoxville. He developed sepsis and died of a stroke forty-one days later, leaving behind his wife Dawn and his daughters Nichole ("Nikki"), Pam, and Mindy.

Dawn Bischoff remembered Jeanne weeping at the gravesite, struggling with a pain mothers have had to bear since time immemorial. "Oh Bobby, it isn't right for you to go first!"

In the summer of 2008, Judge Griffin Bell, Anthony Alaimo's great and most devoted friend—the driving force behind this book— was diagnosed with a terminal illness. He decided to return home to Americus, Georgia, and, with the courage so typical of the man, chose to focus, as he put it, "on the long life I was given, rather than the end game."

In his early eighties, well beyond his biblical "portion" of three-score and ten years, Alaimo became a great-grandfather. Philip and

Pam Alaimo's daughter Julie gave birth to a son, Kaiser, who turned six in 2008.

On January 12, 2009, Jeanne Alaimo, his constant companion and the great love of Anthony Alaimo's life, passed away.

The South is very much a tribal place where sons and daughters dutifully follow the paths their mothers and fathers, grandmothers and grandfathers tread. If Alaimo had any regret, it was that neither Philip nor his grandson Joseph had followed him into the practice of law—for Anthony Alaimo to have journeyed so far with seemingly no one to carry on....

He had pinned his hopes on Joseph Alaimo. When his grandson was a boy, Alaimo had given him a Harvard Law School sweatshirt. On one of their walks on Sea Island's beaches, Joseph remembered promising "Papa" that he would work his way in to Harvard.

Years later, then twenty-nine, Joseph recalled, "He just felt that if it was in him, it could possibly be in me." Joseph added, "I was always a bookish, little kid. My dad, his son, was more of a jock who just hated school. By nature, when it came to reading and writing, I was the A student."

And so Alaimo had his hopes dashed a second time.

Straight out of college, Joseph enrolled in Mercer University School of Law, Griffin Bell and Jim Bishop's alma mater—and quickly dropped out. "I realized I'd signed up for something that wasn't a passing fad," he remembered. "If you're going to go to law school, you've got be ready to do it, from here until eternity."

Perhaps the timing was wrong. In the fall of 2001 the world seemed an unsettled place, particularly to a creative young man trying to find himself. In his own youth Alaimo had gone to work and to war before enrolling at Emory University. He'd even stumbled badly that first semester at Ohio Northern's law school.

Perhaps it was the long shadow Judge Alaimo cast over Middle Georgia, or an unintended cruelty. Joseph was present at the dedication of the Anthony Alaimo Parkway. At one point a man in the crowd turned to him and said, "You'll never be the man your grandfather is." The statement dealt a hurt Joseph would never forget.

Like his father, Joseph regards his grandfather Alaimo with a mixture of love and awe. As a student, whenever he heard a teacher or classmate denigrate the United States, Joseph knew to turn elsewhere for truth. Speaking of Judge Alaimo he said, "I've always looked at him as a beacon of what America can be."

Ironically, the grandson thinks he may have inherited the same rebelliousness that drove Alaimo's myriad escape attempts in the POW camps. For his part, the judge's unswerving sense of fairness and his refusal to impose his will on others may have engendered the liberty both of his offspring feel in choosing, rightly or wrongly, their own paths.

During a 2007 interview conducted by Gabrielle Coppola[3] in New York City, Joseph reflected, "I've come to realize that the very rights my grandfather fought for, the freedom that he, in his mind, constantly fights for, my father and I take for granted."

In Vietnam, they tell the story of a group of orphans who were airlifted out of country at the end of the war. They were flown to West Germany, where they were adopted by German families and grew up immersed in that country's culture and sensibilities. In the 1990s, a magazine decided it would make a great story to accompany them back to their homeland. The magazine assigned a German-speaking American photographer to travel with the adoptees on a visit to the Catholic orphanage in South Vietnam where they'd spent the first years of their lives.

The traveled by airplane, by train, and finally overland, negotiating that country's terrible roads in a van.

---

[3] The author's daughter.

The photographer later recalled how these boisterous, rowdy boys grew serious and silent as the van approached the all-but-deserted orphanage in the dark of night. Every young man was imagining—how could he not?—that he was on the verge of uncovering a precious, long-lost connection to his own mother.

After several rings, an ancient Vietnamese nun shuffled to the door. The boys strained to catch the unfamiliar words as the interpreter explained their mission. The photographer readied the motor drives on her cameras for the climactic moment. Finally the nun understood, nodded, and turned to the expectant boys, many of them now on the verge of tears.

"Your mothers are not here," she said, extending her arms. "Gone, scattered. You will never find them."

One after another, the shattered boys began sobbing.

After a moment, the old nun continued.

"I was the one who held you when you cried, the one who fed you, who cared for you when you were sick, who sang to you," she said. "I'm the one who loved all of you. I am your mother."

The photographer, blinded by tears, took her pictures as the boys embraced the old woman.

And so it seems reasonable to suggest that Anthony Alaimo, by his example, his courage, his love, his respect and mastery of the law, did nurture a long line of offspring—Jim Bishop, David Hudson, Lisa Godbey Wood, and dozens, perhaps even hundreds, of others who have been privileged to know him over the years. He is father to them all.

It is a notion that makes this stern old man smile.

# Chapter 30

"I welcome all of you to the noblest land in the
history of the world."
—Judge Alaimo,
Naturalization Ceremony Address


And so, in his eighty-eighth year, Anthony Alaimo closes the perfect circle of his existence.

On an April morning, he drives across the F. J. Torras Causeway into downtown Brunswick. He parks the pale blue Chevy compact, his "official car," in his spot alongside the courthouse. He rides the elevator to his suite on the second floor, walking past an outsized print of John Chapman's "The Baptism of Pocahontas."

Inside, he dons his ceremonial crimson robe, shines his shoes on an electric buffer, and painfully[1] makes his way through chambers now stripped bare of keepsakes and mementos.[2]

His wood-paneled courtroom is packed with new Americans-eager, smiling, serious of mien, gathered to swear allegiance to their adopted homeland; family members, teachers, and school children; and a welcoming committee that includes the Daughters of the American Revolution, church groups, and the Veterans of Foreign Wars. In short, the crowd is a microcosm of America itself.

---

[1] The judge was recovering from his second knee replacement operation.

[2] When Judge Lisa Wood was officially assigned to Brunswick, Alaimo insisted that she take his own chambers. He moved to a smaller office upstairs.

In the twenty-first century, immigrants seeking citizenship hail from lands far different from those of the Irish, Germans, Italians, and Jews of Alaimo's generation. The world is a much smaller place, a fact reflected in the faces of the men and women arrived in Brunswick from India, the Philippines, the People's Republic of China, Greece, South Korea, India, Kenya, and Vietnam.

After Deputy US Marshall James Nase leads the Pledge of Allegiance, the Judge readies himself to address the assembly. As in the case of his jury calls, Alaimo elevates the naturalization ceremony to an event of sacred status, a living enactment of the fundamental liberties, blessings, and responsibilities of democracy.

His charge to the men and women gathered before him is neither speech nor exhortation, but a simple retelling of his family's history, which, while not unique, may be the ultimate American story:

> My parents, my brothers and sisters and I, were Italian immigrants who were naturalized almost eighty years ago just as you are today. We learned then that the great strength of this country is created by occasions such as this, when men and women like yourselves filled with hopes and dreams, with high aspirations, expectations, and determination, join hands in voluntary association with native Americans in an oath of allegiance to the United States.

> My parents came here with no funds, and nonetheless we had great wealth, that is, the wealth of health, courage, determination, and faith in the American dream, faith in the virtue of hard work and in the satisfaction of a job well done.

> There was really not anything unusual about my parents. They were typical of millions of foreign-born men and women who left their homes in search of something better, and, in the process, so greatly enriched the quality of life in our beloved country.

In this tale, Anthony Alaimo makes scant mention of himself.

He concludes his talk with the admonition that "becoming an American is about much more than fast food, rock music, credit cards, cell phones, and the Internet. Rather, it is about democratic values and choosing our own leaders. It is about hard work, self-reliance, and strong family ties. It is about volunteering to help the poor and the illiterate...about knowing the Constitution and what it stands for. And knowing that wrongs can be righted through our courts...."

Judge Alaimo moves among the new citizens in his red robe, offering smiles and handshakes along with their certificates of naturalization. Then it's off to a side room for homemade cookies, flag-draped cakes, and soft drinks.

In the last years, Alaimo has admitted to growing weary. It is as though the accumulation of years, the losses, and the life experiences have become burdensome.

"Honestly, I've seen enough," Alaimo admitted during a 2008 interview. "I don't look forward to any future experiences particularly."

He then made pointed jokes about becoming a drag on the economy and being driven into bankruptcy over the potential medical costs of "old people who live too long."

And yet, Alaimo never fails to rouse himself from the slough of despond. Like so many of his Greatest Generation cohorts, Anthony Alaimo faces mortality squarely, an aged Ulysses forever pursuing "some work of noble note yet to be done."

When he spoke at the naturalization ceremony, Alaimo's oversized hands came alive, shaping and sculpting his visions and memories in the air of the courtroom. I could picture Santa Alaimo's knees hitting the floor of her bedroom at night, hear her prayers echoing through the tiny apartment in Jamestown. ("In strong, passionate terms she gave thanks to the Almighty every night for the privilege of being in this great land where her children could be educated free of the suppressions of the old world and where we could live in freedom and unlimited opportunity.")

There was Sam Alaimo forever rousing himself to find work to feed his ragged family...Sam painstakingly teaching himself to read Italian, becoming capo di classa at bible study. And Tony's brother, Philip Alaimo, who'd dropped out of school to support the family, coming back to earn his PhD...Philip preaching to his swooning mother at the altar rail of the Methodist church.

Lieutenant Joe Jones, Norris Calkins, and the rest of Alaimo's youthful crew clambered aboard their doomed B-26 in May 1943. Roger Bushell and his fearless warriors broke though the tunnel and the Great Escape marched its way into history. Vincenzo DeMarco, Alaimo's Milanese patron, appeared, doffing his baker's hat in salute.

Rube Garland's raucous belly laugh echoed in the background. Griffin Bell smiled his farmboy's smile, remembering some long-ago mishap or wry adventure. And there, prisoners suffering unspeakable indignities at Reidsville...African-American citizens being denied their rights in Burke County...until Judge Anthony Alaimo could no longer tolerate such stains on his beloved country's honor.

Rising above all these marvelous visions, beyond the courthouse, and into the overarching heavens, one could perhaps glimpse the hand of Divine Providence, or Destiny, at work...

Or simply a silver half-dollar spinning and glinting in the air.

# Bibliography

## Books

Carroll, Tim. *The Great Escape from Stalag Luft III: The Full Story of How 76 Allied Officers Carried Out World War II's Most Remarkable Mass Escape.* Pocket Books.

Gill, Anton. *The Great Escape: The Full Dramatic Story with Contributions from Survivors and Their Families.* Headline Book Publishing.

Greene, Melissa Faye. *The Temple Bombing.*

Harsh, George. *Lonesome Road.* W. W. Norton & Company.

Levi, Carlo. *Christ Stopped At Eboli: The Story of a Year.* Farrar, Straus and Giroux.

Miller, Donald L. *Masters of the Air: America's Bomber Boys Who Fought the Air War against Nazi Germany.* Simon & Schuster.

## Periodicals

"Alaimo Cracks Whip to Correct Problems at Reidsville Prison." *Augusta Chronicle,* February 19, 1981.

"Alaimo Realizes 'Impossible Dream,' Takes Oath Monday as Federal Judge." *Brunswick News,* December 21, 1971.

"Allgood Cited for Contempt, Held Briefly in Detention Cell." *Augusta Chronicle,* February 8, 1978.

"An Innate Sense of Justice." *Atlanta Journal-Constitution,* April 17, 2005.

"Attorney Ask Judge To Take Over Prison." *Savannah News,* March 5, 1981.

"Attorney Jailed Briefly in Protest over Fine." *Augusta Chronicle ,* February 7, 1978.

"Backlog Cure: Tough Rules, Long Hours." *Brunswick News,* January 5, 1984.

"Change of Mind May Have Doomed Moody." *Fulton County Daily Report,* December 17, 1990.

"Court-Ordered Reforms Make Difference at Prison." *Atlanta Journal-Constitution,* August 16, 1985.

"Defusing Reidsville Time Bomb Is a Slow Process." *Atlanta Constitution,* 1979.

"Dept. of Corrections Salutes the Honorable Anthony A. Alaimo." *GSP News,* Fall/Winter 1997.

"Flamboyant Local Lawyer Garland Dies." *Atlanta Journal-Constitution,* November 28, 1982.

"From Hellhole to Model Prison." *Atlanta Journal,* June 6, 1987.

"Garland & Garland 83 Years of Playing Havoc with Atlanta Prosecutors." *Atlanta Journal-Constitution,* October 26, 2003.

"Georgia Judge Helps Out in U.S. Court." *Pittsburgh Post-Gazette,* February 11, 1988.

"In-House Courtroom at Prison Dedicated." *Glenville Sentinel,* November 20, 1997.

"Italians Threaten Pastor." *New York Times,* June 15, 1916.

"Judge Alaimo Praised for Integrity, Accomplishments." *Savannah Morning News,* March 23, 1990.

"Judge Alaimo: A Prison Reformer Who's Been There." *Atlanta Journal-Constitution,* March 1, 1981.

"Judge Ends Suit against Prison." *Brunswick News,* July 1985.

"Judge Gives State Officials 15 Days to Devise Prison Integration Plan." *Brunswick News,* December 13 1978.

"Judge to Receive Legal Honor." *Atlanta Journal-Constitution,* March 31, 2005.

"Learn From Prison Mistakes." *Atlanta Journal,* June 29, 1982.

"Men Sent to Prison in Pollution Case." *Augusta Chronicle,* June 3, 1999.

"Monitor, Judge Use Federal Whip to Spur Prison Reforms." *Atlanta Constitution.* April 17, 1980.

"Nixon Appoints Alaimo Judge." *Savannah Morning News,* November 30, 1971.

"Olympic Torch Touches Glynn County Hearts." *Brunswick News,* July 11, 1996.

"Plant Officials Sentenced in LCP case." *Atlanta Journal-Constitution,* April 27, 1999.

"Prison Life Real to Judge." *Florida Times-Union.* March 2, 1981.

"Prison Officials Cheer Lifting of Court Oversight." *Atlanta Journal-Constitution,* July 25, 1997.

"Reidsville Suit Ends; Job Isn't Over." *Atlanta Constitution,* July 1, 1985.

"Sen. Allgood Jailed for Contempt of Court." *Atlanta Journal-Constitution.* February 8, 1978.
"Slated For Judgeship." *Brunswick News,* November 29, 1971.
"Some U.S. Judges Mark King Day on the Bench." *Atlanta Journal-Constitution.*
"State Prison Finally Gets Some Praise." *Savannah News,* June 30, 1985.
"State Will Comply with Alaimo's Order for Cutback at Reidsville." *Brunswick News,* July 6, 1978.
"The Prison Problems." *Atlanta Journal,* April 1, 1981.
"Tight Prison Security Greets Visiting Judge." *Atlanta Journal,* July 22, 1981.
"Warm Fuzzy Courtroom Occasions." *Brunswick News,* December 7, 1977.
"Was Justice Too Swift at Airport Trial?" *Fulton County Daily Report,* January 31, 1994.
April 20,1996. *Jacksonville Times-Union.*
*Augusta Chronicle,* February 9, 1978.
*Brunswick News* "Section of U.S. Highway 17 Named in Honor of Alaimo." May 21, 1997
*Brunswick News,* December 9, 1992.
*Florida Times-Union,* January14, 1980.
*Journal of Southern Legal History* 12/1–2.

### Other

"A Portrait of a Judge." August 30, 1990.
"Anthony A. Alaimo: Biographical Brief." United States District Court, Southern District of Georgia.
Alaimo, Anthony. Speech. Daughters of the American Revolution, Jekyll Island, Georgia, May 26, 1982.
———. Speech. "Americanism-Hope." December 8, 1992. In "An Evening with Honorable Anthony Alaimo," *The Cloister.*
———. Speech. Ocean Forest Sea Island Group, April 26, 2006.
———. Speech. Veterans of the 450th Squadron, 332nd Bomb Group, September 19, 1985.
Alaimo, Philip, to Tony Alaimo, November 30, 1944.
Cathcart, Bill. "Airborne Justice."
Georgia State Senate "A Resolution." February 8, 1978.
*Gore v. Humphries.* November 9, 1926. Westlaw.

Hudson, David. "Remembering John Sammons Bell: Service and
  Friendship." April 19, 2007.
Loy, Jeanne. Diary.
Mackay, Edward George. Biographical sketch.
Mackay, James Armstrong. Biographical sketch.
McKenzie, Ed, and R. Livingstone. "Dulag Luft."
Naturalization ceremony program, April 18, 2007.
Naturalization ceremony program, April 2008.
Naturalization ceremony transcript, April 27, 2005.
Neary, Bob. *Stalag Luft III: A Collection of German Prison Camp Sketches,
  with Descriptive Text Based on Personal Experiences.* Philadelphia:
  Thomason Press, 1946.
Parkway dedication ceremony program, May 30, 1997.
Stillman, Brig. General Robert M. "The Experience I'll Never Forget."
Vogtle, Alvin "Escape from Stalag VIIA." Transcript.

*Interviews*

Alaimo, Anthony. Interview with author.
———. Interview with Sonja Olsen Kinard. April 14, 2000.
Alaimo, Jeanne. Interview with author.
Alaimo, Pam. Interview with author.
Alaimo, Philip. Interview with author.
Bell, Griffin B. Interview with author.
Bischoff, Dawn. Interview with author.
Bishop, James. Interview with author.
Cullen, Robert. "Black Empowerment" Georgia Government
  Documentation Project, 1985.
———. Interview with author.
Curry, Josephine Alaimo. Interview with author.
Garland, Edward T. M. Interview with author.
Hudson, David. Interview with author.
Martin, Vernon. Interview with author.
Pasciullo, Josie. Interview with author.
Popson, Sandra. Interview with author.
Steed, Robert. Interview with author.
Tjoflat, Gerald Bard. Interview with author.
Winokur, Stanley. Interview with author.
Wood, Lisa Godbey. Interview with author.

## Web Resources

322nd Bomb Group.. Http://usaaf.com/8thaf/bomber/322bg.htm.

91st Bomb Group Stories..
Http://www.91stbombgroup.com/slanetales.html

Alaimo crewmates.
Http://freepages.military.rootsweb.ancestry.com/~hfhm/Kirtland/Main%20class/calkins.htm.

Albert Jenner. Http://mason.gmu.edu/~rrotunda/jenner.htm.

Alexander Solzhenitsyn Harvard Commencement Speech.
Http://www.americanrhetoric.com/speeches/alexandersolzhenitsynharvard.htm.

Alvin E. Vogtle. Http://www.nationmaster.com/encyclopedia/Alvin-Vogtle.

Arbeitskommando*s* camps. Http://en.wikipedia.org/wiki/Arbeitslager.

AT-6. Http://www.aviationshoppe.com/AT-6-Texan.html.

Atlanta population statistics.
Http://www.census.gov/population/www/documentation/twps0027/twps0027.html.

*Augusta National v. Northwestern Mutual.*
web.si.umich.edu/tprc/papers/2006/507/Shahar%20Dilbary%20-%20Famous%20Trademarks%20(TPRC).pdf.

B-26 Bomber Specs.
Http://www.thinkquest.org/library/websitena.html?13831.

B-26 training crashes. Http://en.wikipedia.org/wiki/B-26_Marauder.

Bahia Blanca. Http://en.wikipedia.org/wiki/Bah%C3%ADa_Blanca.

Barrage Balloons. Http://en.wikipedia.org/wiki/Barrage_balloon.

Battle of Bastogne. Http://en.wikipedia.org/wiki/Battle_of_Bastogne.

Battle of Caporetto.
Http://www.historylearningsite.co.uk/battle_of_caporetto.htm.

Bird hunting statute Http://vlex.com/vid/19894510.

Bolzano. Http://en.wikipedia.org/wiki/Bozen-Bolzano.

Burke County Lynching.
Http://www.google.com/search?hl=en&sa=X&oi=spell&resnum=0&ct=result&cd=1&q=lynchings+Waynesboro+GA+lynchings&spell=1.

Bury St. Edmunds. Http://en.wikipedia.org/wiki/Bury_St_Edmunds.

# The Sicilian Judge

Walter Smithwick. Http://goldbamboo.com/yp-ype4426525.html.
Charles A. Schafer. Http://vlex.com/vid/36893057.
Chautauqua Institution. Http://www.ciweb.org/about.html.
Coastal Georgia Regional Development Center.
    Http://www.coastalgeorgiardc.org/.
Col. Friedrich-Wilhelm von Lindeiner-Wildau.
    Http://www.ateal.co.uk/greatescape/.
Colonel Charles Goodrich. *Http://www.b24.net/pow/stalag3.htm.*
Colonel's Island Terminal.
    Http://www.gaports.com/Default.aspx?tabid=356.
De Havilland Tiger Moth.
    Http://en.wikipedia.org/wiki/De_Havilland_Tiger_Moth.
Decca-G Box.
    Http://www.bbc.co.uk/ww2peopleswar/stories/45/a4161845.shtml.
Hurley Jones obituary.
    Http://www.whsc.emory.edu/_pubs/em/2005fall/classnotes.html.
Drane Field.
    Http://www.lakelandgov.net/library/speccoll/manuscripts/military/dra
    nefield_scope.html.
Durchgangslager der Luftwaffe. Http://www.merkki.com/new_page_2.htm.
E. Way Highsmith. Http://www.uga.edu/gm/archives/ArcRho.html.
Edward George Mackay. Http://marbl.library.emory.edu/Guides/guides-
    methodist.html.
Elbert Tuttle. Http://politicalgraveyard.com/b.
Elbert Tuttle.
    Http://en.wikipedia.org/wiki/Elbert_Tuttleio/tuttle.html#RND0X2G
    DR.
"A Brief History." Http://emoryhistory.emory.edu/history/index.html.
Fairchild PT-19. Http://en.wikipedia.org/wiki/Fairchild_PT-19.
Fort Niagara POW camp . Http://pacb.bfn.org/murals/themes/POW/.
Garmish-Partenkirchen. Http://en.wikipedia.org/wiki/Garmisch-
    Partenkirchen.
Newton Longfellow.
    Http://www.generals.dk/general/Longfellow/Newton/USA.html.
Samuel Egbert Anderson.
    Http://www.generals.dk/general/Anderson/Samuel_Egbert/USA.html.
Georgia Republican Party. Http://www.gagop.org.
Gerald Tjoflat. Http://www.ca11.uscourts.gov/about/judges/tjoflat.php.

German POWs in NY state. Http://ww.gentracer.com/powcampsNY.html.

GI Bill. Http://www.gibill.va.gov/GI_Bill_Info/history.htm.

Great Escape. Http://www.pbs.org/wgbh/nova/greatescape/.

Griffin Bell. Http://www.kslaw.com/bio/Griffin_Bell.

Harold E. Cook, 722nd Squadron, 450th Bomb Group. Http://www.450thbg.com/real/biographies/450/038cook.shtml.

Hartsfield corruption case. *Http*://www.law.emory.edu/11circuit/sept96/94-8485.opa.html.

Henry Samuel Atkins Jr. case. Http://vlex.com/vid/38387770.

Hohemark Hospital. Http://www.pownews.com/dulag.luft.htm.

http://beck.library.emory.edu/southernchanges/article.php?id=sc01-6_008.

http://en.wikipedia.org/wiki/GI_Bill.

http://en.wikipedia.org/wiki/Nicholas_Katzenbach.

http://en.wikipedia.org/wiki/Sodality.

http://en.wikipedia.org/wiki/Stalag_VII-A.

http://redstarcafe.wordpress.com/2007/06/26/the-minamata-pieta/.

http://reidsville.georgia.gov/05/home/0,2230,8476793,00.html;jsessionid=76DEF7CAA06D41F30197F43ACE15C48F.

http://www.fleetairarmarchive.net/RollofHonour/POW/StalagLuftIII.html.

http://www.georgiaencyclopedia.org/nge/Article.jsp?id=h-2533.

http://www.huntermaclean.com/firm/14.

http://www.law.cornell.edu/uscode/42/1983.html.

http://www.libs.uga.edu/russell/collections/guthrie/index.shtml.

http://www.newspaperarchive.com/LandingPage.aspx?type=glp&search=james%20spot%20mozingo%20attorney%20darlington%20s.c.&img=\\na0006\6798873\56699502_clean.html.

http://www.newspaperarchive.com/LandingPage.aspx?type=glp&search=robert%20a.%20podesta%20secretary%20of%20commerce&img=\\na0011\6832603\85901419_clean.html.

http://www1.va.gov/vetdata/docs/POWCYO54-12-06jsmwrFinal2ldoc.

http://www3.interscience.wiley.com/journal/112134016/abstract.

Isaac Rosenfeld. Http://books.google.com/books?id=V7D6xS-muIoC&pg=PA123&lpg=PA123&dq=Isaac+Rosenfeld+%22No+man+suffers+injustice%22&source=web&ots=3U79w2d5U0&sig=IK31JG5V_3lDzkqwQVkrnpcqu0o&hl=en&sa=X&oi=book_result&resnum=1&ct=result.

Italian Methodist Church Jamestown. Http://books.google.com/books?id=Hi0VuzVJ_tAC&pg=PA193&lpg

=PA193&dq=italian+methodist+church+jamestown+ny&source=web
&ots=9yNYSTHFXq&sig=kGsGpkNPgLJd7dOV2dS7SzND6Hg&hl
=en&sa=X&oi=book_result&resnum=3&ct=result.

Jack Howell death. Http://www.rougham.org/322nd-mission.php.

James "Spot" Mozingo.
Http://books.google.com/books?id=rJy8eJe7L1sC&pg=RA1-
PA314&lpg=RA1-
PA314&dq=james+spot+mozingo+attorney+bio&source=web&ots=Q
90mzsODcb&sig=VV20lKTBdwg7es3fQCnrUmIkQoE&hl=en&sa=
X&oi=book_result&resnum=1&ct=result.

Jamestown High School.
Http://www.wjcc.k12.va.us/content/schools/jamestown/index.shtml.

Jamestown, New York.
Http://en.wikipedia.org/wiki/Jamestown,_New_York.

Jerry Sage. Http://www.namebase.org/xrut/Jerry-M-Sage.html.

Jimmy Carter's Peanut Brigade.
Http://www.pbs.org/wgbh/amex/carter/timeline/index.html.

John B. Miller. Http://politicalgraveyard.com/bio/miller5.html.

John Gilbert. Http://www.lawyers.com/Georgia/Brunswick/Gilbert,-
Harrell,-Sumerford-and-Martin,-P.C.-873990-f.html.

Josephine Baker . Http://en.wikipedia.org/wiki/Josephine_Baker.

Judge Braswell Dean . Http://thinkexist.com/quotes/judge_braswell_dean/.

Judge Robert Vance murder *Time* magazine.
Http://www.time.com/time/magazine/article/0,9171,969089,00.html.

Kasserine Pass. Http://en.wikipedia.org/wiki/Battle_of_the_Kasserine_Pass.

Kirtland 42-13 Research Project "Norrish Kenneth Calkins.
Http://freepages.military.rootsweb.com/~hfhm/Kirtland/Main%20clas
s/calkins.htm.

La Mamounia. Http://www.mamounia.com/eng/index.php.

Lay of the Last Minstrel.
Http://www.theotherpages.org/poems/minstrel.html.

LCP Chemicals case.
Http://www.time.com/time/magazine/article/0,9171,969089,00.html.

Louis Orth Kelso.
Http://query.nytimes.com/gst/fullpage.html?res=9D0CE1D71339F93
2A15751C0A967958260.

Maschinengerwehr 4. Http:*//wapedia.mobi/en/Maschinengewehr_08.*

Minamata Pieta. Http://wordpress.com/tag/minamata/.

Nicholas Katzenbach.
   Http://www.spartacus.schoolnet.co.uk/JFKkatzenbach.htm.
Operation Torch. Http://worldwar2database.com/html/torch.htm.
"Patton Liberates Stalag VIIA." Http://www.axpow.org/loevskylouis.htm.
Prudentius. Http://en.wikipedia.org/wiki/Psychomachia.
Rabbi Hillel. Http://waldogalan.blogspot.com/2008/05/if-not-you-then-
   who.html.
RAF airfield Bury St. Edmunds .
   Http://en.wikipedia.org/wiki/RAF_Bury_St._Edmunds.
Reuben Garland. Http://www.gsllaw.com/CM/Custom/FirmOverview.asp.
Richard "Racehorse" Haynes.
   Http://en.wikipedia.org/wiki/Richard_Haynes.
Rich-Seapak Corp. Http://biz.yahoo.com/ic/108/108110.html.
Robert A. Podesta.
   Http://query.nytimes.com/gst/fullpage.html?res=9D0CEFDF113CF9
   37A15751C0A967958260.
Roger Bushell/Millionaires Squadron.
   Http://www.pegasusarchive.org/pow/roger_bushell.htm.
*Rogers v. Lodge.* Http://supreme.justia.com/us/458/613/.
Roscoe Pickett. Http://politicalgraveyard.com/bio/pickett.html.
Roy Livingstone Dulag Luft. Http://www.pownews.com/StalagXVIIB.htm.
Ruben Garland. Http://www.gsllaw.com/PracticeAreas/Criminal-Law.asp.
Runaway Train. Http://www.amazon.com/Runaway-Train-Jon-
   Voight/dp/6304084293.
Sea Island/Cloister. Http://www.seaisland.com/footer/presskit.asp.
Sergeant Major Hermann Glemnitz.
   *Http://www.usafa.af.mil/df/dflib/SL3/germans/glimnitz.cfm?catname=De
   an%20of%20Faculty.*
Sheriff John David Davis. Http://bulk.resource.org/courts.gov/c-
   /ca11/787.F2d.1501.85-8289.html.
Stalag Luft III. Http://en.wikipedia.org/wiki/Stalag_Luft_III.
Stalag Luft III abandoned.
   Http://www.manions.com/archive/articles/the_march_from_sagan.ht
   m.
Stalag Luft III. Http://www.b24.net/pow/stalag3.htm.
Stalag Luft III.
   Http://www.usafa.af.mil/df/dflib/SL3/SL3.cfm?catname=Dean%20of
   %20Faculty.

Stalag VIIA. Http://www.moosburg.org/info/stalag/indeng.html.

Starnberg. Http://en.wikipedia.org/wiki/Starnberg.

Sulfur Mining. Http://www.bestofsicily.com/mag/art145.htm.

Swede Hill, Jamestown.
    Https://www.alibris.com/search/books/qwork/5862663/used/Saga%2
    0from%20the%20hills%20:%20a%20history%20of%20the%20Swed
    es%20of%20Jamestown,%20New%20York.

Termini Immerse. Http://www.italianvisits.com/sicily/termini-
    immerse/index.htm.

Termini Immerse. Http://www.bestofsicily.com/mag/art145.htm.

Timken Detroit Axle . Http://www.answers.com/topic/the-timken-
    company.

US District Judge John Wood Jr. assassination.
    Http://www.time.com/time/magazine/article/0,9171,953589,00.html.

USC § 1983. Civil action for deprivation of rights.

Ugo Crivelli.
    Http://lycoming.edu/umarch/Central%20PA%20Methodist%20Pastors.
    doc.

USAAF Washout Rates.
    Http://books.google.com/books?id=P0KiPMJuXkUC&pg=PR11&lpg
    =PR11&dq=washout+rate+world+war+II+pilots&source=web&ots=bP
    ZOYrZdVp&sig=Ufmoi8X-
    n3gzyxWe0S7ORyBfYc0&hl=en&sa=X&oi=book_result&resnum=4
    &ct=result#PPR13,M1.

Vincent Nathan.
    Http://www.prisoncommission.org/public_hearing_2_witness_nathan.
    asp.

Wideawake Airfield. Http://en.wikipedia.org/wiki/Ascension_Island.

*Wiley v. Bolden.* Http://law.jrank.org/pages/13410/Mobile-v-Bolden.html.

Wilmer Mizell. Http://en.wikipedia.org/wiki/Wilmer_Mizell.

Wordsworth. Http://www.bartleby.com/145/ww194.html.

World War II, number of American servicemen serving.
    Http://www.infoplease.com/ipa/A0004615.html.

www.vjolt.net/vol10/issue1/v10i1_a3-Travis.pdf.